DATE DUE

Carnival on the Page

Carnival on the Page

Popular Print Media in Antebellum America

by Isabelle Lehuu

The University of North Carolina Press Chapel Hill *&* London

© 2000

[N]orth Carolina Press

[All] reserved

[set in Monticel]le and Scotch types

[by Tseng Infor]mation Systems

[Manufactured in the U]nited States of America

[The paper in this book] meets the guidelines for

[permanence and durabi]lity of the Committee on

[Production Guidelines for B]ook Longevity of the Council

on Library Resources.

Library of Congress Cataloging-in-Publication Data
Lehuu, Isabelle.
Carnival on the page : popular print media in
antebellum America / by Isabelle Lehuu.
p.   cm.
Includes bibliographical references and index.
ISBN 0-8078-2521-2 (cl. : alk. paper). —
ISBN 0-8078-4832-8 (pbk. : alk. paper)
1. Books and reading—United States—History—19th
century.   2. Popular literature—United States—History and
criticism.   3. American literature—19th century—History
and criticism.   4. Book industries and trade—United
States—History—19th century.   I. Title.
Z1003.2.L44   2000
028'.9'097309034—dc21   99-27582
CIP

Parts of Chapter 5 appeared previously, in somewhat different form, in
"Sentimental Figures: Reading *Godey's Lady's Book* in Antebellum America,"
in *The Culture of Sentiment: Race, Gender, and Sentimentality in Nineteenth-
Century America,* edited by Shirley Samuels (New York: Oxford University
Press, 1992), 73–91, copyright © 1992 by Oxford University Press, Inc.,
and are reprinted here by permission.

04   03   02   01   00   5   4   3   2   1

Contents

Illustrations

Acknowledgments

Many individuals and institutions have contributed directly or indirectly to the completion of this book, and I am pleased to acknowledge their help. I started writing this book as a doctoral dissertation, and I am grateful to the Graduate School and the Department of History at Cornell University for their generous fellowships that supported this project in its early stage. I owe special thanks to Larry Moore, my dissertation adviser, whose critical reading, intellectual expertise, and strong encouragements guided me through the major steps of this work. I thank Steven L. Kaplan, Michael Kammen, Stuart Blumin, Shirley Samuels, and Peter Uwe Hohendahl for the conversations we had on either side of the Arts Quad. Friends and fellow Cornellians also witnessed the genesis of this endeavor. Among them I want to thank Ruth Alexander, Susan Brewer, Martin Bruegel, Tony Farquhar, Susan Semler, and Michael Wilson. The fond memory of our discussions will always remain a big part of that special time when I was a graduate student in the United States.

Although my initiation to the history of the book began in France under the guidance of Daniel Roche, my interest in the American side of that story was prompted by a seminar with the late Stephen Botein at the American Antiquarian Society. Subsequently an Albert Boni Fellowship of the American Antiquarian Society, a Summer Research Fellowship of the Library Company of Philadelphia and the Historical Society of Pennsylvania, and an Albert Beveridge Grant from the American Historical Association provided funds for archival research on the history of reading. Since then my work has greatly benefited from conversations with a large community of book historians. I cannot possibly mention them all by name here, but I am especially grateful to Barbara Sicherman, David D. Hall, and Mary Kelley for their lasting support. Discussions with the late Bill Gilmore and with Rosalind Remer, Ron Zboray, Bob Gross, Leslie Howsam, Charles Johanningsmeier, and Thomas Leonard convinced me that my research was worth pursuing. On the French side, I thank Maurice Agulhon for his intellectual rigor and lasting trust. I also owe grateful thanks to Roger Chartier and Jacques Revel for their wise counsel.

In addition, scholars in other disciplines than history have made thoughtful suggestions. I particularly thank Joy Kasson, Mary Chapman, Betty Bergland, and Joel Martin for their genuine interest and support. A National Endowment for the Humanities Summer Institute on Image and Text at Johns Hopkins University offered provocative discussions and made me rethink what was important in the history of print culture.

Most of all, the assistance of many librarians and archivists made this research possible. I especially wish to thank the staff of Olin Library at Cornell University. At the American Antiquarian Society I thank John Hench, Joanne Chaison, Georgia Barnhill, and the late Joyce Tracy, whose aid with newspapers I deeply appreciated. I also thank James Green and the staff of the Library Company of Philadelphia for letting me handle so many giftbooks. Similarly helpful were the staffs of the Arents Collection of Books in Parts at the New York Public Library, the Rare Book and Manuscript Collections at Columbia University, the Rare Book Collection at the Library of Congress, and the Special Collections at the University of Michigan, Ann Arbor.

Once research gave way to writing and revising, I acquired new obligations. I am grateful to Saint Michael's College in Vermont and the University of Quebec at Montreal for faculty grants, and I thank my colleagues north and south of the border for their help. At both institutions, students have also contributed to the progress of my work by asking pertinent questions about antebellum culture in America. I thank American studies undergraduates at Saint Michael's College and graduate students in U.S. history in Quebec for that fruitful dialogue.

Richard B. Stott read a first version of the entire manuscript, and I thank him for his comments. A special debt goes to Lewis Bateman at the University of North Carolina Press. His unabated enthusiasm for what I was doing has been a surprising comfort during the early stage of my professional career. Mary Kupiec Cayton and Karen Haltunen offered careful readings of the manuscript at different stages of revision. Their incisive comments forced me to clarify my ideas, and I thank them for all suggestions that helped improve the manuscript. John Drendel read most chapters in their final form, and I thank him for his discerning criticism. I wish to extend my thanks to Mary Reid for her attentive copyediting and to Ron Maner and other staff members at the University of North Carolina Press for the care with which they helped me turn a manuscript into a book.

Acknowledgments

Lastly, I want to acknowledge the unlimited aid I received from friends and relatives—in Europe and in North America—during this long endeavor. Jan Albers, Pablo Arreola, Michelle Albanna, Elizabeth F. Burke, Ellen Jacobs, Patricia de Lacharrière, Bertrand Lehuu, Catherine Masurel, and Paula Schwartz have provided emotional support and good distraction. My parents, Maud and Thanh Lehuu, deserve my greatest thanks for their love and trust.

Carnival on the Page

*L'âme d'un historien est celle d'un
lecteur de fait divers.*
Paul Veyne

*What is the use of a book, thought Alice,
without pictures or conversations?*
Lewis Carroll,
Alice's Adventures in Wonderland

Introduction

This study centers on a historical moment of textual transformation. During the pre–Civil War decades, American society saw the emergence of an exuberant print culture, which took a great variety of forms and catered to the tastes of a diversified readership. But for all the multiplicity of popular media and reading audiences, common features stood out. From the miniature giftbooks to the mammoth papers, all the new reading materials shared a festive and somewhat transgressive quality. They performed a collective spectacle in which producers and consumers, publishers and readers, came to participate. This out-of-the-ordinary and carnivalesque tone of antebellum print culture is precisely what spurred these inquiries into a specific passage of American book history.

The essence of print exuberance resulted from both volume and style. The sheer number of popular publications during the quarter century before the economic depression of 1857 resembled a horn of plenty. In fact, the many embellishments in print media of the antebellum period never failed to picture fruits and flowers, which were not only the emblems of femininity but also the emblems of abundance. From the cornucopia of publishing to gastronomic excess, the analogy is not too far-fetched. Critics of the popularization of print were prompt to contrast the abundance of books and the frugality of reading. "Do not read too much," health reformer William Andrus Alcott warned young women in 1840. "The world is almost deluged with books."[1] Just as entrepreneurial publishers attuned their profitable business to the tastes of a diversified readership and concocted a feast of printed words, learned critics called for days of fasting. To counter the protuberance of the publishing market, reformers from all walks of life recommended propriety, discipline, and asceticism. What arbiters of culture were attempting to control, if not eradicate, was a playful culture that cheap books and periodicals were celebrating. For the new publications were characterized not only by their abundance but also by their taste for the eccentric and the off-balanced.

The examples discussed in this book will show that in a variety of ways, yet persistently, a bodily culture permeated the printed page. Whether it took the carnal tone of crime news in the penny press, the uncanny corpulence of weekly leviathans, or even the Catholic images of giftbook engravings, American print culture allowed the body to be omnipresent. Reading matter became a feast for the eye as much as, and perhaps instead of, food for the mind. The materiality of texts, both verbal and visual, and the tactile pleasure they warranted contested the well-established authority of the printed word. It was a carnival on the page, or, to use the definition offered by the Russian literary theorist Mikhail Bakhtin, "the true feast of time, the feast of becoming, change, and renewal."[2]

The new media momentarily turned the world of print upside down. To the seriousness of intellectual pursuits, they offered the challenge of pleasure and laughter. But recognizing the buffoonery and grotesque features of antebellum print media is not significant unless one emphasizes at the same time that this coincided with a threshold in the development of American society and culture. The period often described as the golden age of print was in fact a period of unstable cultural order. To the amazement of contemporary critics and enthusiasts alike, the printed word *staged* a carnival, in the twofold sense of both staging a dramatic representation and entering a phase within the maturing of American culture. Jacksonian America experienced a ritual, a collective passage that marked the discontinuity of historical time. In the words of anthropologist Victor Turner, who studied nonwestern rituals, the phase of history during which print underwent a temporary liberation was homologous to a "liminal period."[3] Much of what follows is an effort at understanding the significance of the ephemeral in-betweenness of the antebellum period, a period long regarded as either an epilogue or a prologue. It was a historical moment when the world of print was betwixt and between order and chaos, when polarities were exaggerated. The concepts of carnival and limen (which means threshold in Latin) are, therefore, useful analytical categories. The convergence of Bakhtin's literary theory and Turner's symbolic anthropology serves here to probe the entire process of transgression beyond the mere identification of transgressive elements in antebellum print culture.[4]

Bakhtin studied the carnival in fifteenth-century Rabelais as both ritual and antiritual. Accordingly, carnival time allowed social hierarchies to be inverted and mocked. As a temporary suspension of all rules, privileges, and moral codes, the carnivalesque stood opposite from official ceremonies and created a space for social innovation.

In contrasting low and high culture, the feast and the fast, the popular and the legitimate, Bakhtin emphasized the subversive power of the carnivalesque in a premodern society. Although he identified remnants of the Renaissance grotesque within the field of realist literature during the subsequent three centuries, Bakhtin was prompt to conclude that by the nineteenth century, grotesque images of the carnival were formalized. Particularly with the beginning of romanticism, the grotesque was interiorized and subjectivized. Once deprived of its original popular vision and social critique, the romantic grotesque, according to Bakhtin, lacked the potential for renewal and regeneration.[5]

By contrast, scholars who have drawn on the work of Bakhtin have identified the survival of carnivalesque tradition in literary inversions and playful contestations of rigid categories. This is, for instance, the approach of Dominick LaCapra, who recognizes not only the critical role played by the image of carnival in modern societies but also the relevance of carnivalesque utopia to history writing. LaCapra's reading of Bakhtin then becomes a call for the new carnivalesque historian who might, like imaginative novelists, laugh at history.[6] Peter Stallybrass and Allon White have also argued that the transformation of the carnival involved far more than carnivalesque residues in later centuries. They have deciphered the reemergence of the carnival in transgressive literature such as the gothic novel as well as in bourgeois hysteria of modern times.[7] Likewise, the interdependence of polarities and the coexistence of opposites that have been emphasized by scholars of European literary history can be found in the new print culture of pre–Civil War America.

Along with the work of Bakhtin and his followers, Victor Turner's theoretical framework holds important clues for the understanding of the transition of the antebellum period. For Turner, the limen is an ambiguous phase in rites of passage. The attributes of liminality elude classification. As he explained, "Liminal entities are neither here nor there; they are betwixt and between the position assigned and arrayed by law, custom, convention, and ceremonial." Liminal entities may be disguised as monsters and have no status. Yet Turner's approach underlined the blend of lowliness and sacredness in the liminal period, a "moment in and out of time."[8]

Since its first publication in the late 1960s and its broad support among academics of various disciplines in the mid-1970s, Turner's antistructural liminality has received mixed reviews.[9] Some have concluded that while reflecting a certain academic fascination for the counterculture of his time, Turner's model failed to be applicable to the study of postcolonial societies.[10] It is particularly in his consensual vision of the "reintegrative communitas"—the third phase of reincorporation subsequent to the liminal period—that Turner is most vulnerable. More recent work in cultural studies, including that of borderland theorists, found fault with Turner's homogeneous and apolitical social imagination. Notwithstanding his shortcomings for postmodern societies, the Turnerian exploration of liminality continues to be pertinent for studying the experimental transgressions of the antebellum period precisely because those were followed by a phase of consolidation, or, in Turner's terms, "reaggregation," in the mid-nineteenth century.[11]

However, some of Turner's critics have furthered the debate over liminality in a significant way. Most insightful among historians is the gender analysis of liminality proposed by Caroline Walker Bynum in a study of women's religious life in the Middle Ages.[12] Bynum challenges Turner's centering of liminality on role reversal and apartness. What was true for gender reversal in male social drama did not occur in the same fashion for women's experience. As Bynum aptly argues, institutionalized liminality such as *béguinages* or lay sisterhoods was perceived not as reversal of but in continuity with women's ordinary experience. Such a persuasive critique should allow for the inclusion of both reversal and continuity in the social drama that is played out in the limen. Following Bynum's critique of Turner's theory, the present study will therefore use the concept of liminality to describe the temporary liberation from normative demands while keeping in mind that structureless behavior in the limen or threshold, that is, the betwixt-and-between zone, might also stem from so-called normal experience. This will prove to be most helpful in analyzing the liminality of women's print culture in the pre–Civil War decades.

Undoubtedly, the legacy of Turner's anthropology rests beyond the dichotomy between structure and chaos in the recognition of existing moments of discontinuity in history. For that reason it is the combined Turnerian and Bakhtinian conceptualization, despite their disciplinary differences, that is instrumental in grasping the characteristics of moments of discontinuity, both in social space and in history. To decipher the transgression at work in antebellum print media involves far more than a celebration of or nostalgia for the carnival. It is rather an exploration into the social fabric of that historical moment.

To that effect Bakhtin reminds us of yet another important link. In deciphering the language of the marketplace in Rabelais's novels, he emphasizes that the carnivalesque merged with the colloquialisms and gestures of the market fair. "The marketplace was the center of all that is unofficial," he noted. "The dates of the fairs were usually adapted to the great feasts of the year."[13] The traditional commingling of carnival festivities with market fairs even continued to exist long after the Middle Ages and the Renaissance. For instance, in his cultural history of advertising in America, T. J. Jackson Lears borrows the vocabulary of the carnivalesque to describe the "magic of the marketplace" and the exotic imagery of nineteenth-century advertisements.[14] Similarly, the festive carnival that burst onto the printed page during the antebellum period was not opposed to but rather belonged to the marketplace. The analysis of its symbolic function will thus require an investigation into the role of successful entrepreneurs in the exploitation, and perhaps also the normalization, of grotesque print media.[15]

This book, therefore, seeks to contribute to a deeper understanding of a very specific historical moment, a period characterized by its own ephemerality as well as the ephemerality of the publications it produced. The pre–Civil War decades played a pivotal role in forcing cultural alignment. Just as the printed page appeared as "a pleasure zone" and a liminal space for publishing innovation, norms of propriety and social markers were introduced into the cultural turmoil to ultimately counter the boundlessness of the age.[16] The following chapters will show that eccentric publishing experiments provoked altogether great pleasure as well as great anxiety when antebellum America witnessed a massive desecration of a tradition of printed words with the onslaught of the marketplace. In the so-called era of the common man, it was not the democratization of knowledge that drew criticism, but rather the emergence of a different, vernacular print culture—cheap, sensational, ephemeral, miscellaneous, illustrated, and serialized—that transgressed the boundaries of conventional media and defied orthodox uses of the printed word. The materials examined here—ephemeral papers, leaflets of memory, books in parts, and lady's books—were quite unlike what had long been understood as books. Whether daily, weekly, monthly, or even annual, they all represented a significant challenge to the traditional definition of a book.

An 1829 federal copyright decision made a clear distinction between books and newspapers in its interpretation of the term "book" in the Copyright Act of 1790. In the words of Circuit Justice Thompson, who delivered the opinion of the court, "A book within the statute need not be a book in the common and ordinary acceptation of the word, viz., a volume made up of several sheets bound together; it may be printed only on one sheet, as the words of a song or the music accompanying it." The issue of literary property was therefore independent of size, form, or shape. What made a difference, however, was the function or use of print. While a book was understood as having a permanent and durable character, a newspaper was perceived as a "fluctuating and fugitive" form, filled with subject matter of temporary use: "The preliminary steps required by law, to secure the copyright, cannot reasonably be applied to a work of so ephemeral a character as that of a newspaper." As Judge Thompson further concluded, "The right cannot be secured for any given time, for the series of papers published day to day or week to week; and it is so improbable that any publisher of a newspaper would go through this form for every paper, it cannot reasonably be presumed that congress intended to include newspapers under the term book."[17]

Deemed ephemeral, and therefore deprived of the protection of the law, newspapers and nonbook publications were not taken very seriously in the 1829 decision. The court obviously could not anticipate the forces it implicitly allowed to be unleashed in the following decades. Free of the constraints of copyright legislation, newspapers and periodicals seized the moment. Their unforeseen triumph in altering American textuality over a short lapse of time speaks to the relevance of popular texts to a society deeply affected by industrial capitalism and urbanization. Of course, the irony of the antebellum production and consumption of nonbook publications is that, in spite of their ephemeral and popular character, they made a lasting impression on the formation of American culture in the nineteenth century. Quite different from the so-called great works of literature, yet not without creativity, popular media fostered changes in the world of cultural goods. In essence, the new print culture was as much an agent of transformation as the result of concomitant changes in the economic and social conditions.

The primary task of the subsequent chapters is to propose a revisionist approach to the formative years of American democracy by chronicling the circus atmosphere that filled the print culture of the time. Historians of the diffusion of information in the nineteenth century have generally regarded books and newspapers as engines of nationalism and social cohesion.[18] This study offers a different perspective: it is less concerned with the notion of a national public—fictive or real—and the expansion of communications than with the playfulness and sometimes rowdiness of the new printed materials and the reading practices they fostered.[19] To be sure, other scholars have already underscored the importance of celebrations, parades, displays, pageants, and street theater in the nineteenth-century culture. They have analyzed the political significance of parades and processions as the popular uses of public and urban space and the site of social contestation as well as the symbolism of class and gender inclusion or exclusion in the civic ceremonies of different periods of American history.[20] Few, however, have explored the link between print and public rituals. One exception is David Waldstreicher, whose study focuses on the period of the American Revolution. He argues that unruly rites of rebellion were transformed into nationalist celebrations through the mediation of print, which served to translate local action into a national future. For Waldstreicher, post-1776 print created assent out of dissent.[21]

By contrast, this study will demonstrate that the festive print of antebellum America was a site for contest. It resembled marketplace festivals far more than official feasts. What was displayed was a parody of the official book culture. Whether it took the form of gargantuan papers for public consumption or individualized spectacles of engravings for private reading, the "print upheaval" reveals the underlying tensions between the new artifacts and the traditional print order they sought to displace. Reading was not just a measurable ability but rather a contested terrain where social differences were exposed and opposite values confronted.

It is hardly to be expected that the present assessment of American cultural transformation will meet the agreement of all book historians and scholars of the nineteenth century. Some will be eager to identify either forerunners or heirs of this carnivalesque print culture in order to challenge the idea of a passage and a formative process. The focus of this study, however, remains the appreciation of a moment of change and renewal, when one joked about the printed word long held most sacred. The resulting cultural rift between popular and legitimate material made reading a controversial activity. There certainly remained a powerful rhetoric that boasted of the democratization of reading in Jacksonian America. But far more than the construction of a common public, the explosion of printed experiments helped draw lines of social differentiation where gender played a critical role.[22] The ephemeral printed word of the pre–Civil War decades thus became the stage of collective representations, transforming a widening reading public not into a homogeneous mass but rather into a multiplicity of publics whose tastes were acknowledged and valued by publishers eager to establish loyalty for their products.

The direction of this endeavor has benefited from studies by both book historians and literary scholars. In many ways it was informed by inquiries in the flourishing field of the history of the book. It certainly reflects the shift of emphasis of the French scholarship of *l'histoire du livre* from books to reading, from quantitative studies of book production, distribution, and circulation to qualitative studies of the activity of reading and the interactions of texts and readers.[23] At the same time, this work departs from bibliographical studies by suggesting that printed materials were cultural goods produced and consumed in a context of other social and cultural activities. Both readers and critics of the popular print culture associated the activity of reading with various forms of public and private entertainment. This study, therefore, tells a story of reading within a broader set of cultural practices, and it poses as part of the future of book history a potential contribution to and dialogue with the history of leisure, the social and cultural history of work and play.

It also shares with literary scholars a concern for the textual fabric of past experience. However, the present approach differs from literary studies because of the deliberate choice of texts that would often be labeled as subliterary or paraliterary, as well as a greater emphasis on readers and their practice of reading than on authors. Moreover, the focus is on the social meaning of the production of popular reading matter in addition to the creation of meaning by an individual reader interacting with a text. For the purpose of contextualizing the practice of reading, the new, popular printed texts and the prescriptive literature on uses of print are set against the mental outlook of men and women readers in a society increasingly transformed by industrialization and urbanization in the pre–Civil War decades.

If compared with the history of other cultural activities, the conclusions here indicate important differences from other scholars' assessments of a cultural bifurcation in nineteenth-century America. For instance, in a delightful study of the theater and the opera, Lawrence Levine describes a gradual shift from a universal common culture to a "bifurcated culture" as elitism developed. He argues that a permanent cultural distinction between highbrow culture and lowbrow culture—and consequent social separation—did not occur before the end of the nineteenth century.[24] By looking at the practice of reading, this study suggests that a cultural chasm occurred much earlier than the case of the theater would let us assume. A cultural hierarchy of highbrow and lowbrow publications was in place before the Civil War, even though social distinctions of reading were probably less immutable than the later classification of other cultural activities because, unlike theatergoing, reading did not require the attribution of a specific public space.

In addition to a discrepancy in the chronology of cultural bifurcation, the argument presented here contrasts with Levine's conclusions in yet another manner: the place of gender in the process of social categorization. While the print carnival encouraged the formation of discrete clusters of newspaper and periodical patrons, gender represented a critical line of distinction in the reading public. In fact, the differentiation of reading by gender was probably even more salient and less permeable as antebellum publishers and readers contributed to the creation of a separate sphere of print culture for women.

This study does not pretend to give an exhaustive account of the abundance and diversity of innovative antebellum publications and the popular uses they fostered. Nonetheless, it covers a variety of formats in order to apprehend the heteroglot exuberance of the carnivalesque print culture from the 1830s to the 1850s. Priority is given to a textual analysis of what was read, whereas readers' diaries, journals, and letters are used only occasionally.[25] This is in no way a rejection of reader-response criticism, but the argument and the material selected for this research preclude such an approach for two reasons. First, unlike book reading, accounts of periodical reading are rare if one excludes those forged by publishers eager to advertise their products. Second, the success, however short-lived, of the new print media is believed to be a more telling response than the isolated comment by individuals.

Chapter 1 presents the genesis of textual transformation in Jacksonian America and analyzes the historical context within which the new regime of print emerged. The exorbitant display of printed materials that opened print to a blend of old and new uses underscores both the transformative power of texts and the in-betweenness of the period. Marked by the transgression of traditional norms and the sacredness of the word, yet not as stratified as it was to become fifty years later, the culture of antebellum America exhibits all the signs of liminality.

Chapters 2, 3, 4, and 5 examine separate case studies of new genres of popular publications. Each of them illustrates how a particular niche was constructed within the literary marketplace and underscores the link between a print medium and its implied audience. Yet together those case studies stress both the diversification of the print culture—the existence of different media for different tastes—and the commonality of all popular forms of printed matter.

Chapter 2 discusses the success of the *New York Herald* in packaging sensational disasters, catastrophes, and crimes as daily news to be purchased for a penny. By publicizing the horrors of private life, James Gordon Bennett's paper participated in the rituals of role reversal and turned the world of print inside out. The mammoth weeklies *Brother Jonathan* and the *New World,* published in New York City in the 1840s, are the subject of Chapter 3. These spectacular leviathans resembled literary museums of oddities and curiosities. Their short-lived accomplishment was to laugh at the printed word and introduce a volatile parade on paper.

Chapter 4 examines a selection of giftbooks that were published in Boston and Philadelphia. These popular "tokens of friendship" combined poetry and prose with delicate engravings for a targeted audience of young, middle-class women. As objects and commodities that served to mediate personal and social relationships, they sealed the bonds between sentimentality and the marketplace. In turn, the giftbooks or literary annuals altered the world of print in the nineteenth century by capitalizing on sensory experience and pleasure reading. Chapter 5 focuses on *Godey's Lady's Book,* a Philadelphia monthly fashion magazine featuring hand-colored steel engravings. These icons of femininity and ladyhood point to the distinctive character of women's textual emergence. The antebellum feminization of a branch of the periodical press reflects not only the cultural empowerment of middle-class women but also the creation of a separate sphere of print culture.

Finally, Chapter 6 looks at this period of print transformation from a different angle than the other chapters. It takes us from lowbrow to highbrow, examining the condemnation of the new media by the learned class and discussing the proper uses of print that antebellum reformers sought to enforce through normative discourse. In numerous advice books for young men and young women, moral stewards enjoined their audience from reading with no other purpose than pleasure. They proscribed popular reading along with the amusements of card playing, gambling, and theatergoing. Admittedly, their intention was not to curb the flourishing business of publishing but instead to ensure that the readers' self-discipline and self-control would counter the pernicious forces of the literary marketplace.

An ideological debate thus arose in the pre–Civil War decades that centered around print innovations and the efficacy of popular reading. Genteel letters were to condemn popular heresies, even though respectable publishing eventually adopted successful commercial features of the "cheap and light" publications. Praised by some as the epitome of democracy and deplored by others as the declension of culture, the new printed artifacts participated in the social formation of antebellum America. As the carnival entered the printed page, it momentarily helped release social tensions and allowed the renewal of the print culture. At the same time, it embodied the coming together of commerce and culture. This book sets out to chronicle that ephemeral and carnivalesque marketplace festival in pre–Civil War America.

CHAPTER 1

The Elusive Reading Revolution

Gertrude was astonished; since the day when she had persisted in leaving
his house, Mr. Graham had never asked her to read to him; but, obedient to the
summons, she presented herself, and, taking the seat which Belle had vacated near
the door, commenced with the ship-news, and, without asking any questions, turned to
various items of intelligence, taking them in the order which she knew Mr. Graham
preferred. . . . He remarked, "This seems like old times, doesn't it, Gertrude?"
Maria Susanna Cummins, *The Lamplighter* (1854)

When the young heroine of the 1854 best-seller *The Lamplighter* de-
cided to take a teaching job and move out of the Graham household,
she defied the patriarchal authority of her protector; her eventual
return in the second half of the novel not only concludes her quest
for independence but also validates the middle-class home and the
ideology of domesticity. Such a turning point in the female bildungs-
roman is appropriately symbolized by the character's reading behavior. Whereas more frivolous girls in the novel are scorned for their
inability to find the leading article or for reading too fast, the educated and sincere Gertrude aptly performs a traditional role.

Maria Susanna Cummins's narrative thus portrays a situation
where reading aloud creates a bond between family members. By
the same token, the gendered character of the newspaper—which
is inscribed with political and commercial news, that is, matters of
the male public sphere—is momentarily mitigated by the artifice of
mixed company and a female voice. This might indicate that beyond
the self-assertiveness and emancipation of female fictional characters, little had changed in the parlors of mid-nineteenth-century

Americans. Scenes similar to the one in *The Lamplighter* could for a brief moment sustain the illusion that a return to old times and a well-ordered world of print was possible. Indeed, the practice of reading aloud continued to be an important female function well into the later part of the nineteenth century.[1] Such portrayals, for which Thomas C. Leonard has coined the term "Parlor Fallacy," exalted the newspaper as the medium of familial interaction, where one read and the others listened. Communal reading of the news in the family home may in fact have become a thing of the past by the middle of the nineteenth century, when self-absorbed readers, alone and silent, failed to interact with one another.[2] Ironically, Cummins's novel itself participated in the making of a much different reading habit, silent and solitary, within the intimacy of the reader's own space. One instance of the solitary consumption of *The Lamplighter* appeared in the 1854 diary of Francis Bennett Jr., a young clerk in Gloucester, Massachusetts, who sat up and read in the novel late at night and even stayed at home from church on Sunday morning to finish reading the book.[3]

The historical context in which the new regime of print emerged thus supported the popular print media that fostered new reading practices while simultaneously allowing for enduring representations of traditional, collective reading. Within the longer narrative of American print culture, the pre–Civil War decades witnessed a passage of print upheaval. The coexistence, and sometimes contradiction, of old and new uses of print points to the in-betweenness of the period, a pivotal phase between, on the one hand, the early republic, when the "mediation of print" made a reader a citizen and vice versa, and, on the other hand, the late nineteenth century, when the "magazine revolution" made a reader a consumer and vice versa.[4] The historical moment defined by the antebellum period constituted an important space for change and renewal in American culture. It permitted publishing innovations to rise and fall and witnessed a multifaceted inversion of the authority of the word. In effect, the silent revolution of typesetting involved something more complex than the simple eradication of tradition and the making of entirely new practices. Instead, the interdependence of opposite uses of print came to characterize the liminal zone of antebellum publishing and its ambivalence toward both the commercialization of letters and the democratization of reading.

The story of what Frank Luther Mott has labeled the "Great Revolution in Publishing" is fairly familiar.[5] By mid-century, one of its enthusiastic chroniclers was Samuel G. Goodrich, alias Peter Parley, author of children's books and successful Boston publisher. Goodrich commented on the changing landscape of publishing in his 1856 autobiography, in which he praised the progress in print as an upward "march of civilization," while emphasizing the lost "reverence" for books and newspapers—no longer scarce—and the new hastiness in the act of reading. His detailed account of the American world of print, what it used to be, and its transformation during the first half of the nineteenth century represents a prime source for the publishing history of the period. "The whole consumption of books in this country is probably not far from seventeen millions of dollars annually!" said Goodrich. "This, of course, leaves out the newspaper and periodical press, which circulates annually six millions of copies, and five hundred millions of separate numbers!"[6] Some scholars believe that Goodrich's estimates of book production even err on the conservative side, while his calculation of the relative increase of American literature, as compared with British literature, might have been too optimistic.

Yet the numbers are telling. It was in the antebellum era and not in the 1880s and the 1890s that the United States faced its first information explosion. Americans had the highest per capita newspaper circulation in the world. In New York City alone, the average per day circulation of dailies in 1850 was over 153,000 for a population of about 500,000; the London dailies circulated far fewer, only 63,000 for a population of 2.3 million. In contrast, it was the success of illustrated weekly magazines that characterized the English history of mass communications.[7] The American democratization of reading prompted comments from many foreign visitors. The British traveler Alexander Mackay wrote that in the 1840s "all Americans read and write" and newspapers are well spread. Frances Trollope had made similar remarks in 1832, noting with her legendary prejudice the ubiquity of newspapers and periodical trash. According to Trollope, from the merchant to the servant, "they are all too actively employed to read, except at such broken moments as may suffice for a peep at a newspaper." However, she also commented on Americans' fondness for novels. Literacy rates remained relatively stable throughout the first half of the nineteenth century. In the early 1850s America's adult white literacy rate was 90 percent, while Britain's adult literacy rate was about 60 percent.[8]

To be sure, the volume of the publishing explosion represents only a partial account of what happened in the pre–Civil War years, as Goodrich was well aware. His estimate of the publishing industry is also testimony to the emergence of new print media, mostly periodicals, that added qualitative changes to the sheer numbers of book production. Goodrich considered the period from 1830 to 1840 an "era of great and positive development," the "era of Annuals," the "era of the establishment of the Penny Press" (whether for good or ill), and also "the era in which monthly and semi-monthly Magazines began to live and thrive among us." He noted a period of prosperity and expansion from 1840 to 1850, "marked by the production of numerous works richly illustrated by steel and wood engravings." From 1850 to 1856, "pictorial-sheet literature [was] brought to a climax in every form, up to the blanket-folio." In addition, this was "the millennial era of Spiritual Literature," as well as "the climax of the Thrilling, Agonizing Literature," mocked by some as "the new Sensation Book" and "a most Astounding Tale."[9]

The concept of a publishing revolution thus indicates radical changes both in volume and in character. Cheap books and periodicals were flooding the country during the second quarter of the nineteenth century. Whereas the eighteenth-century print culture had been the province of gentlemen and clergymen, new printed matter had now begun to appeal to the masses, men and women. In place of rare, expensive, and revered books, a multitude of news sheets, magazines, and inexpensive paperbacks were available in antebellum America. The once well-ordered and controlled world of print had exploded, catering to a multifaceted reading public. Because these popular periodicals might have provided ephemeral entertainment rather than sound knowledge, nineteenth-century Americans perceived the cultural turmoil of the 1830s and 1840s as a mixed blessing. Most of them applauded the widening public access to print, which benefited both men and women. Likewise, they welcomed the instructive and civilizing occupation of reading. Yet praise was not unanimous. Moral stewards and cultural spokesmen voiced fears that the sudden popularization of print endangered a more legitimate culture.

When the written word spread to the "million," the age of Jackson featured something different from a "democratization of gentility." The emerging vernacular print culture revealed an importation of new and older patterns of entertainment and popular beliefs into the printed word, rather than merely a cultural loss or "degentrification."[10] In other words, the transformation of the world of print reflected a process of popularization that had important cultural and social consequences. Although all classes of Americans might have shared the benefits of universal literacy and increasingly affordable reading matter, print itself acted as a catalyst in the antebellum cultural divide. The power of the word was double-edged and split the community of readers as the reading public widened. Behind the powerful rhetoric that boasted of a democratic participation in a unified print culture, nineteenth-century Americans used the printed word to draw distinctions of class and gender.

Both textual representations of popular reading and contextual responses to those representations leave no doubt that a rupture took place in the history of American print culture during the antebellum period. Yet the question remains whether the essence of the change is best conveyed by the term "reading revolution," for the old and the new were both featured in the mid-century culture. Publishing innovations did not cause the displacement of all former uses of print. Neither the outburst of printed material targeted at each audience nor the individualization of reading habits precluded readers' acting out traditional roles as communal readers of a shared medium. In such a case, the idea of a revolution in reading might not be entirely suitable.

The German historian Rolf Engelsing first introduced the concept of a *Leserevolution* in his study of the reading habits of eighteenth-century Bremen bourgeois. Engelsing argued that a reading revolution took place at the end of the eighteenth century as a result of the new availability of books and periodicals. Bremen bourgeois were reading periodicals and newspapers "extensively" by 1800, whereas their countrymen had been reading the Bible, almanacs, and devotional works "intensively" until around 1750.[11] Historians of the American book trade have borrowed the concept and linked the "reading revolution" to other revolutions such as the American Revolution, the industrial revolution, the market revolution, the transportation revolution, or the communication revolution.

To be sure, several scholars have challenged the notion of a definitive shift from intensive to extensive reading and have found evidence for the persistence of intensive reading practices in the period of print abundance.[12] For instance, Cathy N. Davidson argues that reading novels such as Susanna Rowson's *Charlotte Temple* could provide "as much of an emotional or spiritual experience as did the earlier intensive reading of the Bible." Davidson describes a reading revolution in the early republic that featured both a broadening reading public and a new literary genre. She suggests that the novel embodied a subversive ideology and provided the female reader with life experience and that "extensive" reading of numerous novels did not represent a passive form of consumption.[13] Similarly, William J. Gilmore observes that both a communication revolution and a reading revolution occurred when print entered the rural world of the upper Connecticut River valley. Reading became a "necessity of life," an essential vehicle of information, by the early part of the nineteenth century. In turn, the traditional web of community life was irremediably disrupted by the intrusion of print culture.[14]

Generally, however, while arguing that the nature of a reading revolution transcends the simple dichotomy of intensive and extensive, scholars of books and reading have accepted the idea of a "second" revolution of the book (the first refers to Gutenberg), which took place around the end of the eighteenth century and the beginning of the nineteenth century. Historical studies have further shifted the emphasis from the quantitative aspects of the publishing boom to the context in which the multitude of books were received. Most notably, these studies point out the continued primacy of oral communication in an age of print abundance, particularly the undeniable success of the public lecture and the lyceum.[15] Nonetheless, no one would deny that a radical change occurred, even though habits of intensive reading and oral communication persisted in the new era. In effect, the period of transformation between the 1780s and the 1850s has been treated either as an epilogue to the traditional print culture or a prelude to the subsequent mass culture.[16] Variations of the so-called modernization theory have stressed a broad shift from scarcity to abundance, from collective to individual, from traditional to modern, from religious to secular, from intensive to extensive.[17]

But any emphasis on a world that has been lost and sacrificed on the altar of progress risks, first, minimizing the importance of the period of transition and, second, overlooking altogether the continuities with past uses of print and the construction of new sociabilities around the printed word. One objective of this book is to compensate for such disregard by devoting full attention to detailed features of the new print culture. This is particularly important because historians have tended to dismiss the short-lived experiments in unusual media simply as timid forerunners of more noteworthy mass products of the late nineteenth century.[18] My intention is not to argue that antebellum innovations in print were fully realized but rather to point out that it is precisely this in-betweenness of the period that deserves further treatment.

However one looks at it, the reading revolution is rather elusive. Stretched over decades, it resembles what Raymond Williams has called the "Long Revolution," that is, a genuine revolution, transforming people and institutions, yet difficult to define because of its uneven action over a long period and because the values and meanings needed to comprehend the revolution are themselves part of this process of change.[19] During this pre–Civil War transformation American readers negotiated the radical alterations in print culture while at the same time imitating and reappropriating traditional reading habits. But the full significance of the antebellum passage can be grasped only in the context of the longer narrative of print culture, for which it is useful briefly to survey the evolution of books and reading in the colonial era and the early republic.

The American devotion to print resulted from a perennial Protestant commitment to the written word and a republican ideology of virtuous knowledge and educated citizens. In early American history both religious and political pretexts fostered high literacy rates for an adult white population. In comparison with Europe, Puritan New England did not have "dark corners of the land," that is, regions untouched by print culture.[20] The assumption has been that most seventeenth-century New Englanders could read. Kenneth Lockridge, however, has challenged such belief, finding half of the adult male population and most of the women to have been illiterate. Lockridge bases his conclusion on a thorough study of signatures on New England wills from 1640 to 1800.[21] But other scholars have emphasized the distinction between the ability to sign and the ability to read, arguing that more New Englanders could read than could write. Additional studies of New England women's literacy have also brought an upward revision of Lockridge's conservative figures.[22]

Beyond mere questions of measurable literacy, the issue of access to the world of print, whether direct or mediated, has drawn differing views. In contrast to Lockridge, David D. Hall argues that seventeenth-century New Englanders were at ease in the world of print because of the Puritan religion of the book. A common language and a collective mentality bound ministers and parishioners. Hall further observes that the people of seventeenth-century New England "eagerly read street ballads on sensational events, but also treasured Bibles." Since all ages, all sexes, rich and poor, were expected to read the Scriptures, the aura of the Word had permeated collective belief. Hall defines the seventeenth-century print culture as "traditional," as it was entwined with an oral culture and shared by all social classes. The pace of reading was slow, the same books were read and reread, and steady sellers predominated.[23]

While historians of early America still debate the extent of literacy in seventeenth-century New England, they also suggest that literacy levels in other colonies lagged behind those in the Puritan colonies. Nonetheless, literacy rates both North and South, though admittedly with regional variations, rose progressively throughout the eighteenth century. By the nineteenth century, the limited literacy of colonial times had given way to higher levels. Most scholars agree that an almost universal literacy appeared among the northern white population at the beginning of the nineteenth century and that the difference between male and female literacy rates was decreasing. This was mainly the work of a republican ideology.[24]

The revolutionary era is often remembered as an intense period for print, exemplified by the debate over the Stamp Act, the distribution of Paine's *Common Sense*, the seditious pamphlet literature and the intercolonial communication channels, the written Constitution, and the fight for a free press and the First Amendment.[25] In his analysis of the cultural meaning of letters in the eighteenth century, Michael Warner points out that during the 1760s Americans developed a public print discourse that integrated print with an emergent republican ideology and made it indispensable to political life. The rebellious colonists redefined print as "a technology of publicity, having an essentially civic and emancipatory character."[26] In addition, publications represented a virtuous shield against tyranny, corruption, and private vice. Although he tends to overstate the impersonality of an abstract public, Warner convincingly argues that this late-eighteenth-century public print discourse reached beyond the learned few and gave authority to the many. Both the institutions of a representative republican polity and a written constitution further confirmed this authority. The eighteenth-century political public, or emerging public sphere, was a reading public.[27]

Not only a powerful weapon in the American War of Independence, print also provided a common basis for the building of the new republic. American print culture and political culture were deeply interrelated. Universal access to knowledge appeared to be a prerequisite for an independent, virtuous white population, which had to include well-informed republican mothers. Virtuous women of the early republic were, then, the target of advice on what to read and what not to read (presumably fiction).[28]

Since the new republican ideology required informed citizens, newspaper reading exceeded the province of an enlightened elite and became a duty for all white men. Learning in the eighteenth-century republic was thought to be acquisition of extensive knowledge based on wide reading, in imitation of enlightened republican gentlemen such as Benjamin Franklin and Thomas Jefferson. Franklin's middling class of readers comprised neither the many who read almanacs nor the few who read books but rather craftsmen and tradesmen, who required new kinds of books and reading institutions. Franklin's exceptionally wide reading was an archetype of the new extensive reading pattern and a model for republican citizens. And such extensive, secular, informative newspaper reading was in sharp contrast to the intensive reading associated with Christian piety.[29]

By the early decades of the nineteenth century, the American religious and political print ideology was increasingly heterogeneous. Political divisions and the breakdown of Protestant religion into denominations failed to provide Americans with a textual consensus. Ironically, print itself became the very instrument of fragmentation. The explosion of print in the 1820s served new waves of evangelical proselytism and inflamed what Jon Butler has described as the "antebellum spiritual hothouse."[30]

Unlike Europe, where secularism was triumphing, in the United

States it was a religious momentum that carried with it the rise of print culture. As David P. Nord remarks, "Perhaps more than anything else, the missionary impulse—first in purely religious crusades and then in more secular reform movements—lay at the foundation of the popularization of print in the nineteenth century."[31] Both the American Bible Society and the American Tract Society performed pioneering work in mass printing and mass distribution of the written word. Soon all evangelical denominations flooded the country with inexpensive publications: tracts, pamphlets, hymnbooks, magazines, and newspapers. Underlying this growth of popular evangelical literature was the Protestant belief that, in the words of two historians of American religion, "reading was a spiritual necessity, a sacred rite at the heart of personal religion, and that the printed page was itself efficacious."[32] Indeed, the religious press of the nineteenth century successfully combined a fervent Protestant belief in the Word with a democratic urge to multiply readers. Until recently, book historians had not fully examined this emergence of a democratic religious culture in print.

Nathan O. Hatch observes that "virtually nonexistent in 1800, religious periodicals had, by 1830, become the grand engine of a burgeoning religious culture, the primary means of promotion for, and bond of union within, competing religious groups."[33] There was a sort of infatuation with the printed word among these groups. Conversion efforts depended on the quantity of books and newspapers that circulated; the printed word, as much as or even more than the spoken word, became a means of persuasion. Hatch argues that religious movements remained at the cutting edge in the new age of mass communications. They contributed to the introduction of the vernacular and the colloquial in print. The fate of the spoken word was bound to that of the printed word. As one preacher vehemently told his audience, "The Pulpit and the Press are inseparably connected. . . . The Press, then, is to be regarded with a sacred veneration and supported with religious care. The press must be supported or the pulpit falls."[34]

At the beginning of the nineteenth century, the distinctive evangelical faith in the printed word combined with and intensified by the explosion of print generated a vernacular print culture. As the Great Awakening of the eighteenth century had contributed to the transformation of American oratory, so the Second Great Awakening helped increase the consumption of the printed word.[35] Nineteenth-century religious print further transformed the power of the word to disseminate a religion of the heart, more emotional than intellectual, and to contribute to the formation of separate denominations.[36] In place of eighteenth-century print discourse's symbolic representation of rationality and enlightenment, a new print culture—first religious, then secular—emerged in the early nineteenth century to serve the cause of popular belief.

When historians of book publishing have emphasized the breakdown of the traditional world of print and described the shift from cohesion to fragmentation, they have often pointed at technological change as the cause. Yet even historians of technology have begun to challenge this technological determinism. Their conclusions suggest that the popularization of reading stimulated as much as it resulted from technological innovations. The technology of papermaking and printing improved tremendously during the second quarter of the nineteenth century; steam power and rotary presses made it possible to print more reading matter at a lower price.[37] But machinery alone could not create the demand.

Ronald J. Zboray has revisited the argument of technological determinism and observed discrepancies between the actuality of the reading public—which was located primarily in the Northeast—and the publishers' fictive construct of a mass readership of novels. The supposedly "democratic" public did not share homogeneous reading practices or equal access to print in the age of economic inequality. Zboray notes that antebellum innovations in printing technology did not bring a considerable drop in the price of books. A hardcover book continued to cost from 75 cents to $1.25, while the price of paperbacks ranged between 12.5 cents and 63 cents—the most common price being 50 cents. Accordingly, although the publishers' glowing accounts of antebellum book readership trumpeted an alleged democratization of reading, books in fact stood outside the reach of most workers.[38]

Perhaps bound books alone, or novels alone, do not hold the clues to understanding the nature of change in antebellum publishing. Neither the economic and technological context nor a single literary genre suffices to explain the transformation that American print culture underwent from the 1830s to the 1850s. Because the essence of that transformation lies in large part with nonbook publications and their materiality, to grasp the full measure of the democratization of print in the nineteenth century one needs to consider the format as well as the content and volume of popular publications. Whereas literary scholars have analyzed the plots and thematic conventions of popular novels and historians of book publishing have quantified the output of the boom years, the present endeavor is to decipher the somewhat transgressive manipulation of graphic forms in ephemeral publications of this period. Antebellum newspapers and magazines were not only recycling an older popular lore but also conspicuously displaying a distinctive outlook that custodians of culture perceived as debasing the traditional authority of the printed word.

Subsequent chapters illustrate how a process of transgression and inversion was at work on the printed page. The popular print media, while privatizing the consumption of publications, rendered public what was previously thought to belong in the private realm. Likewise, the feminine sphere of letters, which was designed to be separate from and untouched by the masculine sphere of business and politics, was paradoxically co-opted by the marketplace of printed goods, thus complicating the distinction of gendered spheres. Even the act of reading, which was previously associated with the "manly" art of intellectual pursuit, was now suspected of emasculating the self-absorbed reader. The ephemeral role reversal that was played out in print during the second quarter of the nineteenth century therefore has a significance that concerns not only the history of books but also the broader history of culture. For a historical moment, American men and women rejoiced in a gigantic carnival in print, whose purpose was not only to release collective energy during the take-off decades but also to vocalize their appropriation of the power of the word by disrupting the order of print.

The newspapers, magazines, and annuals studied here were for the most part published in New York City, Philadelphia, and Boston during the 1830s, 1840s, and 1850s. As William Charvat has observed, the three northeastern seaports dominated the antebellum publishing industry. Even though the new metropolis of New York was already beginning to take the lead of the periodical trade, the more settled publishing environments of Boston and Philadelphia offered fierce competition against the printing innovations of Gotham well into the 1850s. But the American newspaper, which was born in Boston and matured in Philadelphia during the colonial period, was popularized in New York City in the early nineteenth century.[39] Certainly the United States was still predominantly rural and increasingly turned toward the interior in the course of its aggressive westward expansion. Nonetheless, an analysis of publishing innovations and the character of the new cultural goods warrants a focus on the urban Northeast. It was indeed in the northeastern cities that new fads were introduced before being imitated in other parts of the nation.[40] Sometimes a periodical succeeded in establishing a national distribution, as in the case of ladies' magazines, yet for the most part the construction of new communities of readers began locally around a metropolitan paper.

The very nature of periodicals published at regular intervals is particularly significant for an understanding of the new reading practices. Antebellum America was witnessing the creation of social bonds within the reading audience of a particular daily, weekly, or monthly journal. On his travels in the United States, Alexis de Tocqueville observed the importance of newspapers in American society, saying that a newspaper created an association of habitual readers.[41] Periodicals encouraged new circles of sociability and communities of readers. In so doing, however, the new media were powerful accomplices in the process of differentiating reading publics along the critical lines of class and gender. Hence they provide historians with a window onto the emerging taxonomy and cultural alignment of the mid-nineteenth century.

New publications at the time bore the reprobative label "cheap and light." Of course, cheap printed materials were not completely a creation of the nineteenth century. As early as the era of Cotton Mather, almanacs, broadsides, and various ephemera were feeding the public taste for ballads, sensational pamphlets, and execution accounts. But they remained marginal to the print discourse of the seventeenth and eighteenth centuries and have long been neglected by book historians, who narrowed the meaning of "book" to "valuable books."[42] The nineteenth-century world of print was different both in volume and in character. Had the "cheap and light" publications of antebellum America been little different from their colonial counterparts, their number alone would not have moved them from the periphery to the center. But because they were far bolder in their outlook as well as numerically more visible, they could not be dismissed as marginal.

Whether enthusiastically celebrated or vehemently condemned

at the time, the cheapest and most popular forms of print deserve our attention. The qualifier "popular" indicates that these forms reached a mass reading public, even if their publication was short-lived and the public heterogeneous.[43] Popular periodicals belonged to the people and represented the reading matter of a democratic audience. But antebellum popular culture, if it exalted the democratic ideal, also embodied values of lower status. Those who grew disenchanted with democracy used "popular" to describe contemptible—perhaps even threatening—behavior. Noah Webster defined the word "people" as "the vulgar; the mass of illiterate persons; the commonality, as distinct from men of rank." Similarly, James Fenimore Cooper, the antidemocrat (or quintessential democrat, depending on one's view), associated the word "popular" with the "populace," the "lower sort," the unsophisticated "public." Both Webster and Cooper grew worried about insurgent democracy while participating themselves in the democratization of American culture as popular speakers and writers.[44]

Most scholars of popular culture would probably agree that the "popular" is best defined by what it is not—that is, not learned or refined. At the same time, popular culture in the nineteenth century was not the realm of traditional, customary, indigenous folkways and behaviors that scholars would rediscover with nostalgia a century later. It was not untouched by the marketplace, nor was it untouched by the perennial aura of the written word. American popular culture must be reexamined as a permeable blend of older traditions and newer needs, which testify to a process of cultural reappropriation of and exchange with the learned culture.[45]

By the mid-nineteenth century popular culture bordered on commercial culture. Nonetheless, such a culture was not shared by the entire American people. Popular culture was neither classless nor gender-blind: as "popular," it was set apart, defined through its difference, as one level in a hierarchy of culture. The history of popular forms of print and the reading practices they fostered should therefore include not only a cultural category but also the historicity of a categorizing process. The study of popular culture warrants a recognition of cultural dissent and potential strife. It further sheds light on the emergence of antagonistic cultural spheres in the "era of the common man."[46]

Since the 1960s historians of antebellum America have questioned the "egalitarian myth" of Jacksonian democracy. Labor and social historians have emphasized the inequality of social conditions and the emerging class awareness of the working people during those years of economic turmoil and growing industrialization and urbanization. Whereas social historians observe a polarization of two or three classes, cultural historians emphasize the cultural bifurcation, particularly in the theater, and a hierarchy of cultural levels. Even historians of American religion recognize the growing religious diversity in this period, during which the Protestant consensus was challenged by massive Catholic immigration. Antebellum Protestantism had long since broken up into denominations, and some historians regard the evangelical movement as the ideological work of industrial moralizers, who used religious revivals to disguise fundamental shifts in class relations.[47]

Similarly, the idea of democratic politics has failed to provide a common thread to bind the fragmented past described by social and cultural historians. In the literature on political history, the old story of a "Jacksonian revolution" has given way to new reports of "party politics" and "partisan imperative." Despite repeated calls for historical synthesis, studies of nineteenth-century urban democracy have favored an ethnocultural and class analysis, and inclusive labels have capitulated before quantitative evidence of political warfare. Since the synthesis that Arthur M. Schlesinger Jr. offered in 1945, the age of Jackson has been explained in terms of class distinctions, though with far less celebratory overtones. It is rather the racism of Old Hickory's partisans that has grabbed the attention of researchers.[48]

In this historical context of growing inequality and division, it should come as no surprise that antebellum print culture was tailored according to the various tastes of an increasingly differentiated reading public. When printed matter was plentiful—when "every table [was] littered with annuals and monthly and weekly journals"—and books were outdone by periodicals in the public's favor and purchasing power, popular demand began to constitute a force of production instead of representing readers as passive recipients.[49] Despite the lamentations of those who mourned a bygone era, a lost world of print, and predicted days of doom, the new landscape was not total chaos. A bounty of newspapers and magazines catering to different segments of the reading public displaced the traditionally more univocal print discourse, yet without atomizing society, as some have argued.[50] Rather, the result was the creation of new "textual classes," the building of new associations around common uses of print. These textual classes in turn served as blueprints for social classification by age, gender, social status, and ethnicity. The significance of this transformation raises broader questions about the relation of texts to society or, more specifically, about the relation of textual classes to social classes.[51]

Popular print culture of the 1830s and 1840s included literary genres that were not directly aligned on class but did reflect a process of social formation along class and gender lines. For instance, to explain the birth of the penny press or the new illustrated magazines by the rise of the middle class may not be entirely persuasive, for although the popularization of print reflected a dissemination of the middle-class praise of reading, the particular forms it took constituted a transgression of middle-class practices.[52] Indeed, while most print media of the antebellum era bore the attributes of class identification, their upsurge cannot be tied to the emergence of one social class. In this, the case of American literary production before the Civil War agrees with the conclusions of theorists of the "literary field" and the "institution of literature," who have questioned any simple homology between social classes and literary genres and in so doing have impaired a trademark of an earlier Marxist sociology of literature.[53]

The question, then, is whether popular printed matter was produced for the working class as well as the middle class, or whether material conditions and social status precluded certain groups of men and women from reading the same texts. Antebellum book culture—next to work, residence, and consumption patterns—might have contributed to the distinction of the middle class. However, the new class of printed matter—cheap, ephemeral, pictorial, and serialized—opened print to new, unorthodox uses. Precisely at a time when usages rather than occupation and income were signs of class distinction, American working-class and middle-class men and women came to transform the traditional print culture and simultaneously constructed distinctive cultural configurations within which they defined themselves as groups in opposition to other groups. The breakdown of textual consensus emphasized the intrinsic cultural divide of antebellum society. Instead of blurring growing divisions, the practice of reading contributed to an ongoing process of social stratification.

To complicate things, as reading matter confirmed social distinctions and defined levels of culture, some newspapers and periodicals were marketed in a way that reached diverse social groups. This suggests that cultural reappropriation could occur whenever an audience not originally targeted had access to the new media. The success of ladies' magazines among the Lowell mill girls is a case in point.[54] During periods of economic hardship, however, cultural exchanges were not available to everyone. Book readers could probably afford to share the culture of newspaper readers, but not vice versa. In addition, as whole categories of texts were increasingly gendered, crossing the gap between genders became more difficult. Newspapers remained the fief of men, while fashion magazines became the domain of women. The Civil War would temporarily shake the gender boundaries of reading: on the one hand, for example, *Godey's* increased its circulation among soldiers, while on the other, women were eager to read the papers for news of the front.[55]

Because of possible processes of either distinction or reappropriation, literary genres are not easily identified with social classes. Texts are hardly unmediated expressions of their readers' culture. Moreover, for the first half of the nineteenth century one could hardly expect a unilateral textual representation of the American working class, whose pluralism has been highlighted by labor historians. To refer to all cultural expressions of American workers as the legacy of "artisan republicanism" would be to ignore more diverse roots of the new print culture. The dominant paradigm of the language of republicanism and civic humanism may convincingly explain the resistance of workers to the encroachments of industrial capitalism, but it clearly cannot explain the workers' ardent support for the new marketplace of letters.[56] Not only did the American working-class culture transcend republicanism, republicanism also transcended the working class. In their critique of the new commercial literature, middle-class reformers rephrased the old republican ideology as well. Thus republicanism alone does not hold all the clues to the popular character of antebellum print. Rather, a more complex combination of themes, formulas, and formats contributed to the vocabulary of the new print culture, a culture much in agreement with the "nothing on compulsion" spirit of preindustrial times and

The Elusive Reading Revolution

the playful rituals of the "traditionalists," to use a term from Bruce Laurie's tripartite classification of the working classes.[57]

Instead of linking popular texts with a single political ideology, this study considers the multiple ways people read and used printed matter. Some of the inquiries of this book recall questions raised by literary theorists of reader-response criticism and of the aesthetic of reception. Unlike these theorists, however, my objective is to locate the act of reading, as an active process of producing meaning, within its historical setting. I share with literary theorists the opinion that texts do not exist outside the activity of reading and that they cannot be conceived of as embodying a fixed and authorial meaning to be impressed on passive readers. But I disagree with those who hold that a text may dissolve "into the million and one readings of individual subjects."[58] It is essential to contextualize historically the interaction between texts and readers, since the activity of reading involves the social world of the readers. Past readings or constructions of meaning can then be understood as an interplay of the texts themselves, the mental outlook of the readers, and the prohibitions and precepts inscribed in the texts or expressed through institutions aiming at regulating behaviors.

Tony Bennett uses the concept of "reading formation" to describe the "productive activation," or creative reception, of a given body of texts. As he concludes, "Meaning is not a *thing* that texts can *have*, but is something that can only be produced, and always differently, within the reading formations that regulate the encounters between texts and readers."[59] The best-known example is perhaps the sixteenth-century miller Menocchio's "heretic" reading of the Bible, which was discovered and analyzed by Carlo Ginzburg. In his "productive activation" of the Scriptures, Menocchio likened the creation of the world to the making of a cheese, and angels to the worms that appear in it. His use of texts was "different" from the orthodox reading, rather than "distorted," and was ultimately shaped by the miller's worldview.[60]

The present exploration of popular reading in antebellum America both elaborates on and diverges from Bennett's "reading formations." It differs from literary studies on two accounts: first, it acknowledges the historical process of change that correlates the popularization of reading with other cultural practices, and second, it underlines the collective mode of the cultural configurations and representations. Early-nineteenth-century Americans used print within a context of other cultural practices, both older and contemporary. Their approach to reading in some ways resembled their approach to playing, dancing, drinking, parading, mourning, or praying. They invented new uses of print, imitated older ones, and adjusted their oral patterns of culture to print forms. Popular reading practices in Jacksonian America, therefore, encompassed older practices of piety and entertainment as well as genteel habits. They also blended with and responded to discourses on reading that might be perceived as discursive practices themselves. On the one hand, a traditional print discourse, both religious and republican, had already been internalized and belonged to the realm of *habitus* by the beginning of the nineteenth century.[61] On the other hand, another discourse, critical of popular reading, began to emerge when quite a few Americans took notice of the outbreak of new uses of print. Hence remains of a past world of print might be detected in both the new reading practices and the new print discourse.

The critique of the popular uses of print is more fully developed in Chapter 6. Suffice it to say here that if the elusive reading revolution provoked a reaction from both moral reformers and writers, this reaction was not a completely organized counterrevolution. For one, the cultural arbiters who resisted the popularization and commercialization of letters and advocated a return to a more orderly and unified print culture were themselves using the new genres of printed matter to warn their audience against sinful behavior. Ironically, they too were complacent participants in the profitable market of literature.[62] The position of writers was particularly ambivalent. Some, like Ralph Waldo Emerson or Henry David Thoreau, were outspoken critics of the commodification of literature and proposed a retreat of literary culture from the market economy of books, though they were themselves bound by that economy, nested in what Michael T. Gilmore has called the "imbrications" and "affinities" between the literary world and the capitalist marketplace. Their critique, though, was not pointed at the marketplace per se. As Richard F. Teichgraeber has also suggested, both Emerson and Thoreau utilized the language of the market in their own writing and critique.[63]

One might want to draw conclusions regarding the potential hegemony of the market. Yet the more important point may be that the defenders of cultural legitimacy were crying foul at the spectacle of a different, exuberant, popular print culture. The target of their repeated attacks was the ephemeral material: the newspaper, the magazine, the picture book. Herman Melville, for instance, who himself hoped "to suit at once the popular and the critical taste," bitterly criticized his countrymen in 1851 because they did not care "a fig for any authors except those who write those most saleable of all books nowadays—ie—the newspapers, and magazines."[64] Edgar Allan Poe also expressed his contempt for the new media. When he resigned from his editorship of *Graham's,* he declared, "My reason for resigning was disgust at the namby-pamby character of the magazines . . . I allude to the contemptible pictures, fashion-plates, music, and love-tales."[65] Both Melville and Poe hoped to share the benefits of marketable literature and sometimes courted its readers, but they nonetheless deprecated the popular literature of their day and despised the unsophisticated segment of the reading public.

The present conclusions clearly differ from those of David S. Reynolds, who describes a shared culture in pre–Civil War America, when popular tales in pamphlets and periodicals nurtured the American Renaissance.[66] Whereas Reynolds traces the popular influence on the literary production of Hawthorne, Melville, or Poe, this book looks at the dynamics at work in the layout of the new print media and finds evidence of a definite split between, on one side, the aesthetics of the monstrous and the aesthetics of sentiment and, on the other, the views of the writers of the American Renaissance. While not immune to their zeitgeist, the classic writers—unlike successful editors like James Gordon Bennett and Nathaniel Parker Willis—did not sympathize with the taste of their fellow citizens in the street and in their parlors. The self-proclaimed custodians of cultural orthodoxy claimed a higher status for literature and dissented from the gospel of the market, yet without completely separating themselves from it. To describe the emerging polarity merely as that between an elite culture and a commercial culture, however, would be somewhat misleading, even though the schematic contrast is simple and useful. Given the pervasiveness of the marketplace, the nineteenth-century cultural dichotomy might be more accurately represented by the binary concepts of canonical and trivial, or legitimate and popular.

In any case, the bifurcation was not at all gender blind. Cultural theorists have linked the gendering of culture—"authentic" culture as masculine, mass culture as feminine—with the late-nineteenth-century split between highbrow and lowbrow.[67] But the commodification of print was already associated with the feminine before 1850. The new attributes such as cheapness, ephemerality, miscellaneousness, pictorialness, serialization, even foreignness, were related to the industrialization of publishing. One critic, Alexis de Tocqueville, concluded that "democracy not only gives the industrial classes a taste for letters but also brings an industrial spirit into literature."[68] The association of gender with the new print culture was more than an oblique attack on the alienation of industrial work, however; it was an attack on the character of the new culture itself. When unconventional uses of print were deemed unmanly, when popular publications were associated with the negative metaphor of the "public woman," the textual transformation was regarded as a violation of the social and sexual order. This, in turn, compromised the gendered separation, wrought by industrialization, of public and private spheres. In other words, although printed materials were increasingly customized separately for men and women in order to satisfy the tastes of various publics, the public sphere was threatened to be no longer the exclusive domain of men. As a result, the distinction between the public and the private blurred, and in the midst of border-crossers and ambiguous categories, two antagonistic spheres of cultural production took shape: the legitimate and the popular.

To be sure, the making of these two irreconcilable, yet interdependent, cultural spheres with conflicting perceptions of the printed word—from serious literature to entertaining print media—did not obliterate the consensus in which both were rooted, that is, a belief in the power of the word and a shared legacy of religious and political pretexts. Even though ephemeral publications were intent in their subversion of the authority of the printed word, they too capitalized on its long-established centrality in American culture. Hence the deviance of the popular newspapers and periodicals of the pre–Civil War decades had an even greater impact and accentuated the cultural divide of American society.

With the economic depression of 1857 and its concomitant social turmoil, the cultural bifurcation and the differentiation of reading audiences entered a more permanent phase. If the previous twenty-five years marked a temporary, experimental passage in the transformation of American print culture, then the 1850s marked a consolidation. In other words, the liminal phase that had turned the world of print upside down and produced a carnivalesque and festive laughter came to an end. At the same time, some of its innovations—such as illustrations and serialization—made their way into the sphere of legitimate culture. What followed was, again to use Victor Turner's terminology, the "reaggregation" phase.[69] Accordingly, the print culture of the second quarter of the nineteenth century was a vital interval between the preindustrial, traditional world and the industrial capitalism of the late nineteenth and early twentieth centuries. It could not be construed merely as an epilogue to the univocal republican print culture or a prelude to the culture industry of the turn of the century. In the liminal phase, reading took on a deeper meaning as a symbolic intertwining of associations and exclusions, sociabilities and conflicts, imitation and distinction. While the reading matter itself and its prescribed and proscribed uses testify to a differentiation in gestation, the antistructural liminality of the antebellum era sets it well apart from the state of later American culture.

To conclude, one may ponder the words of Isabella Lucy Bird, the young Englishwoman who was traveling in North America the very same year *The Lamplighter* was published. While making unfavorable remarks on a great variety of topics, she, like many of her compatriots before her, did not fail to mention that "America teems with books." Yet she could only describe cheap forms of printed materials, English reprints, reviews, and magazines. "Every one reads the newspapers and 'Harper's Magazine,'" said Bird, "and every one buys bad novels, on worse paper, in the cars and steamboats."[70] Thus in 1854 foreign visitors continued to comment on both the size of the American readership and the material aspects of the print media. Even though the publishing world was consolidated after the so-called battle of books of the 1840s and *Harper's* ranked among the "quality" magazines, the persistent impression of the ubiquity of "cheap and light" publications would indicate that the ephemeral print phenomenon of the second quarter of the nineteenth century had made a lasting mark on American print culture.[71]

CHAPTER 2

Little Sheets of News and Varieties: The Penny Wonder in New York City

*When the boat got under way, the deck looked like a school or reading
room. The "steamer" proceeded on her quiet course down the bay, while her
passengers were silently engaged with their little sheets of news and varieties. "What
an improvement this upon the past," said an elderly respectable looking gentleman near
me[.] "[F]ive years ago, sir," continued he, "such a lot of passengers would have been
very differently engaged. The men in smoking, drinking, and disputing upon
politics. The women in talking scandal or nonsense. These penny papers
have brought great good, sir, in society. They should be encouraged."*
New York Herald, *November 11, 1835*

In 1835 the *New York Herald* would not miss any opportunity to trumpet the age of democratic reading—and, implicitly, its own success. Sometimes the celebratory tone of the New York daily tended to produce a one-sided evaluation of the new reading public, as this epigraph testifies. When it described the deck of the Newark steamer as a reading room where men and women were silently engaged with their little sheets of news and varieties, the paper saw only good in the new press. It unequivocally presented reading as an enlightening activity, gender blind and performed privately, even in a public space. Such was the appearance, or at least the paper's own rhetoric. Yet a closer look at the *Herald* in its formative years reveals a different appraisal, one that sets the democratic readership at a crossroads between "dreadful pleasures," urban space, and consumer culture.

During the second quarter of the nineteenth century the daily newspaper became the epitome of both a carnivalesque ritual and a market fair, when boundaries were crossed and the private made public. Its fleshly and uncanny content partook of the moment of change that swept through American print culture before the Civil War. More than any other paper, the *Herald* succeeded in weaving a coarse canvas of sensational murders, railroad accidents, and steamboat explosions along with unlimited promotion of merchandise. The penny paper fostered the unprecedented reporting of crime news in the daily press and, by the same token, contributed to constraining criminal literature to the industrial pace of the press and market-oriented publishing. While it offered both local information and affordable pleasure, the new daily adapted earlier habits of gossip and exposure to the new social environment of the metropolis. Its gory and grotesque sheets stood on the threshold where public and private merged, where orality and print coexisted.

It all began with the first issue of the *New York Sun* on September 3, 1833. As the editor Benjamin H. Day stated, "The object of this paper is to lay before the public, at a price within the means of every one, ALL THE NEWS OF THE DAY, and at the same time afford an advantageous medium for advertising." Originally inspired by the English *Penny Magazine* published for the Society for the Diffusion of Useful Knowledge, Day's *New York Sun* was intended to circulate among a low-income reading public.[1] It challenged the former conception of a newspaper as a political editorial by introducing tales, "Police Office" items, miscellaneous stories, and "Help Wanted" notices. Local news and city gossip outnumbered foreign news. The *Sun* eventually claimed to have instituted popular journalism in the United States and to represent the first successful mass-audience journal. To be sure, it was soon imitated by other penny papers, and, most notably, the *New York Herald* emerged as a challenging competitor.

First published on May 6, 1835, the *Herald* claimed to be "equally intended for the great masses of the community—the merchant, mechanic, working people—the private family as well as the public school—the journeyman and his employer—the clerk and his principal."[2] The small four-page paper sold at a penny a day, or $3 a year, and offered both local news and mercantile information, hoping to enlarge its audience to the best men of the country. Its aggressive editor, the Scottish immigrant James Gordon Bennett, emerged as the main leader in the antebellum revolution of newspaper publishing.

Aiming at both readers and advertisers, the "penny wonder" wanted to revolutionize not only the price but also the character and the distribution methods of the American press in the Jacksonian era.[3]

The penny papers, also described as cash press, abandoned the subscription rates of $10 a year that were characteristic of the earlier commercial papers. Instead, they adopted the London plan, a circulation method based on a cash-and-carry policy. The new and cheap newspapers were sold by the single copy or by the week. Carriers on regular routes collected six cents from each customer on Saturday. Thus, without any long-term obligation, the cash newspapers were affordable for a broad, democratic audience. An 1840 editorial of a weekly paper praised cheap newspapers with the following words:

> "Subscribing for a newspaper" used to be something of a circumstance—quite an undertaking, requiring serious deliberation—with those who intended to pay. Those who do not pay, may order all the newspapers published without fear or forethought. Formerly if one ordered a paper, he was booked, for three months, at least, and however he might dislike it, was bound to continue that term, or make more of a muss, than the character of the affair warranted. Now, if one does not like his daily, he has only to pay the boy sixpence at the end of a week, and tell him to cease coming. There is no parade of ledgers, overhauling of receipts, or any such nonsense. It is the nimble sixpence that tells a quick story.[4]

Nonetheless, what best characterized the distribution of the new press was the distant "hallo," the heraldlike tone of the newsboys hawking the papers throughout the city, catching passersby and occasional readers. Often condemned as "little rascals" or "street rats," the ragged vendors of newspapers belonged to the streets as well as to the popular literature of the time. "Every calamity is so much capital to them," remarked one critical observer, "and the more awful or startling it may be, the better for their business."[5] In case of few accidents, business was very dull, and a dearth of news was often replaced by the newsboys' ingenuity. With few exceptions the little fellows were stigmatized by their shameful station in life as young delinquents and, at the same time, shrewd traders. However, a more uplifting perspective appeared in the sentimental stories that featured newsboys, as exemplified by Seba Smith's short story entitled "Billy Snub, the Newsboy," which was published in the 1843 edition of *The Gift* along

The Newsboy, *engraved by Richard W. Dodson*
after a painting by Henry Inman, in The Gift *(1843)*.
Courtesy of the American Antiquarian Society.

with an engraving by Richard W. Dodson after a painting by Henry Inman. In the story, which received the loud praise of little urchins to whom the author read it, the protagonist, Billy Snub, fights the odds of poverty and domestic violence by crying papers with industry and great success.[6] While mingling with both the virtues of hard work and the vices of the harsh and competitive newspaper business, young newsboys walked the pavement, eager to sell the latest issue. Their success was intertwined with that of the newspaper they sold. By lending their voice to the dissemination of the daily news, the young messengers hoped for a better life. In turn, the print form itself was perceived as simply a commodity.

To be sure, the newspaper became an affordable commodity. In sharp contrast to the sixpence commercial papers, the new dailies were available to the common man for just a penny. They were believed to contribute to the enlightenment of society. Unlike the papers of the 1820s—the *Advertiser,* the *Commercial,* or the *Mercantile*—the penny papers of the 1830s and 1840s were the *Star,* the *Sun,* the *Herald,* or the *Tribune.* They crusaded for the public good against political corruption and often claimed to be nonpartisan; their moral mission was to eradicate ignorance and prejudice. They voiced the public's anxiety and perceptions of danger throughout a country apparently in prosperity. For instance, the editor James Gordon Bennett was convinced that abolitionists, Catholics, bankers, foreigners, gamblers, free blacks, and vagrants of all kinds constituted an imminent danger. The purpose of his nativist and racist paper was to reform society and expose misconduct in the metropolis, particularly acts of disorder by robbers, thieves, and paupers from Great Britain. In spite of Bennett's extremist editorials, the *Herald* reached a broad popularity, even among the black community. In a critique of how little support black writers could expect from their own class compared to the success of slave narratives among a white population, playwright William Wells Brown noted that "the *N.Y. Herald* has more subscribers today and gets a larger support from the colored people than *Douglass' Monthly, The Anglo-African* and *The Pacific Appeal* put together."[7] Indeed, the *Herald* was able to appeal to a diversified reading audience by satisfying the needs of a newly urbanized population for entertainment, gossip, and the sense of a community.

While the four-page layout of the penny papers was not significantly different from earlier newspapers, in subject matter the small dailies resembled traditional almanacs, with practical information for everyone—including romance and poems, presumably for female readers. Where earlier almanacs offered wonders, predictions, astrology, moralistic stories, and medicinal cures through a combination of texts and images, so did their nineteenth-century counterpart blend science, hoaxes, and humor.[8] Likewise, the new press

Little Sheets of News

appealed to a popular reading audience, and James Gordon Bennett even commissioned woodcuts about current events in the 1830s, at a time when most dailies regarded pictures as a waste of space. The first instance was in December 1835, when reporting on the great fire of New York City, and more woodcuts came to be used in the early 1840s to show the scene of a crime, a Fourth of July celebration, a funeral, or even a fashionable ball. By the late 1840s, however, the *Herald* followed the practice of most newspapers and put an end to its use of sensational woodcuts.[9]

Unlike the almanac, however, which primarily functioned as a calendar counting time as it passed away, the newspaper was constructed around the timing of a daily narration. Moreover, crime news, the staple of the penny papers, was characteristic not of earlier almanacs but of broadsides and pamphlets. The new journalistic genre thus had ties both to almanacs and to *occasionnels*.[10] The antebellum dailies succeeded in combining the structure of time with extraordinary events. Their chronicle of isolated acts of violence or madness was paced at regular daily intervals, following the industrial regularity of the printing presses. While those events might be regarded as irrelevant to the *longue durée* of history, their publication in daily pennies inscribed them on the historical narrative of everyday life. Thus, without being any less extraordinary in its features, crime news became part of the history of commonplaces.[11]

The variety of the newspapers' content was combined with brevity. Rather than providing a commentary, news was often made up of one sentence giving brief information on duels, murders, fires, fights, drunkards, politicians, etc. These nonreferential sentences gave the reader the freedom to construct the framework of a story. Nonetheless, the act of reading was guided by implicit textual directions for the consumption of the text. For instance, blunt information of a police report embodied the social values of good or bad. The crueler the deed, the stronger the reader's emotion.[12] The narrator could also provide explicit advice for approaching the text in the form of "reading interludes." These were either titles to give the tone or editorials to frame the reader's reception of the message.[13] Editors of the penny press printed information with titles such as "A Most Horrible Murder," "Melancholy Suicide," "Extraordinary Tragedy," "Mysterious Murder," or "Singular Case." Capital characters at the head of an article of tiny print attracted the attention of the public, created sensation, and stressed the moral undertone. On September 10, 1835, the *Herald* gave an emotional heading—LAMENTABLE SUICIDE—to a cool account: "A very respectable woman, the mother of four children, cut her throat yesterday evening, in Spruce Street, and almost instantly died.—The act was done by a razor, while sitting on a chair near the bed side, yet not a drop of blood fell on the bed. She fell back at once and breathed her last in a few seconds. The cause is supposed to be a species of temporary insanity." [14] The precise and unemotional description, which predated photographic realism, intensified the horror of the act. Insanity was the only explanation offered to the reader. The editor also added that this was "the sixth or seventh sudden death happening this week." A recurring pattern of violent death, neutrally reported in a pseudoscientific style, was presented as a true fact; any emotional response in the readers was provoked by the bluntness of the news. This strategy was at the core of the *Herald*'s excellence.

The story of a murder helped the *Herald* take the lead of the press in the mid-1830s, when the scabrous Robinson-Jewett case raised its circulation from 5,000 to 15,000. On April 10, 1836, Helen Jewett, a beautiful prostitute in a house of ill fame in New York City, was killed with a hatchet and her room set on fire. The wealthy, nineteen-year-old Richard P. Robinson, who had been her companion of the evening, was the alleged murderer. The *Herald* began intensive coverage of the "Most Atrocious Murder" on April 11, 1836, and was able to provide its reading audience with "new details" and "full particulars" for weeks. Bennett took the role of journalist-detective and personally visited the scene of the crime to reveal the truth to his readers. He entertained them with minute descriptions of the mutilated body of the female victim, her bedroom, her clothes and belongings. While the investigation dragged, the paper fed the expectations of the readers with the "lives" of both the victim and the suspect. Robinson was finally acquitted after a trial closely reported in the daily press. Even though the mystery was never solved, the case was much publicized and continued to generate new pamphlets and novels, including one in 1849 by George Wilkes, the editor of the *National Police Gazette*, who claimed that the story possessed deeper interest than *The Mysteries of Paris*. Yet before becoming a novel, the story of Helen Jewett belonged to police reporters, and the public craving for information steadily made the success of the *Herald*. [15]

The sensational murder has also received the attention of schol-

Little Sheets of News

THE LIFE OF HELEN JEWETT

ILLUSTRATED

BY THE EDITOR OF THE NEW YORK NATIONAL POLICE GAZETTE,

AUTHOR OF "LIFE OF JOHN A. MURRELL," "JOSEPH T. HARE," "COLONEL MONROE EDWARDS," ETC. ETC.

The Author of Murrell has exceeded, in the LIFE OF HELEN JEWETT, the merit which he displayed in the History of the Massaroni of the West. This may be attributed, in a certain degree, to the peculiar qualities of his last subject, but perhaps is more properly to be accredited to the stronger efforts of a talent, made bold by the favor of the Public. "Helen Jewett" is one of the phenomena of modern literature. Without pretension in its style, it comprises all the qualities of pathos, humor, terror and descriptive tact that belong to an accomplished thought, and its philosophical deductions are reasoned out with a force and point but seldom met with in mere narrative or vain romance. The story possesses, as a novel, deeper interest than the Mysteries of Paris, and we cannot read it without wondering how its strange knowledge was collected by the author, or how he was enabled to methodize it so accurately in the hasty manner in which he must have prepared its weekly chapters for the Press.—*Pathfinder*

PHILADELPHIA:

W. B. ZEIBER, LEDGER BUILDINGS.

Title page, The Life of Helen Jewett,
by George Wilkes (1849). Library of Congress.

ars of the early American press because of its class and gender categorizations. While constructing the murder mystery around Helen Jewett's previous self-representations, the case highlighted the social concern over illicit sex in the new metropolis. The narrative of the urban underworld served a twofold purpose: on the one hand, it permitted the pornographic gaze on the female dismembered corpse, and on the other, it provided an explanation for homicide—that is, sexuality. Thus it spoke to both the public's appetite for penny dreadfuls and its anxiety over the dangers of the promiscuous urban space.[16]

In the early days of mass-audience newspapers, the personality of the editor seemed essential. As one historian put it, the editor was not only a politician but "a public servant, an observer, a social critic and an educator."[17] Nonetheless, even a bold editor like James Gordon Bennett could not make a popular newspaper without the patronage of the people. The broad appeal of the *Herald* was reflected in Bennett's alleged circulation figures. After one year, Bennett claimed a daily circulation of 10,000 and about 50,000 regular readers, which produced a net revenue of $30,000. By 1839 the daily circulation had reached 20,000, and in 1840 a combined daily and weekly circulation totaled 51,000. The year 1840 was marked by the so-called Moral War, in which a coalition of newspapers and magazines spoke out against Bennett's anticlerical and personal attacks. It is worth mentioning that Bennett remained a religious man in spite of his criticism of the clerical establishment, and even though he saw himself as the herald of truth and the enemy of hypocrisy, he was far from being a defender of immorality.[18]

In the Moral War sensationalism was used on both fronts, and although Bennett was not destroyed, he slightly improved the tone of his paper. Bennett claimed a victory in the Moral War and an increase by 2,600 in the *Herald*'s daily circulation. He boasted of a circulation of 30,000 by 1842, with annual receipts of over $125,000. However, historians of journalism have argued that the *Herald*'s circulation dropped by 5,000 daily during the months of the Moral War and declined from 17,000 to 12,000 from 1840 to 1845. Daily circulation did not return to 30,000 until the coverage of the Mexican War between 1846 and 1848.[19] It is highly probable that Bennett inflated his figures, but in a city of about 300,000 inhabitants in 1840, the average circulation of the *Herald* testified to its success.

Scholars have recognized the impact of both the new printing technology and the widening reading public on the rise of the penny press. Frank Luther Mott's early analysis of the growth of newspaper circulation—from 1,200 newspapers in 1833 to 3,000 by 1860—identified the penny press with the industrial revolution. In his seminal work, *American Journalism,* Mott enumerates four factors: demographic growth, the creation of a "nation of readers" through public education and increased literacy, more democratic forms of government that increased popular interest in public affairs, and, finally, the reduction in newspaper prices that made the press available to poorer people. Accordingly, penny papers were mere products of their time. Nevertheless, Mott argues that "the penny paper, revolutionary as it was, did not immediately cause a sharp break with the past in American journalism." [20]

In general, journalism scholars have expanded upon Mott's broad analysis. James L. Crouthamel explains the "Newspaper Revolution" in economic and technological terms. "As the rising fixed costs worked to the advantages of the popular papers with larger incomes, the role of advertising also strengthened the revolutionaries." Unlike Mott, Crouthamel argues that the penny papers took over the functions of the mercantile press. Furthermore, he observes two components in the newspaper revolution: first, a change in style and technique, with the tendency toward sensationalism, and, second, the improvement in technology and news gathering, which treated news as a commodity. However, because of his concentration on the production and the editorship of the penny paper, Crouthamel neglects both the social meaning of the new press and the role of the readers in its making. [21]

Other scholars of popular journalism have further discussed the social constituency of the new press. In *Discovering the News,* sociologist Michael Schudson argues that new social attitudes preceded new technology and transportation development and promoted innovation. [22] In fact, the public's demand for newspapers was a major incentive to increase production. In the case of the *New York Sun,* production with a single-cylinder press failed to meet the requirements of the rapid growth of circulation, and in 1835 steam power was applied to the double-cylinder presses. Even with the introduction of the ten-cylinder press in 1851, production lagged behind the demand of a growing audience in the increasingly populated metropolis until the appearance of the rotary self-feeding press in 1865.[23]

In contrast to previous explanations of the revolution in journalism that emphasized technological determinism, Schudson offers a class analysis of a bourgeois revolution. For him, "The penny papers expressed and built the culture of a democratic market society." Newspapers were not only a product but also an agent of democratization, "spokesmen for egalitarian ideals in politics, economic life, and social life."[24] They contributed to the extension of the market by being a medium for advertisements and in so doing enlarged the potential market. They became a commodity to be consumed. As a commentator remarked in 1855, "The cheap matches and the cheap newspapers were sold in every street. Families before this, had borrowed coals of fire and newspapers of their richer neighbors. With the reduced prices, each family had a pride in keeping its own matchbox, and in taking its favorite daily journal."[25] According to Schudson, the rise of the penny press symbolized and strengthened the new way of being middle class. But his idea of a middle class that included both merchants and artisans in the age of Jackson remains questionable.

Despite a striking difference in their respective class analyses, Dan Schiller also agrees with Schudson's assessment of the penny press phenomenon as a social one. In his revisionist work, *Objectivity and the News,* Schiller defines the reading public of the sensational and cheap press as a working class of hard-pressed journeymen and downwardly mobile artisans, increasingly separated from capitalist industrialists and merchants. Newspapers appeared "to defend the rights of man, through crime news especially, at a time when those rights seemed to be threatened by changing social relations, and when other institutions only turned their backs on cardinal republican values."[26] The penny press was strengthening the unity of American life when inequality and class tensions were growing in mid-nineteenth-century New York City. In contrast to an antagonistic labor press, Schiller argues, the penny papers revived a rhetoric of equal rights, enlightenment, and political independence.[27] Similarly, Alexander Saxton considered the first wave of penny papers in connection with the workingmen's movement in New York City and the formation of the Democratic Party, arguing that the penny press born before the panic of 1837 propagated an urban artisan ideology, democratic and white egalitarian.[28]

Yet to attribute the immediate success and popularity of the new press to the ideology of artisan republicanism fails to take full measure of the diversity of the reading audience and its fascination for the eccentricity of its locality. The political meaning of the penny paper was second to the transgression that the format and content of the newspaper embodied. The emergence of the *New York Tribune,* a cheap Whig daily launched by the reformer Horace Greeley to compete with the *Herald's* Loco-Focoism, confirmed the popular character of the new genre of newspaper publishing across the political spectrum. The meaning of the new press was indeed cultural and was epitomized by the introduction of the vernacular into print. For the penny papers threatened the authority of the printed word not through attacks on the propertied class but through the production of cheap printed matter for the purposeless pleasure of reading.

Certainly Bennett's claims that his audience was more refined than the *Sun's* should be taken with circumspection. However, while the *Sun* was famous for its local news and human-interest stories, the *Herald* also provided commercial news to compete with the mercantile press. Bennett wanted his *Herald* to enter the merchants' houses and to attract them as advertisers as well as readers. His concern was to gain respectability and refine the image of the penny press, which he saw as unduly accused of vulgarity by the intellectual elites of the nation. "The *Herald* has probably, as much as any, contributed to elevate the character and purify the morals of the 'panny papers,' as we are called in contempt," wrote Bennett. "Before we started this journal, the penny papers were generally considered low, vulgar and ignorant."[29] Bennett mocked the *Sun,* which ended up as "much paper used in garrets and cellars to tie up sausages and bundle away old clothes," and contrasted the genteel fate of the *Herald:* "The parlor and boudoir—the counting room and lawyer's office—the banks and the brokers—the workshop and restaurateur, are the places where you find files of the *Herald,* carefully preserved, to be bound up at the end of the year."[30]

In moving from Broadway to Nassau Street, described as Publishers' Row and "a more intellectual and patriotic neighborhood," Bennett wanted to promote his little paper in good society and divert patronage and advertising from the *Sun,* located nearby. He boasted of a great demand for the *Herald* in Gilpin's reading room in the Exchange—the most famous place for New York businessmen—and in the most fashionable boardinghouses. "The *Herald* is the only small paper worth advertising in. Why? Because it circulates among those who can buy and pay for goods, wares, and merchandize."[31] Advertising was essential for the survival of the new press. It represented an important part of the newspapers' capital and helped them remain cheap. Out of four pages, for instance, the *Herald* had two and a half filled with commercial advertisements. Even the part devoted to news contained additional advertisements for societies, meetings, lectures, and the newspaper itself. As Allan Pred has noted, "Very soon after their commencement the penny papers had 75 percent or more of their column space in advertisements."[32]

Indeed, the press evolved simultaneously with institutions of mass publicity. Businessmen, entertainers, and lecturers used publicity in newspapers to enlarge their market, whereas newspapers used sensational events to advertise themselves and broaden their audience. The *Herald,* in particular, attempted to target a mass reading audience by the use of sensational news, and by the same token asked for acceptance among the rich and powerful. "Our only dependence is in the good sense of the mechanics, working-men, and farmers," assured the *Herald,* but it asserted as well its hopes to "double its currency among the intelligent and business people" within its first months.[33] By submitting to the pervasiveness of the marketplace, the paper implicitly reaffirmed the liminal character of the antebellum culture of reading, being between categories and mingling readers and consumers.

The *Herald*'s readers remained anonymous. In contrast to an earlier press, the nineteenth-century newspaper addressed an invisible public. The democratization of print and the multiplicity of newspapers —often more than one for each city or town—resulted in the production of dailies that appealed to and divided particular segments of the reading public. Because of their popular character, the "cheap and nasty" penny papers differentiated themselves from serious reading matter, but they also competed with each other for the patronage of the poor classes of readers. At the same time, they were binding anonymous readers in new and informal associations. Hence the readers of the *New York Herald* were the metropolitan members of what Benedict Anderson calls an "imagined community."[34] They shared the same reading matter while being isolated in their indi-

Little Sheets of News

vidual activity of reading. Their daily simultaneous consumption of the sensational newspaper created an extraordinary mass ceremony, thereby confirming Hegel's observation that newspapers serve modern man as a substitute for morning prayers.[35]

The new mode of circulation also contributed to the privatization of newspaper reading. Whereas newspaper readers formerly borrowed or shared high-priced papers, they now could take their own small copy home for a bit of copper. As the *Herald* stated in its inaugural issue, "There is not a person in the city, male or female, that may not be able to say—'well I have got a paper of my own which will tell me all about what's going in the world—I'm busy now—but I'll put it in my pocket and read it at my leisure.' "[36] The result was a close intermingling of shrill sounds of newsboys and silent reading, busy public space and private stories. One rendering of that cacophony appeared under the pen of Charles Dickens, who offered a sharp critique of the New York daily press in his novel *Martin Chuzzlewit.* Upon arriving in New York City, the main character encountered shouting newsboys: " 'Here's this morning's New York *Sewer!* ' cried one. 'Here's this morning's New York *Stabber!* Here's the New York *Family Spy!* Here's the New York *Private Listener!* Here's the New York *Peeper!* Here's the New York *Plunderer!* Here's the New York *Keyhole Reporter!* Here's the New York *Rowdy Journal!* Here's all the New York papers!' "[37]

The continued publicizing of news was accompanied by the strikingly private character of the news. The antebellum crimes that fed the newsmongers were increasingly stories of private life, melodramatic love affairs, murders of consanguinity, cases of incestuous rape. For instance, the *Herald* began its coverage of the James Wood case on October 2, 1839, with the title "Full Particulars of the Tragical Event in Philadelphia—Elopement of a Daughter and Her Murder by Her Father" and for three weeks gave details on the "Late Extraordinary Tragedy in Philadelphia," "together with a correct history of all the prominent actors therein" and even a "view of the bed-room in which Miss Wood was shot by her father."[38] Similarly, the *Herald* sensationalized the "Horrible Outrage—Unparalleled in Criminal Annals—Capital Trial in Salem, Mass. of Moses Goodhue, for Rape, Committed Upon the Person of His Own Daughter" and, during the same month, the "Trial of Mrs. Kinney, at Boston, for the Murder of Her Husband for Administering Poison."[39] Family crimes made headlines in antebellum America. Although editorials often alluded to a political and social agenda when reporting crimes, the emphasis of antebellum crime literature was primarily on individual and singular acts of dementia, butchery, and monstrosity. The cheap newspapers of a boundless culture now offered a window onto the saga of private life.[40]

The penny press personalized victims and criminals in cases that unfold like serialized fiction or drama and offered new acts every day. Criminals were perceived as "actors" in "domestic tragedies," and the scene of the crime resembled the stage of a theater. Crime reporting even borrowed its headlines from the Shakespearean culture of its intended readers, such as "Blood, Blood, Iago."[41] In the city, news was dramatic material, and Bennett took note of the parallel in an editorial: "If a Shakespeare could have taken a stroll in the morning or afternoon through the Police, does any one imagine he could not have picked up half a dozen dramas and some original character? The bee extracts from the lowliest flower—so shall we in the Police Office."[42]

Writing news meant telling stories, and literary scholars have noted the parallel between the genres of news and novel, between facts and fiction. In a study of the origins of the English novel, Lennard J. Davis has defined an undifferentiated matrix of news/novels in the sixteenth- and seventeenth-century forms of journalism, the printed ballad. Likewise, J. Paul Hunter explores what was read before the rise of the novel and stresses that features of ephemeral journalism and wonder narratives found their way into the eighteenth-century novel in England. By the late nineteenth century, the press also came to provide realistic writers with ordinary characters and everyday experiences. In particular, the city and its newspapers abounded with valuable material for novels. Realism in American literature would owe its character and its first writers—such as Stephen Crane and Theodore Dreiser—to the newspapers' prose and milieu.[43]

Even by the middle of the nineteenth century, journalists were eagerly seeking the "inside story." Participants in highly publicized crimes became well-known personae to the urban public of antebellum America, to the extent that the New York Museum exhibited their wax figures. For instance, the case of Mary, alias Polly, Bodine, who was hanged for the murder of Emeline Houseman (the wife of Bodine's brother) and her child, and for setting their house on fire, was so notorious that P. T. Barnum had a wax figure of her in his museum.[44] The popular demand for portraits and detailed information on the lives of criminals resulted from the growing urban anonymity as well as from the desire to identify the outlaws in the midst of society. Urban dwellers were isolated in the fearful crowd. The antebellum penny press—best exemplified by the successful *New York Herald*—at once combined a new level of exposure of private life with the privatization of the act of reading public print media. News items—*fait divers*—brought tales of private life to public knowledge and provided nineteenth-century readers with a printed spectacle that replaced the pillory, the execution sermon, and the criminal's confession of earlier times.

Human-interest stories offered exposure as a substitute for human contact. As Alexis de Tocqueville mentioned in *Democracy in America*, "Newspapers increase in numbers, not according to their cheapness, but according to the more or less frequent want which a great number of men may feel for intercommunication and combination." Thus the rise of the penny press in the 1830s was due in part to a growing urbanization that created new social and cultural needs. The French critic continued, "A newspaper, therefore, always represents an association that is composed of its habitual readers. . . . The fact that the newspaper keeps alive is a proof that at least the germ of such an association exists in the mind of its readers."[45]

Newspapers provided newcomers to the city with a means of communication as well as guidelines to decipher the urban environment. They represented a substitute for village gossip. They spoke to the reader in an almost intimate manner, as a member of the informal "reading association." Readers, in turn, often sent letters to the editor, who acted as a confidant. The new cultural institution of the daily paper offered a place for dialogue. The *New York Herald* echoed the daily life of New Yorkers, and New Yorkers were reading news of the city. Even though sensational news from other cities was often reported, events concerning New York City usually took priority. In December of 1835 the conflagration of New York City occupied the front page for days. For the occasion a view of the Merchants' Exchange as well as a map of the city were printed, to emphasize the disaster and create sensation. It was the only matter that concerned the citizens. As Bennett reported: "We have abundance of dull news from Washington, but who cared for that?"[46]

Newspapers colored the city. They were daily messengers at all corners and representative voices on the street. But the popular word, which they returned to the street and dwellings, came from the city itself. News was no longer foreign and political, but local and ordinary. The penny press elevated these ordinary events to the level of the printed word. There was a new fascination with police reports, trivial facts from the streets and from private households. The new metropolis seemed to hide plenty of miseries and mysteries awaiting a George G. Foster or a James Dabney McCabe to bring their horrors to light.[47] Echoing the new urban press, Edgar Allan Poe introduced a genre of literary reportage in his *Doings of Gotham*, letters that appeared in the *Columbia Spy* between May 18 and July 6, 1844.[48] Literary scholars have emphasized the importance of "city-mysteries" fiction and images of the antebellum period in the wave of sensational literature that began with Eugène Sue's *The Mysteries of Paris* and G. M. W. Reynolds's *The Mysteries of London* and extended from George Lippard's *The Quaker City* and Ned Buntline's *The Mysteries and Miseries of New Orleans* to Herman Melville's *Pierre*.[49] In comparison, the concern here is not so much the literary production as the role played by the public taste in the transformation of the literary marketplace.

Crime news reported in the *New York Herald* followed a long tradition of "execution sermons," "lives and deaths" of criminals, and "dying speeches," yet with significant differences. As scholars of colonial crime literature have shown, crimes in the seventeenth century were sins against God, and ministers played a central role in the publication of conversion narratives and "last speech" sensations.[50] Execution sermons of early America focused on the salvation of the murderer and referred more to the slope of sin leading to the crime than to the details of the crime and the crime scene. It was not until the late eighteenth century that murder narratives were secularized and the murderer personalized. The narration of the crime itself lengthened, and the criminal became a moral alien. A shift of focus occurred from judgment and conversion to the details of crime, from condemnation to recognition of the criminal. By the nineteenth century, the execution and death of the criminal became secondary to the story of his or her life. Moreover, tales of robbers and bandits gave way to tragedies of private life.[51]

Crime news of the antebellum papers is further distinguished from the chronicle of crimes in the early republic by the rhythm with which it was delivered. The daily occurrences of crime in print created a serialized narration of urban life. Ironically, the antebellum outbreak of crime literature did not correspond to a rise in criminality. Roger Lane's study of criminal violence in Massachusetts confirms an increase in petty criminality, but a decrease in serious crime. Police forces in nineteenth-century cities concentrated more on minor, public-order offenses. Nonetheless, despite actual police statistics to the contrary, the perception of a dangerous underworld accompanied booming antebellum urbanization. The invasion of crime news in New York's cheap newspapers thus reflected not an explosion of criminality in the new metropolis, but rather the growing anxiety of Americans about urban promiscuity and their desire to draw social boundaries between "us" and "them."[52]

In his study of nineteenth-century crime, David Ray Papke examines the forms of "reporting," "imagining," and "remembering" that shaped public perceptions of criminality. In particular, Papke argues that the *New York Sun* and the *New York Herald* competed with the slow and inefficient police and developed a politicized journalism intended to appeal to a working-class audience.[53] The penny papers certainly defined themselves as an alternative police force. They reported extensively on recent crimes and investigated the background of victims and suspects through serialized publication of "horrible details" and "further particulars." Even though crime reporting was considered part of a high moral crusade, the publication of crime stories in the new daily papers satisfied the nineteenth-century heirs of popular lore.[54] The legitimate claims to reform society through exposure of vice and infamy wherever found could hardly overshadow the public demand for titillation and the publishers' profitable capitalization upon the growing sensibility to crime.

The penny papers provided readers with bloody and bodily descriptions, which reflected the carnality that was attributed to the "dangerous" classes of the nineteenth century, including immoral women, blacks, and aliens such as Catholics. In contrast, the middle-class way of life advocated an increasing control of the body. As Richard Brodhead demonstrates by looking at the literature of the pre–Civil War decades, discipline through love displaced corporal punishment. Cultural historians have further underscored that the new humanitarian narrative of the time condemned all sorts of suffering, whether the whipping of slaves, the confinement of the insane, or the cruel treatment of animals. Yet the middle-class quest for refinement and aversion for bodily correction were only matched by the spectacle of pain, or what Charles Dickens called "the attraction of repulsion." [55] A few examples will show the centrality of the human body in popular press reporting.

The 1841 murder of Mary C. Rogers, whose bruised body was found in the Hudson River near Hoboken, New Jersey, yielded extensive news coverage by the *Herald* and other New York papers. It also resulted in the production of fictional work by Edgar Allan Poe in 1842–43 ("The Mystery of Marie Rogêt") and by Joseph Holt Ingraham in 1844 (*The Beautiful Cigar Girl*).[56] Related pamphlets were subsequently published, including *A Confession of the Awful and Bloody Transactions in the Life of Charles Wallace, the Fiend-like Murderer of Miss Mary Rogers,* with a frontispiece that featured Mary Rogers being strangled by one of her beaux.[57] The young woman, who lived on Nassau Street in New York City, had disappeared on a summer Sunday. Both her violent death and her unknown whereabouts in the city created an enigma that the press sought to resolve by speculations about her romantic life, her elopement, an abortion, or even a street gang.

Undoubtedly Poe used the daily reports on the case in writing his tale. But his claims to solve the mystery of Marie Rogêt by use of reason and deduction were antithetical to the desires of newspaper readers. While Poe advocated the work of rationality to a narrow magazine audience, the mass reading public of the daily press sought strong emotions. For instance, Poe offered a refined description of the body of the victim: "About the throat were bruises and impressions of fingers. The arms were bent over on the chest and were rigid. The right hand was clenched; the left partially open."[58] In contrast, the testimony that was originally published in the *Herald* and reprinted a few days later in *Brother Jonathan,* in the form of an interview by the mayor, reported the examination of the victim's body by a Dr. Cook of Hoboken. The question-and-answer style provided the reader with dialogues and blunt descriptions. The passage later edited by Poe appeared in the newspaper as follows: "There was an echymose mark about the size and shape of a man's thumb on the right side of the neck, near the jugular vein, and two or three echymose marks on the left side resembling in shape a man's finger, which led me to believe she had been throttled and partially choked

Murder of Miss Mary Rogers, *frontispiece in*
A Confession of the Awful and Bloody
Transactions in the Life of Charles Wallace *(1851)*.
Library of Congress.

by a man's hand. Both arms were bent over on the chest; and were so
tight and stiff that we had to use some force to straighten them. The
right hand was clenched, and the left was partially open, but rigid." [59]

"Horrible details" and "authentic facts" were the trademarks of
the cheap papers. In particular, the female body of a victim, an un-
fortunate girl or an immoral creature—the body of the "Other," a
marginal figure alien to social order—was a popular subject, and the
editors did not hesitate to provide avid readers with graphic representations. When asked about considerable excoriation on the back
and shoulders of Mary Rogers, Dr. Cook gave the following state-
ment: "I think, [this was produced] by the young girl struggling to
get free, while being brutally held down on her back, to effect her
violation; and therefore, that this outrage was effected while she
was laid down upon some hard substance, a hard board floor, the
bottom of a boat, or something similar." The *Herald* then gave the
substance—instead of more details—of Dr. Cook's examination. The
conclusion was that the victim had previously been a person of chas-
tity and that "her person was horribly violated by more than two or
three persons." [60] By contrast, the lurid part of the account was cen-

sored by Poe's pen. The fate of Marie Rogêt was indeed more polished than that of Mary C. Rogers. "The medical testimony spoke confidently of the virtuous character of the deceased. She had been subjected, it said, to brutal violence. The corpse was in such condition when found, that there could have been no difficulty in its recognition by friends."[61]

Similarly, Poe incorporated bits of the sensational press in writing "The Tell-Tale Heart." However, even though his tale borrowed elements of the trial of Peter Robinson for the murder of banker Abraham Suydam, Poe focused on the psyche of the criminal rather than on the gruesome criminal act. In contrast, the *Herald* and subsequent pamphlet editions published a detailed account of the finding of Suydam's body buried in the earth under the basement floor of Robinson's house. One of the witnesses recalled how they searched the ground with hands and sticks in the area where they felt that there was a body: "I took my coat off, ran my hand down and got hold of the pantaloons, and my finger in the button hole of the left hand side; I could feel the hip; it was all wet, muddy, and slushy, toward the bottom; it was quicksand where his face lay." After having received the directions of the coroner, they pulled the body out; the feet were rather turned up, the hole not being long enough. "I could not recognize him while he lay on his face in the court house, nor could not until his body was washed off, and his face. I then knew at once it was Mr. Suydam; don't know where the body was washed off; I felt sick; he smelt very bad, and I had to go away to get air. The tails of his coat in the ground were thrown back over his head." The body was then exposed at the courthouse "for a short time to the view of such persons as were desirous of seeing it." But the execution of Robinson was "strictly private."[62]

No detail was spared for the reader of newspapers and pamphlets. While Poe underlined his distaste for excesses of popular sensationalism and advocated the use of reason and deduction, the "bloodhound" penny papers capitalized on carnal imagery and satisfied the voyeurism of the reading public. Crime news provided a spectacle to a crowd fond of hangings and executions. As the whipping post and the pillory were increasingly withdrawn from the public eye in an age of growing rationality, lurid printed matter offered a substitute.[63]

Spectacles of the grotesque and the monstrous were enormously popular in antebellum America. Crowds were drawn to curiosities such as the "extraordinary sight of a still-born calf, 'a monster,'" to be exhibited at Barnum's American Museum, or a "black dwarf."[64] Criminals too were considered monsters to be exhibited in public, or at least in print. For instance, the exposure of Madame Restell, the most famous abortionist in New York, included an engraving with her hands drawn as the wings of a bat.[65] The new press emphasized crude display and visibility. It revealed a cultural resistance to refinement and control of behavior, perhaps what Sigmund Freud would call "the return of the repressed."

Writing of the human body in the daily press was transgressing the cultural order and turning the world of print inside out. The filth and miasma of the big city was literally put on the front page. The sewer contaminated the printed word and made its way into the streets, into boardinghouses and tenements, and probably even into middle-class drawing rooms. The cheap papers exposed the bodies of victims of crime or accident, producing both disgust and fascination. Antebellum readers viewed sensational news with both horror and pleasure, for the popular press represented "low" entertainment reminiscent of the carnivalesque.

The revolution that the penny papers effected in print was not only in the publication of deviance and cultural transgression, but also in the temporal framework and the new modes of distribution. Since colonial times, "last speech" broadsides and pamphlets of lurid criminal literature were distributed by peddlers only occasionally. The new press introduced the notion of repetition in time, even in the occurrence of crime. Reading crime news became a daily activity and contributed to the readers' attempts to define their urban community. While discussing the various and singular tastes of newspaper readers, one periodical referred to "the case of the lady who was obliged to consult the celebrated Abernethy, because 'for several mornings past she had not been able to relish her murders'!"[66] The penny papers—and the *New York Herald* better than others— attracted the urban public to read the "top story" of the day. The sensational press introduced a new class of printed matter that represented a blend of mercantile news and traditional popular lore delivered at the regular pace of capitalist production and industrial time. The "subliterary" genre of daily crime literature stood at the threshold of serialization and the capitalist division of labor, while revealing a heritage of earlier storytelling, oral communication, sensational broadsides, and almanacs.[67]

As European travelers visiting the United States had long noted, American newspapers were uninhibited in their sensational treatment of events. European daily newspapers were slower to introduce sensational news, with a lag of twenty to thirty years behind the American press. A sensation mania did not emerge in the popular London daily press until the early 1860s, after the abolition of the old newspaper tax in 1855 had enabled the *Daily Telegraph* to become the first penny daily in British history.[68] Similarly, Paris witnessed the publication of its first daily, *Le Petit Journal,* sold without a subscription, in 1863.[69] The exceptional character of the American popular press was due to the early freedom of the press in the new republic, which established the authority of the printed word, and to the growing demand for informal associations of readers in what historian Arthur Schlesinger Sr. described as "a nation of joiners." At the same time, the cheap newspapers were increasingly distinctive, not so much in their political affiliation as in their popular and sensational character, hawked in the streets by shouting newsboys and filled with detailed crime news. They framed the mysteries of the city and its erotic violence in little sheets of news and varieties that could be had for a penny, and in so doing they commodified both the criminal literature and the metropolitan culture. Furthermore, while gratifying the public taste for murder, melodrama, and catastrophe, the penny papers paved the way to more monstrous printed matter, the so-called mammoth weeklies, and to serialized fiction and drama that imitated the daily police reports.

CHAPTER 3

Mammoths and Extras:
Staging a Spectacle in Print

Large papers. — There is a mania in the United States for papers of gigantick
dimensions. It is said, that one of our already mammoth dailies is still to be enlarged to
an unheard-of extent, so that it will require two boys, at least, to hold it for perusal!
New York Mirror, May 23, 1835

More than half a century had already passed since Connecticut
writer Joel Barlow had criticized cheap editions in his plea for a
national copyright law. "A mean letter & an uncooth page . . . to
catch the Vulgar by a low price," wrote Barlow in 1783.[1] To many
later observers, the same epithet could well be applied to the mammoth newspapers of the late 1830s and early 1840s. Their crude and
poor print quality was matched only by their extravagant propor-
tions and unforeseen style. Yet these Saturday papers of gigantic size
also participated in the American textual transformation and print
cornucopia during the second quarter of the nineteenth century.
They best illustrate the temporary success of the aesthetics of the
monstrous: the new weeklies suddenly launched a "battle of books"
against fair and respectable publishing, only to fade away after their
ritualistic and carnivalesque display.

Historians of publishing have attributed this turmoil to the trade
upheaval caused by the economic depression that lasted from 1837
until 1843. In their accounts the changes in the production and
marketing of literature resulted from the low purchasing power of
Americans. Fierce competition led to unfair trade practices, and the
traditional publishing system briefly broke down. By the early 1850s,

however, the American book trade had returned to stability, and publishing practices became more regulated.[2] In addition to the economic explanation, other scholars have analyzed the literary genre of the new Saturday papers and presented them as the forerunners of dime novels. Because of the lack of international copyright, the magazines were able to pirate English and French novels, publishing them in a double-column format as "Extras" to be hawked on the streets for 25 cents or even less, or to be sent through the mail "without yellow cover and stitching" and "subject to Newspaper Postage only."[3]

Historians have thus examined the competition of foreign and national literary production as well as the birth of cheap paperbound books. Other features of the mammoth sheets, such as their format and textuality, have not received as much attention, although they may hold the clue to the papers' ephemeral success. The sudden and short-lived popularity of the jumbo papers is measured in subscription numbers, which reached high figures of 20,000 or 25,000.[4] These numbers, combined with outrageous style, force us to reevaluate the weeklies not so much as an aberration in the *longue durée* of publishing history as a substantial element of the in-betweenness of the antebellum period. This print phenomenon has a significance far greater than the mere curiosity of an out-of-the-ordinary publication. It demonstrates an attempt by the popular classes of the late 1830s and early 1840s to mock and subvert the traditional print culture. As a festive parody of print, the mammoth papers constitute a historical event with a cultural meaning and reveal the dynamics of cultural realignment in pre–Civil War society. For a brief historical moment, a rupture occurred in the continuity of the traditional system of representation. Texts were devalued and desecrated. The power of the word was contested when print was popularized, the book being broken down into installments, invaded by images, made ephemeral. Reverence for the word became obsolete. The cultural change resembled what Rolf Engelsing describes for the period of the eighteenth-century Enlightenment as *die Erschütterung der Autorität des Buches*—literally, the shaking of the authority of the book.[5] For the antebellum period, however, technology played its part in the process of cultural transformation. Indeed, progress in papermaking, printing, and engraving allowed the popular taste to be satisfied and thus contributed to debasing American print culture. It was as if the technological ability to produce more books was utilized to proclaim the demise of the traditional book and the creation of non-book publications. To be sure, such provocative attacks against the sacredness of the printed word did not remain unchallenged, and by mid-nineteenth century the forces of reaction succeeded in consolidating a newly legitimate book culture.[6]

The analysis presented in this chapter is based primarily on *Brother Jonathan* and the *New World,* both weekly publications competing on the New York publishing scene. *Brother Jonathan: A Weekly Compend of Belles Lettres and the Fine Arts, Standard Literature, and General Intelligence* was first published in July 1839 by Wilson and Company under the initiative of Park Benjamin and Rev. Rufus Wilmot Griswold. Contributors included Nathaniel P. Willis, A. Hastings Weld, and John Neal. Park Benjamin withdrew soon after Benjamin Day, editor of the *New York Sun,* purchased *Brother Jonathan.* Benjamin then launched a competitor, the *New World: A Weekly Family Journal of Popular Literature, Science, Art and News,* on October 26, 1839.[7] Both weeklies were originally published as four-page numbers, in folio editions of about six square feet, but eventually were also offering a sixteen-page quarto library edition. Special jubilee numbers were published as "double double sheet," "quadruple sheet," "mammoth quarto," or even "leviathan" for Christmas, the Fourth of July, or other special occasions. Both *Brother Jonathan* and the *New World* had collapsed by 1848.

Evidence is also drawn from individual issues of the *Universal Yankee Nation—The Largest Paper in All Creation,* published by John N. Bradley and Company in Boston, and the *Boston Notion,* published by George Roberts as the weekly edition of the *Boston Daily Times.* In addition to those publications of the late 1830s and 1840s, this study includes two 1859 mammoth issues of *The Constellation: An Unexceptional Family Newspaper,* published in New York by George Roberts with Park Benjamin as editor. The publications of the late 1850s reveal some legacy of the American popular print culture after the "cheap books war" of the 1840s and the restoration of cultural order and stability.[8]

The approach proposed here is central to the cultural meaning of reading because between texts and readers lies the material appearance of printed artifacts. Using a method at the intersection of bibliography and cultural history, this chapter combines an examination of physical evidence inscribed in the printed matter and the contextual meaning of those book-artifacts within their cultural and historical setting. It particularly takes into account what Gérard Genette calls the *paratexte,* which consists of all elements peripheral to the text: pictorial, typographical, verbal (such as titles and editorials), and other material such as the format and the cover. The *paratexte* is part of the text, but not the text itself, and it implicitly frames the practice of reading. Indeed, the format is as important as the content in the act of reading. It affects the status of the work but reveals also past uses of print and the functions of reading. In other words, a cheap format regarded as the "natural dress of cheap content" embodies cultural values.[9]

The following discussion of the new weeklies is threefold. First, their format is examined as the epitome of grotesque corpulence and a visual representation of bodily deformity, which was characteristic of a manly popular culture and a taste for street festivals. Second, the internal organization of the Saturday papers, which resembled a literary museum of oddities and curiosities, is analyzed in continuity with changing expectations of the reading public. Finally, the literary content of the weeklies is examined, particularly the serialization of popular literature in their extras. Eagerly read by the public, yet denigrated by critics who stressed the foreign origin and immoral character of such publications, the extras or supplements to *Brother Jonathan* and to the *New World* also contributed to the transformation of literary production. Moreover, while they all originated with the weekly papers, the leviathans and the extras proved not to have the same life expectancy. The mammoth weeklies hardly survived beyond the 1840s, whereas by comparison the extras were granted a flourishing afterlife. They set a pattern for serialized fiction in newspaper format and paperbound books that was imitated by more respectable publishing firms such as Harper and Brothers. Because of the enormous success of a once-despised class of printed matter, the popular publications progressively made their way into mainstream publishing.

Illuminated Leviathans

Titles emphasizing the American character of the periodicals appeared as a simple disguise for cheap reprints of foreign literature in the age of a nascent movement for American literary nationalism. "Brother Jonathan" was also the sobriquet used before the introduction of Uncle Sam to designate both a typical American and America itself. It began in the seventeenth century as the British nickname for Roundheads, or Puritans. By the nineteenth century "Brother Jonathan" referred to a Yankee and the American national character. In 1825 John Neal, one of *Brother Jonathan's* later coeditors, published a three-volume novel in England entitled *Brother Jonathan*, after the main character, a Yankee named Jonathan Peters. It might have been the origin of the title of the weekly. The masthead ornament of the *New World*, on the other hand, represented Columbus approaching the shore of the Virgin Land with Indians greeting him. The tone was definitely grandiose, and the *Universal Yankee Nation* followed the trend, introducing a title ornament in July 1841 that featured an eagle with flags embracing the sea, a ship in the center. Symbols of progress included a railroad locomotive on the right, a factory with smoke on the left, and a herald riding a horse toward the West on the far left. The weekly paper was a patriotic allegory.

Leviathans were biblical monsters, symbols of apocalypse. The weekly newspapers that called themselves "mammoth" or "leviathan" were thus proclaiming their monstrosity. Gigantic character was to replace republican sobriety and frugality. It was not the first time that huge papers existed. The early 1830s had witnessed large-size newspapers, the "blanket sheets" of about two by three feet that unfolded to a four-foot width. As one historian noted, these commercial subscription papers "obviously were intended to be spread out on the library table at home, or across the counting house desk." [10] They were a sign of economic success. Yet soon the fashion shifted back in favor of the small papers. The *New York Daily Sentinel,* a celebrated labor paper, announced in 1832 that a reaction was taking place. "Seven-by-nines are springing up in every city like mushrooms, and people are beginning to find that seven inches multiplied by nine of genuine democracy is a far better accompaniment to their cup of tea or coffee, than three feet square of toryism." The *Daily Sentinel* saw this "return to nature" as characteristic of the "march of mind." [11] Likewise, the penny papers sold by newsboys in the streets of New York City from 1833 on, and in other large cities thereafter, were a reasonable size, 8½ by 11 inches.

However, the large-size papers reappeared in the late 1830s and early 1840s, this time as a symbol of boldness and exuberance. The standard size of the "satanic press" happened to be two by three feet, or even four feet long and eleven columns wide. Mammoths of 500 square inches were soon outstripped by those of over 1,000 square inches, and the *Yankee Nation* announced the publication of a sheet "containing exactly EIGHT THOUSAND FIVE HUNDRED AND FORTY SQUARE INCHES."[12] To my knowledge, the American Antiquarian Society holds the largest one, a quadruple number of the *Universal Yankee Nation* of 4 feet 5 inches wide by 10 feet 8 inches long, or 6,784 square inches. In an 1839 letter to his friend and editor Rufus W. Griswold, Henry J. Raymond of the University of Vermont relates the unmistakable reaction that mammoths induced when unfolded in a post office: "The subsequent reception of that up-to-the-sky-to-be-lauded, biggest-of-all-possible-newspapers, and most beloved of all brethren, '*Brother Jonathan*' made me resolve . . . to dispatch an Epistle to your address about the quickest. . . . The appearance of this hugest of mammoths caused no small stir among the good citizens of this unaccustomed-to-large-sight-seeing place."[13]

The size of these newspapers alone indicates that the practice of reading a weekly was different from that of reading small books. Individual reading may have been particularly difficult. Reading mammoth sheets required a collective environment and shared sociability. In February 1840 the *Boston Notion* came up with a new masthead ornament portraying a group of people, which included men and women, gentlemen and laborers, reading an issue of the *Notion* held by two giraffes. Humorous imagery made expansive use of the colossal size of the weeklies, showing, for example, readers standing on ladders, or sandwich men walking on stilts in the streets. One engraving in the *Universal Yankee Nation* portrayed possible practices of reading a mammoth weekly in Boston. Men were shown holding huge papers in the middle of the street, while a *Double Double Universal Yankee Nation* was hanging from a balcony for people to read from the street![14]

Mammoth sheets were antithetical to private reading. They were conceived for display, for exposition in public spaces and in the streets. They were a blend of posters or broadsides and newspapers. The leviathans' dimensions recalled those of some playbills and circus show bills. They were essentially exhibitionist, representative of what we know to have been the popular taste in the age of P. T. Barnum. The illuminated jumbo papers were meant to appeal to the same antebellum audience that flocked to mermaids' exhibitions and Tom Thumb shows. The taste for hoaxes, exposure, and freak shows was not restricted to the museum. It had pervaded the sensational press by mid-century.[15]

Masthead ornament, Boston Notion,
February 1840.
Courtesy of the American Antiquarian Society.

The publication of such "monstrous sheets" was made possible by
a new technology, praised by some publishers as evidence of American progress and received by others as a mixed blessing. The eighteenth century had witnessed a significant increase in newspaper dimensions with the growing availability of larger sheets of paper. But
it was not until the development of cylinder papermaking machines
in the 1820s and 1830s, followed by the introduction of Fourdrinier
papermaking machines in the 1840s and 1850s, that hand manufacture gave way to mechanization. In addition, the introduction of
steam power and Napier-type Hoe presses allowed the industrialization of printing. The price of newsprint also fell during this period,
from 16 cents a pound in 1830 to 8.3 cents in 1860. One historian
has argued convincingly that the technology of papermaking was a
social and cultural product rather than a determinant. The greater
demand for cheaper and more abundant paper was an incentive for
technological improvement, such as the use of chlorine bleach for
processing rags in the 1830s and their subsequent replacement by
wood pulp by the 1850s.[16]

The size and number of images in these papers were similarly

Our Place of Business—A Section of State Street, in Boston,
engraving in The Universal Yankee Nation—Mammoth Quarto,
January 1842. Courtesy of the American Antiquarian Society.

inflated. Special issues for Christmas and the Fourth of July tried to escape the regularity of industrial time and contributed to the perpetuation of preindustrial festivities and commemorations. The jubilee numbers belonged to the popular culture that drove crowds to parades on the Fourth of July and to Christmas maskings and "fantasticals."[17] The mammoth sheets and leviathans were an integral part and echo of the urban street culture before the Civil War. Illustrations pointed to the festive character of American popular print, when images pirated the word and challenged its authority.

The pictorial double sheet of *Brother Jonathan,* for instance, advertised "upward of 100 engravings" for its December 25, 1840, issue. And the July 4, 1848, issue of *Pictorial Brother Jonathan* was a perfect example of the power of images. The jubilee number totaled eight pages of text filled with images. The front page provided four full-size "Portraits of Distinguished American Statesmen: From Recent Daguerreotypes by Plumbe"—namely, Thomas Hart Benton, Henry Clay, John C. Calhoun, and Daniel Webster. Pages four and five offered a splendid two-page cut of 22 by 44 inches, "measuring nearly SEVEN SQUARE FEET!" Representing a famous event of the Mexican War, the "Storming of the Castle of Chapultepec by the American Army under General Scott" on September 13, 1847, it was advertised as "the largest fine wood engraving ever printed in the world" and "a grand experiment in the illustration of American patriotism and valor." Page six had a full-width cut, "The Celebration of the Glorious Fourth of July in New York, with Sketches of the Grand Military and Civic Procession at Different Points." (The parade thus entered the street literature!) The issue also published scenes of the carnival in Paris by the illustrator Gavarni, and the last page offered a collective oval with several women's portraits, including one of the famous actress Fanny Kemble Butler. The whole issue gave the appearance of a gigantic gem, a horn of plenty, a spectacle.

The format and character of the leviathans emphasized a popular taste for exaggeration and grandiloquent imagery rather than middle-class gentility and refinement. Social and cultural historians have recently called our attention to the "manliness" of American working-class culture before the Civil War. Along with gambling, drinking, theatergoing, and prizefighting, the act of reading mammoth sheets belonged to a male conviviality, an urban street culture.[18] The monstrous sheets represented a kind of "printed rowdy," at odds with the antebellum privatization of reading and the cult of domesticity. Along with the material appearance, however, the subject matter of the weeklies reflected the coexistence of opposites so particular to the carnivalesque.

Literary Museums of Oddities and Curiosities

The first issue of the *Universal Yankee Nation* on January 9, 1841, expressed the editors' intention to give variety in "The Mastodon of American Newspapers." They assumed that the readers of miscellaneous newspapers desired "a vast collection of useful, interesting, and amusing reading, adapted to all minds, all classes, all tastes, ranging from 'grave to gay, from lively to severe' through all the world of literature, science, art, and the concern of daily life—facts, fancies, sermons, anecdotes, essays, poetry, mathematics, popular stories, horrid murders, commercial news, whims, scraps, oddities, etc. A paper of this sort, should be as various as the *notions* in the pack of a Yankee pedlar."

The magazines were designed to ease the transition from a rural preindustrial past to the new urban industrial environment. They were tattlers with the "weekly gossip" as editorial. They offered an incongruous assemblage of short stories and miscellaneous news. Memorabilia or *faits divers* such as "A Learned Dog," "A Carriage without Horse," "A Good Toast," "A Name," "Beautiful," "Blood," and "Barbarious Age" were isolated details of four to ten lines, juxtaposed on the page without any logical interconnection. They subverted textual totality and negated historical time. For instance, good advice ("To Kill Mosquitoes") appeared between foreign news of South America and rumor from Texas.[19]

Yet it was not unintentional. The concept of ill-assorted parts versus the whole was at the root of the miscellany. The literature in the *New World* was indexed under the following categories: "Editorials, Original Tales, Sketches, Translations, &c., Popular Literature, Extracts from N[ational] Works, Pictorial Illustrations, Foreign Files, The Scrap Book, Literary World, Theatrical, Musical World, Political World, Patchwork, Science and Art, Naval and Military, Foreign Summary, and finally Poetry, Original and Selected." The periodical was just a collage of past and present, of remote and nearby information, a mélange of facts and fiction, a compilation of odds and ends. The cultural meaning of this heterogeneous literary content is close to what Richard Hoggart called the "cornucopia," or the "working-class baroque."[20] Popular printed matter became a literary museum of oddities and curiosities that resembled Barnum's American Museum. Humor seemed to have been the only common thread in the literary patchwork.

As justification for publishing miscellanies, the weeklies often claimed that they endeavored to offer something "that will suit all tastes." In an age of increasing differentiation of reading audiences, however, the image of common reading pertained more to rhetoric than reality. "Family Journal" appeared in the subtitle of these mammoth sheets, and they advertised reading for father and mother along with the children. The newspapers themselves often told stories about each member of the family being interested in a specific department of the weekly, whether it was ships' arrivals and auctions for men or obituaries, weddings, and fiction for women.[21] As a miscellany, the weekly paper catered to the disparate interests of an entire family and presumed that unit to be in existence. But the idea of the weekly newspaper providing every member of the family with reading, although persuasive, was mostly nostalgic.

Antebellum America, in fact, witnessed a decline of family reading and an increase in individual reading, particularly in the new urban environment. Historians of novel reading have discovered that young single men represented a prime market for books of fiction.[22] Similar evidence for magazine reading appeared in apprentices' diaries. Edward Jenner Carpenter, a nineteen-year-old apprentice to a cabinetmaking firm in Greenfield, Massachusetts, revealed a whole network for exchanging papers with his friends through the mail. He even mentioned in an entry on February 2, 1845, that he sent his "big brother Jonathan" to his friend David E. Alexander—a rare reference to a mammoth's readership. Later in the 1850s Francis Bennett, a fifteen-year-old apprentice at a dry goods store in Gloucester, Massachusetts, collected his "pictorial" every week, probably *Gleason's Pictorial Drawing-Room Companion,* an illustrated magazine published from 1851 to 1859.[23]

Whereas records of readers's response are scant, it can be inferred from the reformers' idealization of family reading that the practice was waning and that the benefits of collective reading needed to be emphasized. "A book is tenfold a book, when read in the company of beloved friends by the ruddy fire, on the wintry evening; and when our intellectual pleasures are associated with domestic affection." Conversely, the young men who scattered to clubs and taverns and preferred male sociability to the pleasures of the home embodied a threat to morality. "Nowhere is the volume of holy wisdom more appropriate, than when read aloud in the household assembly."[24] Cultural arbiters advocated a return to an earlier, idealized community of readers, where instruction and entertainment were intertwined, where reading aloud was preferred to either silent individual reading or noisy street rowdiness. They advocated family reading, intensive reading, and restraint in a time of print abundance and grotesque buffoonery.[25]

In this period of textual transformation and changing practices, it would not be entirely surprising to detect remnants of past reading habits not only among moral reformers but also among popular readers. One particular example demonstrates the ingrained definition of what a book ought to be. It would seem almost paradoxical that the reading public that was fond of newsprint and printed ephemera would want to keep those papers as permanent reading matter. Such was the case, however, with the practice of binding magazines to form a book. First the *New World* and then, two years later, *Brother Jonathan* published a quarto library edition along with their folio edition as a response to the reading public. "The immense quantity of interesting Current Literature which from week to week has hitherto been presented in the pages of the Folio Paper, has brought us, from all directions, expressions of regret that the matter thus furnished is not printed in a shape convenient for preservation."[26] The readers' desire to preserve and bind together magazine issues, to make their own books, suggests that the transformation of American print culture did not presuppose a tabula rasa but instead allowed old and new practices to coexist in this liminal phase of being in-between. Although print was becoming discontinuous, miscellaneous, and ephemeral—that is, different from traditional print—antebellum readers had appropriated the authority of the word for their own social and cultural needs. The historical moment of change and renewal that the carnivalesque print culture brought to American society did not preclude the fusion of popular and official culture. Some features of book culture, therefore, were carried over into the new miscellany culture. And popular publications in turn introduced new features, such as serialization, into the mainstream world of publishing.

Mammoths and Extras

Extras of Fiction and Drama

The practice of serialization initiated by the dailies' police reports and prevalent in the supplements to the new weeklies was soon adopted by major publishers. Scholars of literary publishing have noted the emergence of extras, or special issues of the weekly papers, as forerunners of paperbound books and dime novels.[27] However, the heyday of the extra deserves further attention. It corresponds to the historical transformation of the modes of production, of which serialization was an important part. Indeed, the sphere—or what sociologist Pierre Bourdieu would define as the "field"—of cultural production and consumption underwent structural changes and re-alignments. For Bourdieu the "literary field" is a microcosm with a specific structure and specific laws, a space of objective relations between producers, writers, critics, and readers, yet not unrelated to the broader political field.[28] As a response to both a structuralist—or formalist—analysis of texts and an earlier Marxist sociology of literature, this approach has the advantage of combining text and context, internal and external readings. It suggests that conflicts and alliances within the literary field are bound to the whole field of power relations in society. Yet external factors affect the structure of the field only indirectly, for, according to Bourdieu, "the field refracts."

Consequently, the notion of field facilitates the conceptualization of the forces present in the period of antistructural liminality of pre–Civil War culture. In the midst of the carnivalesque spectacle, this passage in time marked the confrontation of opposite cultural entities. The production and dissemination of a commercial culture involved the competition of new merchants of popular reading with an older class of cultural custodians, ministers and moral stewards. The emergence of cheap and light printed matter forced the adjustment of internal mechanisms and structures within the literary field. As a sphere of popular literature developed under the people's patronage and with the complicity of entrepreneurial publishers, the institution of criticism emerged. In view of the growing commodification of letters, literary critics raised their voices in defense of an earlier cultural orthodoxy and against merchants of cheap books and a craving reading public. The literary marketplace became a battleground between promoters of trivial or commercial literature and those of serious or legitimate literature.[29] The competition within the literary field also reflected a geographical dualism: on the one hand, the well-established literary dominance of New England, and on the other, New York literary figures such as Park Benjamin, Rufus Griswold, and Nathaniel P. Willis, who boostered magazine publishing in the new metropolis.[30]

In light of the cultural realignment at work in antebellum America, which involved not only the mediation of literary production by literary critics but also the reformers' condemnation of popular practices, one would hardly expect the popular voice to make its way to the printed page. To be sure, American popular taste was filtered by those who controlled the means of literary production. Neither the producers nor the consumers of printed matter could escape the commodification of texts. However, public taste governed the market in antebellum America, and popular demand became one of the forces of production.[31]

One case in point is the use of serialization, which was far from being new by the nineteenth century. Serial forms of publication had long been associated with the poorer public, and earlier European publishers had serialized or intermittently produced texts such as the ballad. By the eighteenth century serialization was used in magazines.[32] The publishers' strategy to maintain their readership through serialization intensified by the early nineteenth century. It became a major mode of literary production associated with capitalist division of labor between authorship, printing, publishing, and distribution.[33] By moving from ephemerality to continuity through installments, serialized publications at regularly scheduled intervals redefined the sense of time.[34]

This was a question not only of publication frequency but also of subject matter. In contrast to newspapers, whose content tended to be up-to-date events, happenings, and the latest news, the story papers featured exotic places and faraway times. An overview of all stories serialized suggests an exercise in intertextuality and a propensity for blending contemporary literature and older fare. For instance, *Brother Jonathan* and the *New World* extras included perennial tales, legends, and historical romances such as "Naval Tale," "Historical Legend," and "Romantic, Chivalric and Supernatural" legends.[35] Particularly popular were stories of a medieval land with queens, noble knights, and magic, an ambivalent world of splendor and chaos. The cheap reprints of *Letters of Mary, Queen of Scots*, edited by the English historian Agnes Strickland, *Francis of Valois, Or the Curse of St. Valliar. A Tale of the Middle Ages*, by the American journalist

Edmund Flagg, and legends of English popular uprisings like Jack Cade's rebellion in 1450 played no small part in the process of popularizing history and conveying an idealized version of the medieval past in the nineteenth century.[36] Likewise, the Middle Ages were the setting of numerous European historical novels, such as Sir Edward Bulwer-Lytton's *The Last of the Barons,* on the Wars of the Roses, an extra for which the publisher of *Brother Jonathan* "confidently anticipated a sale of at least 50,000 copies." [37]

Indeed, Bulwer-Lytton, along with Charles Dickens, the Frenchman Eugène Sue, and the Irishman Charles Lever, was among the foreign authors whose popular works were easily pirated in the supplements because of the absence of international copyright law. Of Bulwer-Lytton's novels, both *Brother Jonathan* and the *New World* published the complete edition of *Zanoni; Or, the Secret Order,* which sold respectively 26,000 and 33,000 copies, while *Brother Jonathan* also published *Eva; A True Story of Light and Darkness.*[38] In 1841 the *New World* serialized Dickens's *Barnaby Rudge,* which appeared the same year in the *New York Tribune.* The *New World* supposedly sold 50,000 copies of the first American edition of Dickens's *American Notes* in its extra of November 1842.[39] *Life and Adventures of Martin Chuzzlewit* appeared in *Brother Jonathan* in March 1843, and in a new format of the *New World* in 1844. The *New World* also offered the first American publication of Sue's *The Mysteries of Paris,* before the publisher Harper and Brothers joined the race by publishing the famous novel by installments in 1843. Following the success of *The Mysteries of Paris,* the *New World* serialized Sue's *The Wandering Jew* in 1845.[40]

Even though European works were more profitable, because they could be reprinted without remunerating their authors, American production was certainly not excluded from the extras. In 1842 *Brother Jonathan* published *The Dancing Feather; Or, the Amateur Freebooters,* by Joseph Holt Ingraham, while in February 1843 the *New World* published Longfellow's "The Wreck of the Hesperus" as well as "Lights and Shadows of Factory Life in New England," by A Factory Girl. By 1842 the *New World* advertised the publication of "Original American Novels" in its extra series, in particular *The Western Captive; Or the Times of Tecumseh,* by Seba Smith; *The Conspirator, a Novel,* by An American Lady; and Walt Whitman's *Franklin Evans, Or the Inebriate. A Tale of the Times.*

However, drama seemed even more popular than fiction, considering the titles of works published in the *New World* and *Brother*

Jonathan extras. The *New World,* for example, published *The Tragedy of Count Alarcos,* by Benjamin Disraeli, and *Glencoe; Or, the Fate of the MacDonalds,* a tragedy in five acts by Thomas Noon Talfourd, in one extra; *John of Procida or the Bridals of Messina,* a tragedy in five acts, and *The Rose of Arragon,* a play in five acts, both by James Sheridan Knowles; *Blue Beard,* a story in five acts by Ludwig Tieck, translated from the German by J. L. Motley; and *Money,* a comedy in five acts by Sir Edward Bulwer-Lytton.[41]

The centrality of theatrical publishing in the antebellum period corresponded to the popular practice of reading melodrama. Plays were published in extras and supplements but also appeared in cheap paperbound editions after popular performances at the Park Theater in New York City or at the Chesnut Theater in Philadelphia. Incidentally, Samuel French, who began publishing plays in New York in the 1850s—most notably the widely distributed *French's American Drama* and then the *French's Standard Drama* series—was selling mammoth weeklies in the late 1830s. The alliance between drama and print in fact ran far deeper than the professional careers of some individuals, and historians of playwrights have located in the late seventeenth century the beginning of ideological relations between print and the stage.[42] By the nineteenth century, plays were read or recited, revealing practices of oral reading at a time when reading was becoming a more private and silent activity. These popular publications of tragedy and melodrama confirmed a common cultural configuration between reading, theatergoing, and even acting. Thomas Chamberlain, an English immigrant worker in New York City, wrote in his diary of the 1840s that his infatuation with the theater and the opera led him not only to attend numerous performances but also to play a role on stage.[43] Reading drama was immensely popular and therefore was included in a general critique of popular amusements. In one reformer's words, "dramatic pleasures" resulting from reading drama were considered useless in comparison with the realities of science.[44]

In the end, it is almost ironic to observe the eventual failure of the mammoth sheets, while their supplements and extras succeeded in launching the market of paperbound books. The demise of the weeklies has been attributed to various factors, including the competition of other magazines and the appearance of Sunday papers, changes in the postal legislation that limited the size of newspapers and increased rates for magazines and pamphlets, and the expansion of the movement for American literary nationalism and the discussion of international copyright.[45] Nonetheless, as this chapter has emphasized the exuberance of the Saturday papers both as illuminated leviathans and literary museums of oddities and curiosities, it would be difficult to overlook that character in an attempt to explain the papers' downfall. The aesthetics of the monstrous that were at the root of the weeklies' success were also contributing to the shortness of their existence. By the 1850s "mere bigness was already out of date."[46]

Publishing success had shifted from the bigger to the handsomer, targeting the middle class, while a cultural consolidation was taking place and distinctions of various reading audiences were crystallizing. Family journals designed for all members of the household were staples for the transition period from the country to the city, as an extension of village gossip. But once home journals, produced and consumed by women, became a medium of domestic literature and advice, while special books and magazines for children appeared, and daily newspapers offered miscellaneous news and fantasy, and even published a Sunday supplement, then a mammoth weekly "to suit all tastes" was no longer adapted to the market. Furthermore, the subscription rate of $3 remained a luxury for the average laborer, who made about $1 a day and could only expect to work about 200 days a year. The spectacular leviathans had a cultural meaning that in the end precluded a middle-class and genteel reception, but also a price too high "to catch the Vulgar." It was only for a short moment of change and renewal, in between phases of cultural stability, that a grotesque popular culture took to the streets and turned the world of print upside down.

CHAPTER 4

Leaflets of Memory:
Giftbooks and the Economy of the Gaze

We say again, we hail these Annuals as the harbingers of better days . . .
while they are designed to be rich in poetry, thought, feeling, and sentiment; yet
they are valued chiefly for the kindly emotions and cherished memories which they
awaken. And when we find them on the center and parlor tables of our kindred
and friends, we know that in every such family are the loved and valued—
hearts, somewhere, that vibrate responsive to kindred hearts.
The Laurel Wreath (1846)

While mammoth sheets and paper leviathans were parading in the
streets of New York City, printing presses in Philadelphia and Boston were orchestrating a different, yet no less extraordinary spectacle. From the late 1820s to the mid-1850s, small books of duode-
cimo size were published annually for holiday rituals of gift giving
and quickly became a showcase of preciosity, combining lavish engravings, consolation poetry, and pressed-leather binding. The thousand different giftbooks that came to ornament many parlors and
private chambers illustrate another aspect of a changing print culture and the in-betweenness of the antebellum period.[1] Although
more surreptitiously than the sensational penny papers or the weekly
papers studied in previous chapters, the new literary annuals significantly altered the world of print in nineteenth-century America. *The
Gift, The Pearl, The Gem, The Bouquet, The Souvenir, The Forget-me-not,*
and *The Remember-me* were unusual books whose function extended
well beyond the words printed in them and whose reading took on
new meanings. This chapter will explore both the content and the

economy of giftbooks in order to understand the fad they generated in the antebellum decades. While most nineteenth- and twentieth-century critics have classified the antebellum annuals as ornamental, light, frivolous, and escapist, the present study proposes to reevaluate those "leaflets of memory" as sacred objects in a new domestic religion.[2]

Gifts and Tokens

Elegant holiday presents offered American literary and artistic production for prices ranging from $3 to $15. Viewed either as a book of prints, a book of poetry, or a book for personal bonds, the giftbook was in fact far more than a book. It was primarily a gift and a sign of taste and social status. When the Boston publisher Samuel Griswold Goodrich alluded to the "Age of Annuals" in his 1857 *Recollections of a Lifetime,* he described the giftbooks as "messengers of love, tokens of friendship, signs and symbols of affection, and luxury and refinement."[3] Himself the publisher of the successful annual *The Token* from 1828 to 1842, Goodrich knew well both the economic and the symbolic value of giftbooks and was eager to respond to it. He was far from being alone. Indeed, American writers and engravers were prompt to take notice of the giftbook market. With the well-known exception of Thoreau, few literati minded being associated with such florid publications.[4] For instance, Edgar Allan Poe admitted in an 1829 letter to Carey and Lea, the publishers of *The Atlantic Souvenir,* that he wanted to be counted among their contributors: "I know of nothing which could give me greater pleasure than to see any of my productions, in so becoming a dress and in such good society as 'The Souvenir' would ensure them."[5] To be sure, praise was not unanimous, and to some contemporaries the gaudy character of the annuals did not signify progress. Ralph Waldo Emerson was one of those critics. As he noted in his journal in April 1852, "The Illustrations in modern books mark the decline of art. 'Tis the dramdrinking of the eye, & candy for food; as whales & horses & elephants, produced on the stage, show decline of drama."[6]

While revealing his elitist contempt for popular taste, Emerson's assessment of illustrated books rightly underscored the shared character of print and stage in the age of P. T. Barnum. It was precisely the exuberance of their visible features that made the Garlands and the Keepsakes a publishing novelty and a temporary commercial success. During the second quarter of the nineteenth century, before they lost to the competition of cheaper publications and before photographs of the late 1850s outdated their fine engravings, the giftbooks represented the astute commodification of American print culture. Moreover, the age of annuals marked the important relationship of the sister arts, poetry and painting, and their mutual influence. It further highlighted the experimental nature of antebellum publishing, which blended past and present, European style and American art, sacred images and secular words. In representing all of those interactions, giftbooks embodied the very liminality of their time, and the ritualistic gestures they fostered strengthened the yet unsealed bond between print and consumption.

Book historians have begun to consider books as physical objects with weight, bulk, and dimensions regardless of their content. As one historian noted, a book "can be held in the hand, clasped to the breast, stuffed in a pocket, stacked on a shelf, laid on a table, or tossed in the air; it can be purchased, lent, stolen, given away, or burned."[7] A book can serve a variety of purposes, and the meaning of reading can only be grasped in a context of other cultural and religious practices. Giftbooks also had multiple uses, and the act of reading was intertwined with the practices of gift giving, status striving, and even simple gazing. Giftbooks provided beholders with great pleasure in the spectacle of precious binding, fine design and format, and splendid engravings. Whether in society or in private, reading or contemplating a giftbook was an emotional experience. Hence the act of offering giftbooks was part of an economy of sentiment, an exchange of beautiful luxury goods for memory and love. Likewise, the display of giftbooks on the center table of the drawing room or the parlor was both a moral and a social act, one that wrapped signs of social distinction in the banner of the crusade for social improvement and the power of sentiment. Thus the activity of reading a giftbook transcended the simple act of deciphering a literary text.

For the most part, giftbooks have been remembered as anthologies of nascent national literature with lavish steel-engraved illustrations. Those delicate repositories of American art and letters have received the attention of scholars interested in the authorship of American works. Giftbooks have been cited in relation to the early contributions of artists and literary men of the new republic—at the expense of lesser production by the so-called scribbling women. It is not the intention of this chapter to redeem the flowery, sentimental content of what a scholar has called "lilies and languors," the vanilla-flavored and honeyed stories of the fashionable annuals. The present objective is rather to locate giftbooks—including their "canonical" texts and their sentimental literature and iconography—in a context of the production and consumption of objects with symbolic value. Giftbooks are analyzed here as physical objects, commodities that belonged to a world of goods and served to mediate personal and social relationships. Giftbooks were not primarily texts designed to convey transcendent messages and ideas. They were things with an economic value and a social life. They were produced, purchased, offered, possessed, displayed, contemplated, read, copied, admired, and praised. They were also loaded with values involving aesthetics, rituals, gender, and class.[8]

The symbolic value of giftbooks may be best exemplified by the anonymous poem, "The Gift," which first appeared in *The Token* for 1829 and was later reprinted in *The Forget-me-not* for 1855. The first six lines are as follows:

> I come with a gift. 'Tis a simple flower,
> That perhaps may wile a weary hour,
> And a spirit within a magic weaves
> That may touch your heart from its simple leaves—
> And if these should fail, it at least will be
> A token of love from me to thee.[9]

Altogether a flower, a spirit, and a token of love, the book as gift was a "transvalued" object, to borrow a concept from anthropology.[10] Gift-books held more than an economic value in the market economy of nineteenth-century publishing.

Annuals are usually classified as serials, because they appeared at regular intervals in the fall for Christmas and New Year's presents. Yet they did not have the ephemeral character of magazines and newspapers. They could be described as hybrid publications, blending features of periodicals and books. They had the format and the value of books, but they were very special books, appearing under the same title from year to year with a different content, at least most of the time.

American literary annuals were designed after the English keepsake and the German *Taschenbuch,* whose broad success depended upon steel engraving. The European annuals of the 1820s and 1830s were an adaptation of the literary almanacs and pocket books that had existed in Europe since the beginning of the eighteenth century. There was nonetheless an important distinction: whereas the eighteenth-century almanac tended to be a calendar with factual information, including chronicles of the preceding year's events and genealogies of the reigning sovereigns, the nineteenth-century annual was composed entirely of poetry, prose, and engravings. The English *Literary Souvenir* and *Friendship's Offering* were anthologies, "cabinets" of poetry and romance, while all the "useful" information was removed. Similarly, the new American annuals bore no resemblance to almanacs.[11] Their content was timeless, even though their seasonal publication recalled the practice of celebrating sacred holidays with illuminated manuscripts and religious books.

Books and Social Rituals

Antebellum giftbooks thus belonged to a long tradition of offering books, particularly the ritualistic New Year's gifts, although their early success made some giftbooks year-round presents entitled "a Christmas, New Year, and Birth-Day present." As special presents books served to initiate or reaffirm a bond between the giver and the recipient; they gave symbolic form to the patronage system. They were preferable to other presents because of their assumed social and sexual neutrality, which was so important in the early modern world of encoded objects.[12] The anthropologist Marcel Mauss studied the practice of gift giving as part of a larger social situation. Mauss recognized forms of giving as gestures in a system of symbolic exchange. He described the practice of gift exchange and reciprocity in contrast to a market economy and "economic" practices. More recently, Pierre Bourdieu has questioned such a contrast between gift exchange and commodity exchange and considered gift exchange as a particular form of the circulation of commodities.[13] In light of Mauss's and Bourdieu's remarks, giftbooks may be considered a prime example of the intricate junction between traditional ritual and modern consumption. Indeed, the development of a market economy in antebellum America did not appear to extinguish the traditional custom of giving books as Christmas and New Year's gifts. Instead, it revived older uses of print while expanding the marketplace. While some cynics would probably conclude that the pretense of "giving" just hid a commercial transaction, the giftbooks' entanglement of the symbolic capital and the economic capital holds significant clues for understanding antebellum society and culture. As products of the nineteenth-century economy of sentiment, giftbooks highlight the workings of cultural designs in a market economy.

In nineteenth-century America, books ranked high on the list of potential gifts. According to T. S. Arthur, the author of the sensational *Ten Nights in a Barroom* and several conduct-of-life books, a book was the ideal gift because it could be both "given and received without violation of delicacy" and might also be a "refining and elevating influence."[14] Books were likewise praised by Eliza Leslie, successful writer of juvenile tales and short stories in giftbooks and *Godey's Lady's Book* as well as editor of both *The Gift* and *The Violet*. In her *Behaviour Book: A Manual for Ladies,* published in 1853, Leslie advised her readers concerning the etiquette of giving and receiving presents: "Young ladies should be careful how they accept presents from gentlemen. No truly modest and dignified woman will incur such obligations. And no gentleman who really respects her will offer her any thing more than a bouquet, a book, one or two autographs of distinguished persons, or a few relics or mementos of memorable places—things that derive their chief value from associations."[15]

Books represented legitimate presents and were enhanced by association not only with the donor but also with writers and distinguished artists. Giftbooks, in particular, were vivid galleries of arts and letters and offered a range of celebrities to be associated with. Once given as a present and personalized through the inscription in the presentation plate, the giftbook was made the possession of one person and served as a pretext for personal bonds between the donor and the recipient. But its content, designed for exhibition, could be shared with a society of readers and beholders. The nineteenth-century giftbook retained some of the traditional values attached to books as collective property. Its artistic and poetic knowledge was a gift likely to be transferable.

"The Souvenir," a story by Eliza Leslie first published in *The Pearl* in 1830, and then in *Affection's Gift* in 1832, illustrated the symbolic value of the giftbook as an instrument strengthening interpersonal bonds. The story is about a souvenir giftbook offered by Mr. Woodley to his daughter Amelia for Christmas, but selected by her brother Oswald in a bookstore on Christmas Eve. The function of the book as reading matter is hardly mentioned: Amelia read all the stories in one evening. The emphasis is rather on the delicate engravings modeled after famous paintings. In the story the plates were carefully examined, and the author narrated the ceremonial reception of the giftbook: "To describe the delight of Amelia on receiving this elegant present, is impossible. She spread a clean handkerchief over her lap before she drew the book from its case, that it might not be soiled in the slightest degree, and she removed to a distance from the fire lest the cover should be warped by the heat. After she had eagerly looked all through it, she commenced again, and examined the plates with the most minute attention. She then showed them to her little brother and sister."[16] The contemplation of images in the giftbook was a major source of pleasure for its reader-beholder. The souvenir was first a token of paternal and fraternal love, but it soon became a friendship offering when Amelia discovered that her brother's young friend, Edwin, was skilled at drawing but lacked models to copy. Amelia eventually presented the souvenir to Edwin, who in turn illustrated her album with copies of the engravings. Leslie's story was meant to teach the lessons of friendship to her young readers. In addition, "The Souvenir" reveals the main function of reading as beholding and the role of the object as the symbolic intermediary in the creation of personal bonds. The giftbook was an object associated with a person, and it created a circle of sociability.

To be sure, the act of giving a book to a young girl was hardly a novelty of antebellum America. What was new was the type of book. The Bible had long been the most common book offered as a gift, and it remained so in nineteenth-century America. Giving a Bible was sharing the gift of God. One example of such belief can be found in a memorable episode of Susan Warner's 1850 bestseller, *The Wide, Wide World,* which involved the purchase of a red Bible. Before the central character, Ellen Montgomery, took leave of her dying mother, they proceeded to a bookstore to purchase a Bible that Mrs. Montgomery wanted her daughter to keep with her on her travels. The gift of a Bible signified a rite of passage from girlhood into womanhood: the sacred text was to accompany Ellen in the "Wide World." The purchase of the Bible was made possible by the selling of Mrs. Montgomery's ring in a jeweler's store; buying a Bible for the young girl thus was part of an exchange economy. Once in the bookstore, Ellen had to make a choice among a dozen different Bibles. "Such beautiful Bibles she had never seen," said the narrator. "She pored in ecstasy over their varieties of type and binding, and was very evidently in love with them all." She had to compare "large, small, and middle-sized; black, blue, purple, and red; gilt and not gilt; clasp and no clasp." Her mother dissuaded her from the choice of a large royal octavo Bible, and from a miniature edition in two volumes, gilt and clasped, with excessively small print. Finally Ellen selected a beautiful red Bible of moderate size and sufficiently large type.[17] Throughout the description of the purchase and the reception a day later, when the Bible was brought in, Warner emphasized the materiality of the Bible as a commodified object and the beauty of the book, both inside and out. Such an episode in the novel epitomized the blend of the new consumption ethic with sentimental morality and piety. The Word of God appeared as a commodity, not only passed from mother to daughter but purchased outside the home.

Likewise, a "friendship's offering" in the shape of a book belonged both to a system of circulation of commodities and a system of social relations. It linked a flow of objects mediated by money to a construction of sociability. The gift of a literary annual reenacted the ritual presentation of a special book to a young lady, and in so doing retained a few attributes of the act of offering a Bible. The distinction between religious books and giftbooks was further lessened by the commodification of both genres, which were primarily valued for their beauty. By merging the sacred with the profane, giftbooks themselves came to offer a new format of devotional literature for private practices of piety. The popular "messengers of love" and "tokens of friendship" thus appeared as both derivative of and substitute for religious artifacts. They epitomized the transition from a religious to an increasingly secular print culture, while participating in the making of a domestic religion. At the same time, the icons and magical commodities that giftbooks constituted were not separated from economic exchange in nineteenth-century America.[18] They closely conformed to the order of the marketplace. For instance, the economic logic of new editions would allow the gesture of gift giving to be repeated on various occasions, thus altering its cultural designs. It is therefore from the dual perspective of culture and consumption that giftbooks constitute a window onto their encoded times.

Giftbooks did not belong in the bookcase on the wall of a drawing room, where only standard authors found sanctuary. Rather, they could be found on the center table, which, according to one historian, "stood in massive, marble-topped dignity in the precise center of every parlor or drawing-room of the period."[19] Such a central piece of furniture held many things, including, in particular, books directed toward the women of the household. Mark Twain described such a parlor in his postbellum *Life on the Mississippi*. The parlor was set in the South, but it could as well have been in New York: "In a parlor, fifteen feet by fifteen—in some instances five or ten feet larger; ingrain carpet; mahogany center-table; lamp on it, with green paper shade . . . ; several books, piled and disposed, with cast-iron exactness, according to an inherited and unchangeable plan; among them, Tupper, much pencilled; also, 'Friendship's Offering,' and 'Affection's Wreath,' with their sappy inanities illustrated in die-away mezzotints . . . ; current numbers of the chaste and innocuous Godey's 'Lady's Book.' "[20]

The giftbook became an essential companion of the center and parlor tables of middle-class homes. It belonged to a parlor set along with center table and lamp and enhanced the status image of the owner. Parlors were the essential "setting of domestic relations," which established claims to social status. Karen Halttunen has persuasively argued that the parlor of the middle-class home was "a middle social sphere," a front room between the urban street and the more private rooms of the house. The parlor represented a woman's "cultural podium," where she would exert her influence. Nineteenth-century parlors were carefully furnished, and their display served to reaffirm social pretensions. Among the new artifacts of the middle-class way of life appeared the carpet, the sofa, and the piano. Giftbooks too were consumer goods that helped define the middle-class household and demonstrate good taste—that is, moral standing.[21]

Visual Texts and Aesthetic Uplift

Even though status striving represented an important function of giftbooks, this did not undermine the symbolism and ritual practices surrounding them. Rather than simply signifying "conspicuous consumption," the social function of the giftbook as ornament was blended in a moral context.[22] The display of giftbooks on center tables was perceived as a social and moral act that might be even more influential than reading itself. *The Young Lady's Friend,* a conduct-of-life book for young girls written by a woman, advised female readers on the social etiquette of books and "reading societies":

> When you receive your young friends at your own house, you should consider yourself responsible for the direction which the conversation takes; and, if it is becoming uncharitable or unprofitable, you should feel bound to give it a safer and better impulse. The introduction of a beautiful annual, or portfolio of prints and drawings, will often answer the purpose; and the fashion of strewing centre tables with books of fine engravings has a moral use which makes it very valuable. I have seen the breath of scandal stopped, and an unpleasant topic changed, by the timely opening of one of these volumes."[23]

In antebellum society, where the love of gold seemed to have displaced the love of kindred, annuals were hailed as the harbingers of better days. They spoke the "language of love," reviving the old customs of Christmas as a jubilee day when "mutual kindnesses and gratulations were given and returned." Annuals expressed a certain nostalgia for the practices of the old times that the "noise and clattering machinery of busy life have drowned."[24] In such a context, the giftbook was seen as a moral tool because it was beautiful. This was indeed a period when the uplifting power of beauty was increasingly perceived as a motive in the age of reform. Neil Harris has described how a growing number of nineteenth-century Americans came to believe that art and religion were interdependent. According to Harris, European travel helped dissolve the traditional suspicion of the arts by Protestant Americans, who gained a new sensitivity toward great art in Catholic societies. This was the personal experience of Fanny Hall, Francis Parkman, Nathaniel Hawthorne, Harriet Beecher Stowe, and Bayard Taylor.[25]

Besides the tourists and the artists, some Protestant ministers also grew more respectful of cathedrals and masterpieces. Diane Apostolos-Cappadona has defined as "Christian romantics" educated clergymen who recognized the alliance between art and religion: for instance, Cyrus A. Bartol, Henry Ward Beecher, Horace Bushnell, Orville Dewey, or Samuel Osgood.[26] They parted with a long tradition of both Platonic philosophy and Protestant theology that for centuries had elevated words and hearing at the expense of images and any tactile perception of the divine. In growing less iconoclastic, the Christian romantics recognized that worshipers could be helped by the visual arts to move toward the invisible, the sacred. Paintings then were regarded as appealing to religious sentiments. Such beliefs were shared by the transcendentalists, who considered that beauty led to contemplation and spirituality, although for them human art continued to be inferior to nature. Henry David Thoreau, for instance, wrote that beauty was "the garment of virtue."[27]

From the traveling artists and the transcendentalist philosophers to proselytizing ministers and the moralizers who sought the beautification of cities and parks, a growing consensus emerged in favor of the development of American art in a variety of forms. A substantial number of Americans of the pre–Civil War decades believed in the power of art to contribute to moral uplift. It is therefore in this context that art reproductions of antebellum giftbooks take on their full meaning. They reveal the inspiration drawn from masterpieces of religious iconography at a time when American-born artists were celebrated and the moral crusade for beauty secularized. The convergence of all those attitudes is best demonstrated by a visual example. Washington Allston's *The Mother and Child* was painted in 1828, purchased by the Boston Athenaeum in 1829, and eventually lost; it was a new version of his 1816 painting titled *The Virgin and Child*.[28] Although it recalled the Renaissance representations of the Madonna and child, particularly those of Raphael, Allston's original painting received mixed reviews. Contemporary critics found the mother too matronly for a Madonna. Allston himself agreed and re-titled the painting *A Mother Watching Her Sleeping Child*. By 1828 his Raphaelite inspiration gave way to a secular and domestic setting of a nurturing mother with a sleeping infant.

Born to the South Carolina rice aristocracy and educated at Harvard, Allston has been described as America's first romantic painter, his colorist talent earning him the title of "the American Titian" in America and abroad.[29] In contrast to his early career as a history painter in England between 1801 and 1818, his later works upon returning from Europe were more intimate, with "imagistic aspects."[30] Allston considered *The Mother and Child* one of his best works and granted Seth Wells Cheney permission to engrave the plate, which the engraver also rated his finest.[31] It appeared in *The Token* for 1837 with yet another title, *The Mother,* along with "The Mother's Jewel," a poem by Hannah Flagg Gould, the New England poet who was

The Mother, *engraved by Seth Wells Cheney after*
a painting by Washington Allston, in The Token *(1837).*
The Library Company of Philadelphia

best known for her verses for children.[32] If the visual representation
had lost both the halo of Christ and its scriptural referent, the companion verbal text by Gould restored the spirituality of the scene. It
served to frame a secularized religious image into a celebration of
motherhood and a prayer for private devotions: "Hence unto Him
be my little one given! / Yea, 'for of such is the kingdom of Heaven!' "
Scriptural words thus joined with the image to secure the ties between Christian piety and domestic intimacy.[33]

Both visually and verbally, motherhood and childhood were recurring themes of antebellum giftbooks, which largely utilized the

Childhood, *engraved by John Cheney after*
a painting by Thomas Sully, in The Gift *(1840).*
Courtesy of the American Antiquarian Society.

religious pictorial vocabulary of the old masters, particularly early-
sixteenth-century Raphael and mid-seventeenth-century Murillo
paintings.[34] Numerous sentimental plates entitled *Infancy, Innocence,*
and *Rosebud* portrayed rosy cheeks and soft curls. *Childhood* was the
title of one engraving by John Cheney, Seth Wells Cheney's older
brother, after a painting by Thomas Sully, the portraitist often called
"the American Lawrence" because his style recalled that of Sir
Thomas Lawrence. The plate was presented as frontispiece for the
1840 volume of *The Gift*, along with a poem by Charles West Thomson. Its delicate touches were to enshrine the perfection of happiness

Emblematical title page, after Parmigiano, in The Token *(1828).*
The Library Company of Philadelphia.

as it appeared in childhood's eye and childhood's heart, "untainted by vice and unsullied by art." [35] The passing moment of childhood's freshness and beauty was also an emotional reminder of the fragility of life, particularly at a time when consolation literature and mourning rituals reveal a greater sensibility to the loss of loved ones. [36] Increased life expectancy somewhat paradoxically made each death more painful. From the sleeping infant to the weeping mother, nineteenth-century literature and art did not lack euphemisms for death. Angels' heads and cherubim even supplied a tenuous link between home and heaven. Antebellum giftbooks thus came to excel in their display of sentimental iconography. The emblematical title page of *The Token* for 1828 offers such an example of sentimentality. It presented a grace surrounded by cherubim after a painting by Parmigiano, thus appropriating religious imagery to celebrate in a secular medium maternal love and the power of sentiment.

Beatrice

All giftbooks' engravings were not derivative of religious icons, however. Historical and literary references were also pretext to the illustrations. For instance, references to Renaissance Italy through the persona of Beatrice were numerous in antebellum America. Whether the name alluded to the Dantesque Beatrice and the Christian sublimation of erotic love, the story of Beatrice Cenci, which combined incest and murder, or Cellini's Beatrice, who reappeared in "Rappaccini's Daughter" by Hawthorne, her angelic beauty or dramatic death were offered to the public gaze. Indeed, Beatrice was, in the words of poet and critic Christopher Pearse Cranch, "a thoughtful poet's dream of woman's dignity and grace." [37]

It was between 1816 and 1819 that Allston painted his *Beatrice,* which Bryan Jay Wolf describes as "an image of pre-Victorian sentimentality—a virginal girl with side-turned head in a moment of devotional pause—to express, ostensibly, a state of innocence 'primeval' and unarticulable." [38] Allston's distinctive talent in representing young ladies' reverie has been appropriately labeled romantic. However, for Wolf the cross and gold chain against the rounded fingers of Beatrice's hand show a confusion between earthly and divine, between eroticism and spirituality. In contrast, Elizabeth Garrity Ellis argues that "Beatrice symbolized the redemptive journey of the imagination, from loss to spiritual transformation through love." [39]

She traces the roots of Allston's small picture to three sources: a portrait of his deceased wife, his study of *The "Bridgewater" Madonna* by Raphael (ca. 1508), and his friendship with the English romantic Samuel Taylor Coleridge, who rediscovered the forgotten Dante. Coleridge's friendship certainly affected Allston's literary approach to the visual arts, as he believed in the power of art to represent poetry. Of course, what better subject to prove it than Dante's *Divine Comedy,* which for the transcendentalists constituted the triumph of poetry over prose and of spiritual truth over doctrine.[40] The message might even be publicized through a giftbook, which served the express function of allying words with images.

Thus Allston's *Beatrice* was engraved by John Cheney for *The Token* (1836) and was accompanied by an eight-page unsigned text, "Dante's Beatrice." Although the painting was praised for faithfully representing the exquisite beauty of Beatrice Portinari, whom Dante had immortalized in poetry, with her fair hair braided with pearls, it was not the only image of Beatrice during the antebellum era.[41] John Cheney engraved another Beatrice, after a painting by Daniel Huntington, which was first used as the frontispiece for *The Gift* in 1844 and then was renamed as *Fair Inez* in both *The Gift* of the following year and *The Ruby* for 1849. This image portrayed a dark-haired maiden with drooping eyes, not unlike the Greek goddesses, Florentine girls, and Indian fruit sellers who represented the dark heroines of nineteenth-century romantic literature and art. Her beauty stemmed in part from her exotic and foreign figure, thus echoing tales of seduction. While the material form of Beatrice held sensual qualities, she was framed in moral terms by writers and poets. In the context of American conservatism of the nineteenth century, printed words were indispensable to mediate the visual experience of the beholder. The great beauty and early death of Beatrice led her to become a symbol of true womanhood and a vision of perfection. Nonetheless, just as her celestial being was to inspire emotion and elevate the soul, her portrait of light and dark shades, which linked love and death, was offered to the gaze of the reader-viewer.

By mid-nineteenth century visual texts were still telling stories, as Henry James noted, and in the case of Beatrice, the public could tap into numerous tales of horrors to fuel its imagination.[42] In a perceptive study of ideal sculpture in nineteenth-century America, Joy Kasson devotes a chapter to narratives of female victimization and visual representations of the tragic death of beautiful women. One

Beatrice, *engraved by John Cheney after a*
painting by Daniel Huntington, frontispiece in The Gift *(1844).*
Courtesy of the Historical Society of Pennsylvania, D7714.

example was *Beatrice Cenci* (1857), a sculpture by Harriet Hosmer, who presented Beatrice as a Christian, with a rosary in her hand. As Kasson reminds us, "Behind the sentimental stories of spiritual triumph lurk untold tales of rape and murder."[43] The Renaissance Beatrice Cenci was indeed a symbol of sorrowing beauty and terrible fate. Held captive and sexually abused by her father, the young girl killed him and was subsequently executed for parricide in 1599. Her tale of family and shame later inspired Percy Shelley's verse play, *The*

Leaflets of Memory

Cenci. But it was a portrait, falsely attributed to Guido Reni, that had intrigued the English poet when he saw it at Palazzi Colonna in 1819. Ultimately, the coming together of word and image told the story of Beatrice as a fallen angel. Hawthorne too was fascinated with the so-called Guido portrait, where he seemed to recognize "Rappaccini's Daughter," and later recalled the event in the seventh chapter of *The Marble Faun.*[44]

Hawthorne's Beatrice tale was set in Padua in the late 1520s. Sighted in the enchanted garden or botanical laboratory of her father, Dr. Rappaccini, Beatrice became the obsession of Giovanni Guasconti, who perceived her alternatively as Dante's Beatrice and poisonous Beatrice, either angel or devil. An abundant critical discourse has been devoted to "Rappaccini's Daughter" because of its ambiguity of good and evil, of medical science and religious dogma.[45] Suffice it to say here that, through the narrator's critique of both Calvinist orthodoxy and Unitarianism, Hawthorne's intriguing tale drew a parallel between the philosophical debates of the Renaissance and the religious controversy of New England in 1844. His story of Rappaccini's daughter, at once a redeeming Beatrice and a tempting Venus, echoed other literary texts, including Genesis, while emphasizing the power of recollection and memories of sensory experiences, which merged past and present.

In the same way as Beatrice Rappaccini, alias Cenci, alias Portinari, Cheney's engraving allegorized the tragic heroine in one of America's leaflets of memory. Giftbooks of the pre–Civil War era in fact gave many faces to the name of Beatrice, which in turn were used to portray nameless images of female beauty and illustrate various stories.[46] From representations of feelings to feminine objects, pretexts to images of women were unlimited. Young women in a state of reverie illustrated *Apprehension, Resignation, Contemplation, Hesitation, Reflection, Imagination, Mourning,* and *Penitence,* as well as embellishments of *The Necklace, The Toilette, The Glove,* and *The Love Letter.* In consequence, the female portrait became a recurring feature of the giftbooks' pictorial content. Whereas early productions exhibited engravings of landscape, maritime, historical, and genre painting, by the late 1830s annuals rarely appeared without at least one female portrait, frequently recycled in subsequent publications.[47] This succeeded in establishing the gender of the targeted reading/viewing audience and in classifying giftbooks as "ladies' books."

The importance of female portraiture in giftbooks is particularly striking given the fact that, by contrast, men far outnumbered women in portrait collections of the nineteenth century.[48] This point has not received much attention from scholars, who instead have emphasized the nineteenth-century bias that ranked portraiture as a second-class art and a far less respected genre than historical painting.[49] In a study of *The Token* and *The Atlantic Souvenir,* David S. Lovejoy notes that "there was no interest in reproducing portraits of specific people."[50] Indeed, formal portraiture held an aristocratic character and would have been at odds with the democratic spirit of the times. Although Lovejoy sees little presence of two portrait painters, Thomas Sully and Chester Harding, in the case of Sully the evidence is more compelling. Of the more than two thousand portraits he painted during his seven decades as an artist, a great number were widely reproduced in issues of *The Gift,* a competing giftbook to *The Token.*[51] Along with other artists, Sully had his portraits engraved for giftbook illustrations and vignettes of title pages, thus joining in the mass production of female portraits. The emblematic female image was indicative of the intended audience, but its repetitive presence contributed to the representation of sisterhood. Next to the many Beatrices illustrated, Helen, Agnes, Annette, Miranda, Viola, Rebecca, Isabella, and Lesbia formed a vivid company. It was, in fact, no mere coincidence if the theme of sisters was particularly popular in giftbooks, both in stories in verse and prose and in group portraits of two or three young women.[52] The visual and verbal texts of antebellum giftbooks testified to the conjoining of the sister arts of painting and poetry. Sometimes a third muse joined in the sentimental allegory of painting, poetry, and music.[53] Trios of young women were then reminiscent of representations of the three graces of giving, receiving, and returning, thus echoing the rituals associated with giftbooks.

The frequency of feminine icons designed to appeal to women patrons and recipients resulted in the feminization of giftbooks and the creation of a separate sphere of print culture. Not only did the texts and images represent women, but, more important, they showed women reading. Such was the case in *The Valentine,* painted by Washington Allston in 1809–11 and engraved by James B. Longacre for the 1828 edition of *The Atlantic Souvenir.* The image was presented in the giftbook along with a poem by Lydia Maria Child, the author of the historical romance *Hobomok.*[54] Allston's precious painting itself was based on a drawing of his first wife, Ann Channing Allston, who

The Valentine, *engraved by James B. Longacre after a*
painting by Washington Allston, in The Atlantic Souvenir *(1828).*
The Library Company of Philadelphia.

died in 1815. It particularly moved the Brahmin society of Boston
during the 1839 Washington Allston retrospective. The painting of
a woman deeply engaged with reading did not fail to provoke comments by Margaret Fuller and Oliver Wendell Holmes.[55] While Boston intellectuals, both male and female, were drawn to the aesthetics of women reading, many female readers of *The Atlantic Souvenir*
could already find particular affinities with the young woman portrayed. Namely, her simple, dark dress called attention not to her
body but to both her face and the letter she was reading. "There's
subtle power in every line of that bewitching Valentine," wrote Lydia

Maria Child. Instead of catching the eyes of the beholder and involving her with the picture through an "I-You" relation, the subject was self-absorbed: "What are thy thoughts, thou placid one?" the poet asked.[56] The young woman's gaze was focused on the page, thus inviting the beholder to engage in a similar activity.[57] Such representations of women reading delicately supported verbal appeals for the expansion of women's letters, thereby contributing to the transformation of antebellum culture.

The Price of Pleasure

All in all, giftbooks' images were not random illustrations. In fact, the adjoined text was usually ordered by the editor for the purpose of providing an appropriate commentary for a previously selected engraving. The sequence of production leaves no doubt about the primacy of visual representations. The importance of the giftbooks' appearance was not overlooked by the publishers, who were committed promoters of the new literary annuals. While giftbooks have been cited for initiating the practice of paying writers for their literary contributions, a closer look at the cost books of Carey and Lea for *The Atlantic Souvenir* and of Carey and Hart for *The Gift* reveals that contributors and editors represented only a secondary expense in the giftbooks' economy.[58] From 1826 to 1845, payments to writers remained fairly stable, between $500 and $700 for a total of about 320 pages of prose and poetry combined. The cost of contributions to *The Gift* and of Eliza Leslie's editing together represented an average 6 percent of the total cost of production of the annual. By comparison, the total cost of contributions to *The Atlantic Souvenir* averaged $570 but decreased on a percentage basis as the size of the edition moved from 2,000 to 10,500.[59]

Far more than the new practice of paying literary contributors—which already set *The Gift* above the majority of giftbooks—other expenses were responsible for the costly production of the books.[60] Given the relative stability of the price of paper and printing during this period, it was no doubt the combination of engravings and binding that constituted the bulk of the expenses. For instance, in the cases of both *The Atlantic Souvenir* and *The Gift*, engravings amounted to about 20 percent of the total cost of production. Binding represented about 30 percent of *The Atlantic Souvenir*'s budget and nearly 40 percent of *The Gift*'s budget.[61] Thus engravings and binding—that is, the signs of distinction of giftbooks—added up to 50 or even 60 percent of the total production costs. From the late 1820s to the 1840s, the production rate per book remained over $1, even when the size of each edition increased. This was due to the cost of binding, which was not reduced by larger editions, and to the continuing rise in the cost of engravings. The latter was the result of increased competition for the handsomest pictures and the best engravers.[62]

With retail prices ranging from $3 to $15, giftbook publishing may have appeared to be a profitable business. In reality, of course, the profit margin of the publisher was directly affected by both the wholesale value and the cost of production. Scattered data for wholesale values suggest stable prices and publishing profit that remained proportionate to the volume of sale.[63] Various strategies were introduced to cut costs, such as selling used plates for illustrations or recycling some of them in later publications. Nonetheless, the costs for literature, paper, printing, and binding were hardly reducible. Only engravings could significantly affect the cost of each giftbook, but their popularity precluded any decision to limit their number. In the face of rising prices for illustrations, then, the best methods of assuring greater profits would have been either to increase the volume of sales or to raise wholesale value per item. Those options were to be ruled out primarily because sales of each edition reached a ceiling by the 1830s, as the market became saturated and competition from other annuals intensified. In addition, the alternative of raising wholesale value would have been at odds with the intended middle-class target. Hence the wrapping of the same text in different qualities of bindings, from cloth to calf, emerged as a strategy allowing publishers to cater to a public fond of distinctive objects.[64] By the 1840s the volume of editions was smaller, but the range of bindings and formats was wider. This marketing strategy gave the illusion of uniqueness and exclusivity in the age of mechanical reproduction. Publishers stressed the beautiful finish and preciosity of the giftbook, which was perceived as a symbol of taste and status.

So even in a context of greater economic pressure, publishers continued to fill giftbooks with what their targeted public cherished most: engravings. They spared no pains in making splendid books, ornaments for the parlor table. Yet in the age of reform, pleasure derived from the illustrations was described in terms of moral and social usefulness. While critics scorned that annuals were conceived merely as a source of entertainment, both producers and consumers

chose to sustain the economy of the gaze. The question, nevertheless, remains whether small books, however beautifully illustrated,
could be "pure" tokens of love, untouched by the economic system that generated them. Just as publishers were to capitalize on
the beauty of their printed goods, the negative effect of monetary
transaction might simultaneously tarnish and devalue that beauty.
Indeed, annuals were thought to redeem the impersonal and materialistic world; they were presented in contrast to rather than dependent upon the marketplace. At the same time, they were charged
from the outset with those very values of acquisitiveness and immediate gratification. To conclude along with the critics of the time that
the success story of giftbook publishing indicated a declension from
Protestant asceticism to immoral hedonism would give little credit
to the public's own motive. If reader-beholders of giftbooks engaged
in an act of consumption, they did so not so much to celebrate the
world of commerce as to value "expressive goods" that had aesthetic
and spiritual significance. As a refined artifact, the giftbook offered
a sense of beauty that was intended to move its beholder and therefore testify not only to her aesthetic taste but also to her virtue and
sensibility.[65] The gendered economy of sentiment hoped to restore
an earlier spirit of reciprocity to a society transformed by the market
economy. The irony was that once feminized and entrusted with the
benevolent mission of gift giving and sentimental exchange, these
embellished books implicitly bore the marks of commodities and
could no longer escape the capitalist system they were designed to
alleviate. To recognize the hegemony of the market, however, in no
way diminishes the multifaceted role of giftbooks, which still centered on emotional enjoyment, whether it served an individual or a
social need.

Gustave Flaubert introduced a wonderful description of the pleasure of turning the pages of a keepsake in *Madame Bovary*. The heroine, Emma, had entered a convent at the age of thirteen, where
she received a religious education, sang sentimental songs in music
class, and surreptitiously read novels. She read Walter Scott, historical romances, and also keepsakes that her schoolmates had received
as New Year's gifts. "She quivered as she blew back the tissue paper
from each engraving: it would curl up into the air, then sink gently

down against the page. . . . There were portraits of unidentified aristocratic English beauties with blond curls, staring out at you with their wide light-colored eyes from under straw hats. . . . Others, dreaming on sofas, an opened letter lying beside them, gazed at the moon through a window that was half open, half draped with a black curtain."[66]

It was with the bracket lamp above her head, in the silence of the dormitory at night, that the young Emma was reading the keepsake annual, beholding the pictures, and dreaming. "It was very exciting," said Flaubert. Like Emma Bovary, any reader-beholder could be lost in the intimate spectacle of a giftbook, although American portraits were more likely to represent the face of innocence and true womanhood than aristocratic beauties. It was almost as if the act of reading and gazing resembled an enchantment. As object, the giftbook held a magical charm, like an amulet or a talisman. In fact, *The Talisman,* an annual published in New York from 1828 to 1830, claimed explicitly to possess mystic virtues. The sentiment of friendship, gratitude, respect, or love was indestructible so long as the book was kept. "There's magic in the web of it."[67] Historians have noted the deployment of books as magical talismans and aids to divination. The Bible, in particular, served symbolic and unorthodox purposes such as "swearing oaths, registering births, curing the sick, making decisions, predicting the future, and warding off devils."[68] Likewise, "tokens of friendship" were charged with magical properties and virtues quite apart from the literary texts that were printed in them. Unconventional uses of print and belief in the magical power of books thus survived well into the secular and rational age. The antebellum giftbook seen as a "commodity fetish" combined a commodity form with precapitalist residues of sensuous magic and aura.[69]

From rituals of friendship to comfort for deathwatches to feminine icons and fetishes, the antebellum leaflets of memory fostered cultural practices far more diverse than the mere presentation of literary anthologies. While it belonged to a genre of printed matter born in Europe and in vogue internationally, the American-made giftbook had a multilayered significance that needs to be analyzed in the particular historical context within which it developed. The success story of that ephemeral publishing venture reflected not only the commercial spirit of the period but also the ambivalence of American society toward sensory experience and pleasure reading.

Banknotes, featuring feminine emblematic images,
from the Bank of Alabama, Huntsville, and the
Connecticut River Banking Company. Longacre Collection,
The Library Company of Philadelphia.

Both the power of sympathy and the interplay of words and images conflated in a new type of book during the historical moment when a religion of the heart helped remodel a book culture that itself was originally rooted in the Protestant religion of the book. This was not just a reading revolution but also, as Joy Kasson suggests, a "viewing revolution."[70]

Of course, the key participant in that transformation was the female reader-beholder. Young women were not only the recipients of giftbooks but also the subjects of their engravings. Because of their exclusion from economic competition, women were thought to be the moral guardians of American society and the angel in the house, albeit a consuming angel. At the same time, through their overwhelming presence in giftbooks' illustrations, women feminized American print culture. Their newly gained visibility in pictorial texts was so effective that feminine emblematic images, such as cherubim

Leaflets of Memory

and graces, appeared on banknotes next to steamboats, railroads, and eagles, thereby sealing the bonds between sentimentality and the marketplace.

In sum, the material culture of antebellum giftbooks succeeded in telescoping the symbolic and the economic values of books. The cultural meaning assigned to them as agents of improvement and harbingers of a better society was more than a façade for status markers. Belief in aesthetic uplifting determined the way these delicate symbols of love and taste were produced and marketed. For all those reasons, giftbooks were objects to be treasured. Yet, while their outlook posed as gender-defined, their monetary value was a constant reminder of their exclusive character. Not many a brother, husband, or lover could afford to pay at least $3 for a little book. Moreover, not all women were represented in print: only white ladies appeared in the engravings. Giftbooks thus precluded a lower-middle-class and working-class audience. They remained signs of social and sexual distinction, catering to only one stratum of the reading public. During and after the economic depression of 1837, when the motto of the so-called battle of books was "cheap," the emphasis in giftbook publishing was rather on splendor and delicacy. The luxurious appearance of giftbooks seemed at odds with the egalitarian and utilitarian values of Jacksonian America, yet they were scorned along with other print media by those who censured "cheap and light" books. These miniature books had in fact transformed the printed word into a feast of images. In spite of their preciosity, giftbooks were popular, but for only a passing moment. Once the feminine engravings were reproduced in ladies' magazines that reached a wider and less affluent public, the age of annuals came to an end. Daguerreotypes emerged as the new keepsakes, to be offered or possessed in memory of a loved one, and the society that came of age with the Civil War turned to other sights to replace the gaze of leaflets of memory.[71]

CHAPTER 5

The "Lady's Book" and the Female Vernacular in Print Culture

A clergyman of New England, distinguished for piety and learning, writing
of the "Lady's Book" as the favorite periodical of his wife, observes—"If it belongs to
the department of 'light literature,' it is light *in the sense that it* illuminates."
"Editors' Table," *Godey's Lady's Book,* June 1847

As the previous chapters have indicated, antebellum publications were ephemeral, eye-catching expressions of an ebullient period. *Godey's Lady's Book,* the most popular periodical for women both North and South, is another example of America's innovative and festive print culture during the pre–Civil War decades. In the words of a contemporary commentator, it was "The Banquet of the Boudoir."[1] Although the ladies' magazine long outlived the penny press, the mammoth papers, and the giftbooks, it too reflects the transitory nature of antebellum publishing. The rise of *Godey's Lady's Book* from the 1830s to the 1850s testifies to the subtle complicity between the magazine's producers and the reading audience they sought to satisfy. The antebellum magazine is therefore representative of a specific historical moment of cultural turmoil. Its heyday, however, faded with the 1857 depression, which was soon followed by the war. The postbellum magazine was altogether a different publication, thriving on sewing patterns and household hints.

In contrast to its late-nineteenth-century offspring, the pre–Civil War magazine still relegated commercial ads and the world of goods to the back of its issues.[2] Instead, what it successfully marketed were the colored prints interleaved between fiction and moral fare. Borrowing from the feminine engravings that first appeared in giftbooks, yet literally adding color to their images, prints portraying elegant and delicate ladies came to enhance the new American women's magazines during the 1830s and thereafter. Often torn from the issues to decorate middle-class homes, these hand-colored steel engravings represented a major commercial feature of antebellum women's periodicals. They were unanimously praised, superseding the sentimental and lachrymose stories in the public taste. Yet even though these images represented an intrinsic component of nineteenth-century American print culture, scholars have repeatedly neglected them and considered them almost as an anomaly in the narrative of historical progress. As one historian concluded, the fashion engraving represented "a particular wrinkle of early American civilization."[3] This chapter will examine the textual construction of *Godey's Lady's Book* during its formative decades and assess the historical significance of portraying women in a monthly magazine. As the paramount example of the rise of women's periodicals, *Godey's* further illustrates another aspect of the festive carnivalesque in print culture and the transformation of public taste before the Civil War.

The ladies of Louis Antoine Godey's magazine, more than the features of other periodicals, illuminate the construction of femininity in antebellum printed material. First published in 1830, the famous Philadelphia magazine continued uninterrupted monthly publication for over sixty years. Few books about pre–Civil War culture have failed to mention *Godey's* as the epitome of sentimental literature and frivolous taste. Scholars have sometimes cited the magazine's ornaments as part of the style and economic astuteness of women's periodicals. However, most studies have focused on the literary contributions by Edgar Allen Poe, Nathaniel Hawthorne, Ralph Waldo Emerson, Harriet Beecher Stowe, Lydia H. Sigourney, and Catharine M. Sedgwick, among others, as a way of redeeming the triviality of the fashion magazine. More recently, feminist scholars have been concerned with legitimizing sentimental literature and reassessing the protofeminist functions of lachrymose stories for women readers. They have emphasized the role of Sarah Josepha Hale, crusader for female education and editor of *Godey's Lady's Book* from 1837 to 1877. But feminist critics too have chosen to ignore the frivolous ornaments apparently at odds with republican simplicity and the "matriarchy of the kitchen." In their accounts, nineteenth-century magazines were designed for readers, not viewers. Consequently, the visual and frivolous aspects of fashion and pictorial embellishments have rarely been deemed worth mentioning.[4]

The cultural centrality of a ladies' magazine with a national distribution that claimed 150,000 subscribers by the time of the Civil War deserves further attention.[5] Its icons of femininity and ladyhood also belong to a reexamination of nineteenth-century American culture, because they point to the distinctive character of women's textual emergence. The visual texts of the magazine represent not only an additional object of textual inquiry but, more important, a window onto the commercialization of sentimental literature and a measure of the internal tensions within nineteenth-century representations of gender.

Godey's Lady's Book regularly claimed in its editorials and advertisements to be "literary and pictorial," "useful and entertaining." One must therefore inquire into the complex relationship of images to texts and explore how illustrations both underwrote and undermined the sentimental message of the magazine's stories and editorials. In addition, the introduction of pictorial texts into a broader discussion of sentimentality offers a way to transcend the ongoing debate between the antisentimentalist critique and the revisionists. Ann Douglas has reiterated the value judgment of nineteenth-century cultural arbiters, seeing sentimental literature not only as a lesser genre but as a corrupting means of self-indulgence and the epitome of consumerism. Her unambiguous approach recalls the Frankfurt School's critique of mass culture.[6] At the same time, Douglas's critique of a feminine and mass culture provoked a revisionist approach to sentimental novels. Jane Tompkins, in particular, has convincingly deciphered the "world-shaking" designs of novelists and the readers' empowerment as inscribed in popular novels of the nineteenth century.[7] Yet revisionists have been limited to the private works of popular literature, and skeptical historians still wonder about the influence of sentimental power beyond the private realm. If the Christlike death of Little Eva in Harriet Beecher Stowe's *Uncle Tom's Cabin* best epitomized the work of sentiment, it did not hinder the "peculiar institution." Despite Abraham Lincoln's subsequent praise, Stowe's printed words alone could not eradicate the institution of slavery. The economic and political system apparently remained unchanged with the advent of popular and sentimental literature.[8]

Nonetheless, the case of *Godey's* suggests that the transformative force of popular literature was a public event. Middle-class female readers were not merely passive consumers of sentimental periodicals but rather played an active role in the transformation of American culture. Nineteenth-century reading of sentimental literature led not only to the construction of meaning in individual lives but also to the public transformation of print culture. Women in antebellum America in fact achieved significant cultural gains. They introduced a popular and feminine aesthetic and forced the traditional print culture to make a space for woman's voice, even if that space was conceived as a separate sphere. They publicly altered antebellum culture, while contributing to its stratification and categorizing. The antebellum feminization of a branch of the periodical press reflected the specificity of its targeted audience, while enforcing the division of gender through the production of separate texts.[9]

The nineteenth-century visual and textual representation of women was both progressive and restrictive. The early American republic witnessed the production of publications especially designed for women but confined them within the boundaries of a feminine aesthetic. Ultimately, even though ladies' magazines that published fashion plates as a way to attract female subscribers retained the stigma of popular printed matter, illustrations themselves were increasingly accepted in the world of publishing in the decades preceding the Civil War. In this respect, the white middle-class women readers of *Godey's Lady's Book* contributed to a major change in American culture.

A close analysis of the magazine's engravings will illustrate the cultural meaning of sentimental figures in antebellum America. For this purpose the engravings are considered not so much as direct representations of the image that nineteenth-century white middle-class women had of themselves, but rather as texts that the reader-viewers were appropriating, enjoying, and approving. It may seem obvious to us that a magazine targeting a female audience would offer fashion plates. However, a careful reading of *Godey's Lady's Book* reveals the historicity of the hand-colored steel engravings that featured duos and quartets of ladies.

The Coming of *Godey's*

To be sure, *Godey's Lady's Book* was not the first illustrated magazine for women. Colored fashion plates had been published in *La*

Gallerie des modes in Paris from 1778 to 1787, and several English ladies' magazines of the late eighteenth century featured discussions of fashion and sometimes a fashion plate next to the text. The early American republic followed the example of the mother country and witnessed the production of periodical publications specially designed for the "fair sex," in contrast to the absence of women's subjects in newspapers. Even monthly repositories of polite literature such as the Boston *Miscellany* and the Boston *Atheneum, or Spirit of the British Magazines* hoped to increase their circulation by attracting women. Nonetheless, fewer American magazines imitated English ladies' magazines in publishing a fashion plate as part of a market strategy. For instance, the Philadelphia *Ladies' Magazine and Repertory of Entertaining Knowledge,* which appeared from 1792 to 1793, copied large portions of the London *Lady's Magazine* but apparently lacked money "for such additions as the engravings, patterns, and pages of music" especially attractive to subscribers.[10]

Fashion images did not make an appearance in American magazines for women until the 1820s and 1830s, as though prejudice against fashion was the result of the emancipation of the young and virtuous republic from the influence of corrupt Europe. The first American periodical for women to issue a colored fashion plate was the Philadelphia *Album and Ladies' Weekly Gazette* in June 1827. Its editor, Thomas C. Clarke, also founded the *Ladies' Literary Port Folio* in 1828, with the same attraction of a fashion plate.[11] But soon afterward *Godey's* achieved preeminence with colored fashions and other embellishments. While offering a symbiosis between traditional European fashion publications and American giftbooks of the late 1820s, *Godey's* set the pattern for a definite genre of magazines soon to be replicated. Its success was so persuasive that images of steel-engraved ladies became a significant feature of the pre–Civil War publishing landscape.[12]

It is worth noting that the commercial use of fashion plates was controversial. For the first seven years of its existence, *Godey's* made the fashion engraving and the discussion of fashion a priority. However, when the conservative reformer Sarah Josepha Hale took over the editorship of *Godey's* in 1837, she vehemently condemned fashion and only reluctantly retained the magazine's famous fashion plates for the sake of the public. Hale had already confronted the question of fashion plates in her own Boston publication, the *Ladies' Magazine,* before merging with *Godey's*. She had criticized the display of fashion as a symbol of extravagance and European luxury ever since her publishing beginnings in 1828. Nonetheless, she was forced to compromise with the public's demand because of economic necessity and finally introduced a fashion plate in the November 1830 issue of the *Ladies' Magazine*. When she gave up the use of fashion plates for good in 1834, just at the time of fierce competition in the publishing world, her *Ladies' Magazine* simultaneously declined in popularity.[13]

In effect, even though editors and publishers produced the magazines, they had to reckon with the readers' aesthetic dictates, which made images central to the economy—including production and consumption—of antebellum feminized print culture. While the public's demand was a major force of production, the dissemination of engravings in books and magazines was also due in part to the technology available by the second quarter of the nineteenth century for the reproduction of images. Cheaper than copperplates but much finer than woodcut, steel allowed an intensive reproduction of illustrations. It satisfied both the public and the publishers, who aimed at a profit through mass production and lowering of the item price. However, since the steel-engraving plate needed to be printed separately from the text, it was more expensive than a woodcut. The golden age of steel engraving from 1825 to 1845 has been described as the successful period of illustrated publishing for the middle classes, who were particularly fond of "semi-luxurious" illustrated books.[14] *Godey's Lady's Book* was both a product and an agent of that publishing golden age. Yet the experience of *Godey's* contained its own specificity because of the size of its reading public, the duration of its popularity, and the context of American culture, which emphasized republican simplicity in contrast to European luxury and elitism.

Interestingly, the magazine's fashion plates were admired and appropriated by its subscribers even though they were juxtaposed to and controlled by stories containing the dress reformers' message, which championed sincerity and condemned the hypocrisy of fashion. Nineteenth-century women readers were probably interested in the fashion of dress exhibited in *Godey's,* but their satisfaction resulted primarily from the portrayal of women in full-page watercolored engravings. The issue, then, is not so much the character of fashion and its progressive acceptance in American society as it is female imaging. Accordingly, the style of the fashion represented in print is historically less important than the very fact that women were represented in print at all. Dresses, hats, and petticoats did matter for *Godey's* readers, but the analysis of their debut in print goes beyond mere discussion of fashion. The publication of feminine and sentimental figures in *Godey's Lady's Book* testifies to the contribution of the reading public to the construction of a popular print culture.[15]

Nineteenth-century readers were buying a synthesis of pictures and narratives when they subscribed to *Godey's*. Potential conflict was embedded in the juxtaposition of visual and verbal texts. For *Godey's* was a composite text in which images were controlled by words and assimilated into the discourse on sentimentality, while at the same time possibly undermining the authority of the text and allowing autonomous readings.[16] Images gave a specific character and added value to the magazine. However, while the fashion engravings were as important as, or even more important than, the editorials in terms of commercial strategy and readers' pleasure, they were integrated into the magazine and assumed the power of the printed word. For instance, images were for "telling stories," and fashion plates represented conversation pictures when labeled with captions such as "It is a secret."[17] Images, then, were reminiscent of a time of oral and visual communication, and such elements of a residual culture long undermined by textualization were incompletely incorporated into print culture.[18] Under a cover of harmony with the written word, images were subversive. They challenged the legitimate culture without representing an alternative culture per se, for they had acknowledged the power of the word. In turn, the written word attempted to dominate images that, once controlled, could serve the instructive function of print. *Godey's* was a vivid example of such a strategy.

Godey's Ladies

Godey's Lady's Book published twelve issues a year. From about 48 pages in the 1830s and early 1840s to about 60 pages in the late 1840s and over 92 pages in the 1850s, with some issues up to 120 pages, the "Book"—to use the magazine's self-reference—changed shape over time. Any change was presented as an improvement by the editors. With the increase in size, some new features were introduced. The magazine of the 1830s was essentially made up of stories, poems, musical composition, fashion intelligence, and a hand-colored fashion plate every three months. Additional departments were introduced in the 1840s, such as a ladies' work department or health and beauty advice. Woodcuts of needlework, crochet, and hair design increasingly appeared within the text. The constant policy of the magazine was to augment the number of pictorial embellishments at the same rate as the number of pages. In the 1850s *Godey's* doubled its size, and advertisements on back covers emphasized the "immense increase of reading matter without reducing the number of full page steel engravings."[19] Such a strategy is easily explained: illustrations were profitable.

Indeed, Louis Antoine Godey, widely known as "the Prince of Publishers," was a shrewd entrepreneur.[20] Born in New York City in 1804, Godey was more or less self-educated. He combined an early penchant for books with a financial instinct. Not only was he a creator and a builder, but he considered himself a gentleman. He was devoted to the "fair ladies" and fathered the popular monthly magazine for their delight, while sensing its commercial value. He saw a source of profit and secured it with extensive use of advertising and self-congratulatory letters. Louis Godey skillfully courted his reading audience by using Barnumesque strategies and by boosting the public image of his magazine. Thus what one historian once said of antebellum entertainment such as melodrama or P. T. Barnum's museum was also true of popular reading matter, especially women's magazines: "Success was as much a matter of preparing an audience as pleasing it."[21] For instance, Louis Godey told his readers that the illustrations constituted the main expense of the magazine: he could run *Godey's* at lower cost without the "embellishments." But he would generously continue to satisfy the readers' demand for visual texts. In fact, such a big investment resulted in a secure profit from subscriptions. Therefore, from the very first years of its publication, *Godey's* advertised the quality of the plates and the number of engravings per issue rather than the quality of its literature.

Throughout its existence the magazine's most distinctive feature was the watercolored fashion plate. The plates were colored at home or in the shop by women hired specifically for the purpose. Watercoloring had traditionally been an essential feminine accomplishment.[22] At the same time, it seems particularly ironic that the emergence of a female identity in print was made possible by the use of cheap female labor at the protoindustrial level. At one point Louis Godey had 150 employees for hand coloring alone. He informed his readers that "the mere coloring of the prints cost us nearly three thousand dollars per annum."[23] *Godey's* sometimes experimented with other techniques; for example, the first mezzotint fashion plate was published in February 1847. But in general the pattern was set by hand-colored steel engravings. The production of the plates thus reflected a historical moment of manual reproduction, one of proto-industry within traditional settings that resisted the shift toward mechanical reproduction already operating in the printing industry.

The images in *Godey's* retained the unique aura of artisanal labor in the face of commodity production. The magazine's female workers sometimes used another color for a dress when the first ran out, leading to complaints about the discrepancy between one reader's fashion plate and her neighbor's. The publisher denied mass production and ingeniously justified the variety by arguing for the uniqueness of a woman's complexion: "We now colour our plates to different patterns, so that two persons in a place may compare their fashions, and adopt those colours that they suppose may be most suitable to their figures and complexions." [24] Undoubtedly the fate of the "Book" was attached to its embellishments, and its success seemed to vanish once its illustrations appeared old-fashioned. To be sure, illustrations became essential to most magazines after the Civil War, and *Godey's* vaunted "steel against wood" as a proof of luxury and a strategy for survival. However, its images began to look provincial, and by the late 1880s halftone electrotypes supplanted the magazine's historic engravings.[25]

During its antebellum heyday, *Godey's* displayed fashion engravings in addition to a variety of illustrations—engravings of landscapes, genre paintings, and religious scenes—recycled from contemporary giftbooks. The fashion plates were not only more valuable but also technically different. They seemed unfinished, more like drawings without volume and body, projections waiting for a finish and color, or just suggestions or models, prepared canvas awaiting women's own construction of meaning. This was not surprising, given the specificity of female education, which had long stressed intuitive and emotional qualities at the expense of mental capacities. In contrast, the functional curriculum of female academies in the early republic had little room for an ornamental education, which had traditionally emphasized the "elegant accomplishments" such as drawing and embroidery as a badge of upper-class status. Yet well-minded middle-class reformers who promoted functional education for wifehood and motherhood failed to eradicate such decorative accomplishments and could only incorporate them in their moral

The "Lady's Book"

reform for female improvement.[26] Drawing was based, after all, on the skill of reproduction rather than creation. Education in drawing seemed particularly appropriate for working women—supposedly well adapted by nature to the manufacture of articles of taste and fancy—and a safe path away from vice and misery. As one teacher of drawing put it, "The natural refinement and delicacy of the female mind renders it a fruitful soil, that should not be neglected or let run to waste, when its cultivation might realize such rich advantages, not only to themselves, but to their country." The advantages of education in drawing for girls became essential and second only to the formation of religious principles.[27]

The fashion plate, the hallmark of *Godey's*, represented more than just the dresses. The costumed figures posed against a decorated background, indoors or outdoors, with furniture, wallpaper, and drapery fabrics. The fashion plate itself was a setting for parlor theatricals and intimate staging. Whether standing or sitting, the ladies in the engravings kept the same empty expression on their faces. The mouth was closed; the eyes looked down or at another figure. The engraving was a distant spectacle offered to reader-viewers. In contrast to portraits, *Godey's* ladies did not pay attention to the spectator; they looked at each other and were involved in their closed society or separate sphere. In addition to the direction of the eyes, the orientation of the heads was interesting. The ladies held their heads quite artificially, with a sort of mask, as if heads were accessories like hats. They were not supposed to represent the source of female energy, for women's movements were directed not by intellect but by sentiment. Even more significant were the gentle, clean hands of these ladies. The hands acted out dialogues in the fashion plates; they were directed to other figures or they held objects, most likely flowers or handkerchiefs, but often books or engravings, presumably from *Godey's Lady's Book*. The world of *Godey's* represented the "civilization of the hand" as opposed to the machine.[28] The fireplace or home was women's sphere, a haven separated from industry and social evil. The fashion plates thus reaffirmed the nineteenth-century cult of true womanhood. Moreover, the gentle white hand holding an object was a symbol of leisure and property. *Godey's* pictured a world of objects to be possessed and appropriated, and in so doing it defined itself as another object in middle-class interiors.[29]

Unlike other objects, however, *Godey's* engendered a new vernacular. Words and images complemented each other and made a whole,

Fashion plate [untitled], Godey's Lady's Book, *July 1845.*
Courtesy of Olin Library, Cornell University.

an imaginary, speaking body. The publication of fashion engravings reconstructed in print an alliance between gesture and voice, simulating an oral performance. Color, the most visible component of pictorial signs, gave the fashion plate its "flesh and body." [30] Feminine writing could not exclude feminine imagery, which already incorporated a male-dominated discourse about the female body. While masculine writing did not presuppose the juxtaposition of pictorial representations of the male body, female literary culture was compelled to incorporate physical images of women. Because of the social sanction against women's speech and writing, silent and gestural women used images in their *prise de parole.* Women as "tongue snatchers" took the word and molded it to their image and likeness, while implicitly surrendering to a female-as-object discourse. [31]

In the engravings the details of dress were secondary to the decor, the situation, the pose. A fashion plate entitled *Taking Tea in the Arbor,* for example, was a staged representation of a private scene. The description of the plate, which had been included in the first article during the early years of the magazine, was moved to the last pages of the issue soon after Sarah Josepha Hale became the editor. Hale's conservative feminism failed to rid *Godey's* of its fashion images, but at least frivolous discussions of fashion were relegated to either the "Editors' Table" or the "Editors' Book Table," thereby isolating the engraved figures and private scenes from their prompt-book. Only the curious reader would discover that one figure was wearing a "morning-dress of white cambric, of exquisite quality, the skirt trimmed with double rows of muslin puffing," while the other had a "walking-dress of rich jasper silk."[32] For most reader-viewers, however, the specificity of the fashion matter may have been less important than the theatricality of the scenes in the plates.

The theatricality of social relationships was newly accepted in the late 1840s and 1850s. Parlor theatricals reflected the social representation of middle-class gentility.[33] Similarly, *Godey's* staged theatrical performances directly on the page for its readers. The "Book" was an ersatz theater for a large audience, and its theatrical prints curiously recalled a long tradition of books of theater. The visual effect of theater was communicated through the numerous illustrations of the major scenes of the play. The role of the engraving as a two-dimensional theatrical stage was confirmed by its presentation through a medallion, which re-created the environment of a theater and projected the stage in the back, while it simulated the intimacy of a performance for the solitary reader.[34] The fashion engraving was conceived as the theatrical exhibition of a domestic scene in which the space was similar to the parlor in nineteenth-century middle-class homes, between the private rooms and the public street. Meanwhile, the description was that of a performance, as indicated by the commentary: "Apart from its interest as a faithful report of fashion, in the arrangement of the scene and its actors, our artist has displayed unusual good taste."[35]

The fashion plate also standardized female duos and quartets. The repetitious presentation of almost identical figures, like a species, was a pictorial reconstitution of the "sisterhood" of middle-class women.[36] They participated in intimate relationships, sharing secrets or chitchat about fashion. Furthermore, the sequence of repetitive images created a cinematic montage, generating meanings independent from the editorials or adjoining stories. The figures thus offered a potential autonomy from the written text. The reader-viewer was allowed to interact with the freed visual texts, contemplating them silently as icons of a private and domestic religion. At the same time, the visual representation of gender provided all readers with a shared experience and served as a blueprint for the formation of a group consciousness.

But not all American women had the opportunity to appear in the new feminine print culture, which was molded to the likeness of ladies, not mill girls. The mill girl was not given a voice in the cultural formation of antebellum America; she had to embrace the views of the ladies, whose portrayal appeared in a dream world. Even though the ideology of domesticity was not alien to working women, *Godey's Lady's Book* was designed as a magazine for the middle class, and it claimed the respectability of its audience. Both the style of the stories and the engravings emphasized an air of gentility, with "taste and refinement."[37] To be sure, *Godey's* also delighted working-class readers. The factory operatives of the Lowell mills, who are often cited by historians for their compliance with the moral values and paternalism of their employers, preferred amusement and entertainment to serious lectures. As their militant publication, *Voice of Industry,* suggested, "The trashy, milk-and-water sentimentalities of the *Lady's Book* and *Olive Branch,* are more read than the works of Gibbon, or Goldsmith, or Bancroft."[38] Certainly working women were appropriating a magazine that originally targeted leisured women, and in so doing they subordinated class to gender formation.

Godey's confined women within narrow boundaries while providing them with a separate medium for their voices. The female reader-viewer received a book of her own and became visible. The reading audience of *Godey's* contributed to the configuration of the female subject while using the language of the female object. Thus the presence of feminine images in antebellum print culture was both conformist and subversive. Even though *Godey's* justified publication of the plates in condescending terms of a traditionally different feminine taste, more sensitive and emotional than intellectual, thereby acknowledging the inequality of the female ornamental stratum of literature, the feminine print culture could also provide a forum for agitation. Just as nineteenth-century women's power originated in the cradle of the family circle, religious associations, and the community of sisters, the separate sphere of print culture represented a center of power, a platform for the voiceless, and a channel for the formation of an authentic feminine speech. The intrusion of a female vernacular into print culture overlapped with the antebellum crusade for beauty and a softening of American Protestant piety and was similarly rooted in the empowerment of white middle-class women in the decades preceding the Civil War.[39]

Crusade for Beauty

Sarah Josepha Hale's editorials provided the "embellishments" of a conventional female miscellany-repository with a moral and conservative frame. After compromising with the public taste for fashion plates, Hale was able to make *Godey's* a commercial success.[40] The complementarity of images and texts drove sales. The valorization of images assured the continuity of the market, while the written texts worked for the legitimation of the magazine. Images added value to the product and made it an expensive commodity. At the same time, they represented a didactic means of conveying messages to women. Publishers of illustrated magazines did not admit plainly that they satisfied the public's demand for images, but they used the rhetoric of the antebellum crusade for beauty and the appeal to the senses through images. The discourse surrounding the publication of pictures was not about the triviality or idolatry of beautiful images, but about the directness of pictorial messages that served the cause of beauty, piety, and morality.

Publisher and audience emphasized the beauty of the magazine, defining a sensual reading through the pleasure of visual texts. There seemed to be a conflict between the need for enlightenment through books and magazines and the conception of reading as enjoyment. Reading as mere pleasure was scandalous and immoral.[41] It seemed reminiscent of a hedonist class, at odds with the new republic. The editors of *Godey's* were aware of opponents who described the fashion magazine as the amusement of a class, and therefore they developed strategies to redeem the visual pleasure of the text. For instance, advertisements for *Godey's* emphasized the work of sentiment:

> Many persons, who seek no further than our title, presume that the "Lady's Book" is intended merely for the amusement of a class, and that it does not enter into the discussion of those more important questions connected with the realities and the duties of life which every well-informed *woman,* mother and daughter, should be acquainted with. But such is not the fact. It is now, as it has ever been, our constant care to combine, in the pages of the "Lady's Book," whatever is useful, whatever is elevating, whatever is pure, dignified, and virtuous in sentiment, with whatever may afford rational and innocent amusement.[42]

To the argument that periodical reading was leisure and entertainment—in other words, a private vice—reformers and writers cited the need to encourage female literacy and combine it with maternal instruction and public virtue.

Godey's epitomized the nineteenth-century shift from a primarily devotional to an increasingly secular literature, blurring in a single medium the sacred and the profane. Godey probably intended such an effect by calling his magazine the "Book," often without quotation marks. *Godey's Lady's Book* was meant to be a woman's Bible and could complement the large family Bible. Critics of Louis Godey even referred to the magazine as "Godey's Bible" or "God-ey's Bible."[43] The act of reading was presented as a domestic occupation, a private or familial relationship, comforting and feminine, within the intimate space of the home. Images, in particular, were central to the spirituality of nineteenth-century Americans, and altered antebellum practices of piety. Protestantism was progressively renouncing traditional objections to images. The second quarter of the nineteenth century witnessed a definite movement in favor of the fine arts and a growing relation between art, morality, and religion. Art was regarded as a refining instrument for social improvement, and women as the special guardians of artistic riches.

During the three decades before the Civil War, Americans experienced different attitudes toward Catholicism and artistic extravagance in the expression of religious spirituality. Protestants began to consider the possibilities of painting as an appeal to religious sentiments. As described in the previous chapter on giftbooks, belief in aesthetic uplift was growing. Art was seen as softening brutish feelings, and beauty was trusted with the power to redeem an increasingly impersonal and materialistic world.[44] To a certain extent American Protestantism now accepted as a means to piety artifacts that had been associated with alien faiths. Art also played an important role in nineteenth-century middle-class culture once the disestablishment of churches and the development of domestic religion made the family the center of spiritual formation. Art came to decorate middle-class homes, while visual images were increasingly perceived as symbols and as a religious language.[45]

The issue at stake is the place of the female vernacular in the antebellum transformation of religion and the evangelical movement. The moral crusade for beauty was gender-specific. Art was feminine courtesy and gentility par excellence, the civilized society versus the urban crowd and the savage beasts. Women and art joined in a civilizing influence. In particular, the female gentility embodied in the imagery of mother and child revealed both the feminization of American religion and a softening of American Protestantism. Antebellum Protestant piety was feminized and came to resemble a sensibility usually associated with Catholicism.[46]

The embellishments in *Godey's* were icons for new practices of piety and allowed contemplative reading. While not a fashion plate, one particular engraving entitled *The Coquette* deserves our attention, for it reveals the work of sentiment and the manipulation of pictures in addressing the fashionable. The pictorial scene remains mysterious in itself and requires the details of the written story. The practice of reading as the work of a detective deciphering a message uses the power of the story for unveiling the mystery of the image. The description holds the attention of the reader well into the text before presenting clues to the detailed illustration.

According to the narrative, the woman pictured was a beauty, but not a good wife. As the complete opposite of "The Constant" or "true womanhood," she preferred to entertain a society of admirers rather than keep a house, and she made her husband unhappy.

> She sat alone in their own room one morning, after he had gone out, with the cold gray light of reality breaking round her. She had gone to a jewel box for some trinket, her favorite in girl-hood, and had found, beneath half-forgotten ornaments, the miniature of her husband, his gift at their betrothal. She had drawn a lounging-chair to the table, in an indolent, careless mood, thinking to check reproachful thought in the preparation of a dress for the evening. Her pet spaniel was watching curiously, from her knee, an intrusive visitor from a neighboring apartment. The seductive languor of early spring filled the whole atmosphere, and sad, regretful memories came stealing over her with its softness.[47]

This enlightening scene led the woman to self-examination, humiliation, reproach, and finally repentance. In other words, both the commentator on the image and the illustrator of the story are describing a conversion experience. It does not matter whether the image or the story was produced first; the nineteenth-century reader-viewer was in the presence of both. One cannot avoid seeing similarities between the miniature of the woman's husband and the

The Coquette, Godey's Lady's Book, *March 1851.*
Courtesy of Olin Library, Cornell University.

medallion in which she is portrayed for the reader. There was a play around the power of images, of revelation and potential redemption. The engraving could well be a religious icon, a pious object of domestic religion. Reformers believed that an image provided a direct, immediate, emotional message. It was meant to touch the heart of every woman and was charged with moral power. An image carried an ideological message and could spread the spirit of domestic love and social peace. "What better lesson could a long story teach?" Pictorial texts were used by sentimental reformers as the embodiment of simplicity and spirituality.[48] The editor of *Godey's* as well as its contributors recognized the primary function of the pictures as a way to attract the audience and were aware of the secondary role that texts played in the magazine.

However, the image had almost a fetishistic character and cult value. Its sensual language represented an open door to idolatry and potential deviance from the moral crusade. The pictorial texts of antebellum women's magazines were a double-edged sword; most reformers therefore recommended a well-controlled use of visual signs. While some reformers were ardent opponents of periodicals such as *Godey's*, the liberal ministers who competed with women writers of domestic fiction for the emerging literary market shared the cultural tools of secularization.[49] They tended to frame images with typographical constraints and reduced the polyvalence of the message by adding the printed word. They monitored and "illustrated" the images with editorial comments and titles. Figures were disciplined by words, but the efficacy of such a submission remained questionable. As visual representations multiplied in antebellum print, written discourse began to accept a new dependence upon images for conveying messages. Even the conservative Sarah Josepha Hale overcame her long prejudice against the display of fashion as a symbol of extravagance and luxury. Hale came to advocate the manipulation of images for the service of reformist ideas rather than the total elimination of images. The history of *Godey's*, then, reveals the victory of the commercial strategy and the adaptation of the reformist discourse to the market. Images that would have been burned in an earlier era were now framed by an ideological discourse; rather than being destroyed, they were controlled and charged with discursive meaning.

Fashionable Mothers

By the mid-1840s each issue of *Godey's* included at least four "instructive" embellishments, religious or secular, in addition to the monthly fashion plate, miscellany in the work department, and models of cottages.[50] However, as the ideology of domesticity began to infiltrate all pictorial texts, fashion plates increasingly depicted domestic and sentimental scenes as well. Attractive watercolored engravings appeared to be an appropriate medium for moral messages. They were *tableaux vivants,* staging motionless women in domestic scenes. For instance, the comment on the engraving *A Domestic Scene* in the August 1845 issue read: "Our readers will notice a striking improvement in the style of our recent fashion plates. We give, this month, the latest fashions for ladies and children, in the form of a domestic scene, which serves at once to exhibit the last fancy in dress, and the most recent improvements in the form of the cradle, easy chair, foot-cushion, etc. Where fine touches of art can be thrown in 'after this fashion,' we hold it our duty to see that it is done."[51]

The fashionables went home instead of going to the party or the promenade. They were conforming to the cult of true womanhood. Sentimental mothers were to substitute for coquettes, and fashion was tailored to the ideology of domesticity. Hence the fashion plate began to resemble other images of domestic and sentimental scenes, such as the engraving entitled *Maternal Instruction* that was published in the March 1845 issue in support of Sarah Josepha Hale's female education campaign.[52] Sometimes domestic engravings filled the gap when the magazine had no fashion to offer. One significant case was a delicate engraving in the issue of February 1845 entitled *Infancy,* which epitomized the sentimental culture of antebellum America: "In lieu of the fashion this month we have given a coloured steel engraving—a novelty at least, be its success what it may; we can only add that it is doubly as expensive as the fashions." The sleeping infant with the black kitten was a fine illustration of domesticity and motherhood, presented as a luxury in comparison with fashion plates. However, repeated requests brought back the fashions, for the sentimental cult of domesticity with no fashion at all was less popular among subscribers than "sentimentalized" fashion.

One final point bears comment. The many engravings that women —and perhaps men as well—tore from the issues to enhance their homes and apartments offer convincing evidence of the nineteenth-

A Domestic Scene, Godey's Lady's Book, *August 1845*.
Courtesy of Olin Library, Cornell University.

century public taste. The plates were highly valued by subscribers.
For instance, *Godey's* reported a story emphasizing the prominence
of its fashions; one man had "cut out the fashions lately and sold
them for as much as the whole number cost him, and then had his
females improved to the amount of a whole year's subscription by the
interesting contents."[53] In an era of commercialized goods, the demand for paintings and images to post on the walls of private homes

Maternal Instruction, Godey's Lady's Book, *March 1845.*
Courtesy of Olin Library, Cornell University.

was increasing. The possession of objects, particularly pictures with
the power of representing reality—and sometimes sameness—was a
means of confirming status in an apparently mobile society. Thus,
more than Sarah Josepha Hale's sentimental and moralistic editorials, the steel-engraved ladies of *Godey's* made the emerging feminine
press a lucrative business.[54]

At the same time, *Godey's Lady's Book* helped entrench a separate
sphere of antebellum print culture. The magazine's visual texts were
didactic. They were repetitive and they set a pattern, an archetype of
ladyhood. Color prints provided women readers with lessons of man-

Infancy, Godey's Lady's Book, *February 1845.*
Courtesy of Olin Library, Cornell University.

ners, behavior, and dress as well as entertainment. But more important, the engravings made nineteenth-century women "visible" and
outlined the female subject and the female distinctiveness in print.
To be sure, the world of *Godey's* was a society of white middle-class
Protestant women in private homes—a world that could occasionally be appropriated by other social groups.[55] The aesthetic specificity of the magazine reflected the particular identity of its reading
audience and the details of women's experience. It confirmed a process of social and gendered differentiation and a historical moment
when images designed as messengers of moral reform could simply
be contemplated for pleasure.

We could not understand the work of sentiment and the emergence of a feminine voice in American nineteenth-century culture
if we ignored the sentimentalists' confrontation with and eventual
acceptance of visual texts. Originally at odds with the ideology of republican simplicity and sentimentality, visual texts came to serve as
medium and midwife for the dissemination of the culture of sentiment. Ironically, it was the triumph of the market of printed images
that strengthened the private women's sphere—separate from and

redemptive of the public world of commerce. If the engravings in *Godey's* were the magazine's best selling point, they allied producer and consumers. The pictorial commodity-text was profitable to the former and pleasing to the latter. Furthermore, it had a resonance within the whole culture of antebellum America. The lessons of these visual texts were conformist and reaffirmed the ideology of domesticity, maternal instruction, and the power of sentiment. Although women's pictorial representations shared in the construction of sentimentality and domestic femininity, they effected a significant change in the American public sphere as well, thus complicating the binary of the separate spheres. The use of a visible language to translate middle-class women's existence represented in itself a resistance to the traditional authority of the printed word. By intruding into the dominantly male print culture, and thus transgressing the boundaries of gender, the female vernacular took part in the exuberance of the carnivalesque market fair and the liminality of the antebellum period.

Even though the relationship of visual texts to editorials remained tense and unstable in *Godey's,* gendered visual representations were successfully incorporated in antebellum print culture. In turn, the feminization of American culture facilitated the introduction of illustrations in a great variety of nineteenth-century books and periodicals, including prayer books and Bibles. Traditional texts were altered to comply with the public taste and reflect its infatuation with a tangible spectacle.[56] For instance, the New York publishers Harper and Brothers published an *Illuminated and New Pictorial Bible* between 1843 and 1846. Harper's Bible was extensively illustrated with 1,600 engravings by Joseph Alexander Adams and sold in fifty-four parts, at 25 cents each, in order to reach a larger audience and cover the enormous cost of illustrations. Framed as a showcase of delight, each engraving contributed both to the pleasure of the reader and to the desecration of the culture's most authoritative text. When one could buy just the Book of Genesis for the engraving of the Garden of Eden, reading the Scriptures became a far different experience from earlier practices. Just as Antiochus entered Egypt with an imposing army and elephants in 1 Maccabees, the elephant entered the Word with phenomenal display in pre–Civil War America.

EXTRAORDINARY COURAGE OF ELEAZAR.

I. Maccabees, *in* Harper's Illuminated and
New Pictorial Bible *(1843–46). Courtesy of Rare and*
Manuscript Collections, Kroch Library, Cornell University.

There is little doubt that Emerson, who had scorned the production of elephants on stage, would have equally condemned the grotesque illustrations of Harper's Bible. But he was also aware of the
inevitable quest for images in his times, which he conveyed in an isolated sentence in his journal: "Our age is ocular." [57] The proliferating
images in printed matter—from steel-engraved ladies and biblical
scenes to the verisimilitude of criminals in the *National Police Gazette*'s
woodcuts—did not go unnoticed by contemporary critics, who saw
them as the epitome of the popularization and deprecation of culture. As defenders of a cultural orthodoxy, their attacks on popular
reading became more vocal by mid-century. Their highbrow definition of books and reading is the subject of the next chapter.

CHAPTER 6

A Useful Recreation:
Advice on Reading in the Age of Abundance

'Tis therefore an economy of time to read old and famed books.
Nothing can be preserved that is not good. . . . Be sure, then, to read no
mean books. Shun the spawn of the press on the gossip of the hour. Do not read
what you shall learn without asking, in the street and in the train. . . . If you
should transfer the amount of your reading day to day in the newspaper
to the standard authors, —but who dare speak of such a thing?
Ralph Waldo Emerson, *Atlantic Monthly,* January 1858

The fugitive journal and popular books of the day served the sole purpose of dilettantism, according to Ralph Waldo Emerson. Easily found, yet ephemeral, they simply qualified as rubbish. "Never read any book that is not a year old," was Emerson's first practical rule.[1] Of course, the transcendentalist was not alone in casting such a severe judgment on the print culture of his time. A growing number of learned Americans came to share the opinion of the New Englander. They did not embrace the so-called golden age of publishing as an unequivocal blessing but rather voiced a jeremiad of days of doom in an age of grotesque exaggeration. In light of the carnivalesque exuberance of the print culture described in previous chapters, the critique offered by these cultural arbiters takes on its full meaning. Before the chaos of a boundless print wilderness and the tempting feast of words and images, they argued for a return to a more traditional order of print with fewer books and greater moral discipline. To them, the availability of printed matter did not just foster popular enlightenment but made reading a controversial activity. These middle-class custodians of culture, both men and women, perceived the age of print abundance as a fall that could only be redeemed through the habits of frugal reading that characterized an earlier age of scarcity. As Emerson had already pointed out in his 1837 Harvard address to the Phi Beta Kappa society, "Books are the best of things, well used; abused, among the worst."[2]

This chapter explores the discourse on popular reading constructed by a broad range of highbrow critics—ministers, physicians, literati, and labor advocates. Unlike previous chapters, which examined the materiality of the lowbrow print culture by looking at the ephemeral publications that were read and cherished in the antebellum period, this last chapter is concerned with the ideas of those who positioned themselves against popular books and the reading practices they encouraged. As readers themselves, of course, critics could not simply advocate the repression of the carnivalesque festival. Their calls for Lent may be regarded as an implicit recognition of the importance of the carnival and an effort to counterbalance the feast with fasting. The interdependence of the polarities of high and low further suggests that in spite of their sometimes sharp attacks on popular print culture, the custodians of legitimate culture also belonged to this threshold of time, betwixt and between, where the categories were ambiguous. They certainly reacted to the spectacle of unforeseen and out-of-the-ordinary printed artifacts, of which some were "cheap," others "light," and most saturated with images. However, critics of lowbrow print were themselves partners in the production of letters and remained ambivalent toward the literary marketplace.

Antebellum reformers directed their prescriptive literature at youth. Their moral guidance appeared in small books entitled *The Young Man's Guide* or *The Young Woman's Guide, Advice to Young Men on Their Duties and Conduct in Life* or *Advice to Young Ladies, Lectures to Young Men* or *Lectures to Young Women*. Most American men and women who lectured and wrote about the uses and abuses of reading were white, middle-class, educated New Englanders, affiliated with various Protestant denominations, and often supporters of Whig doctrine. They were also involved with a broad range of reforms, from temperance to health reform to abolitionism. These fervent crusaders sought to delineate normative standards governing all departments of life, and the activity of reading, long encouraged by a Protestant and republican reverence for the written word, did not escape their scrutiny. They accentuated the warnings against "cheap and light" reading and offered new prescriptions for serious reading, as they saw the traditional notion of reading as a duty give way to reading as a pleasure. The quality of reading matter was to prevail over quantity, although reforming the readers' uses of print meant more than simply categorizing literary genres.

The discussion of reading in conduct-of-life books, often twofold, reveals a striking ambivalence: if practiced with restraint and with a purpose, reading was regarded as a useful recreation, but excessive reading for mere pleasure was morally wrong. Books and reading, therefore, appear in discussions of amusements as both "innocent" and "dangerous."[3] The polarity between good and bad reading, intensive and extensive, collective and individual, masculine and feminine, fills the reformers' chapters on reading advice. This underscores a nascent cultural bifurcation at a time when moralizers began to see in the popular uses of print an inversion of legitimate behavior. The new print culture and the reading practices it fostered represented a transgression to be condemned along with card playing, gambling, and theatergoing. But in contrast to the latter, which were public recreations, reading was often performed privately, and its critique marked a new venture into controlling the private behavior of individuals.

To be sure, the condemnation of popular practices of reading was not a novelty of the nineteenth century. Colonial ministers had long preached against wrong reading, while themselves reckoning with a marketplace for "wonders" and "merriment."[4] What was different about the antebellum advice on reading was the extraordinary use of printed matter by those who denounced the excesses of popular reading. If they forcefully attacked the new media and advocated proper uses of print, they also offered equally sensational and lurid descriptions of dangerous reading. Indeed, successful features of the popular print culture were to make their way into mainstream publishing by the 1850s.

Lectures and books were addressed to youth because reformers believed that youth revealed the virtue or corruption of society. In their view, the strength and safety of a community relied on the character and intelligence of its youth.[5] Ministers and lecturers addressed

A Useful Recreation

young men as a distinct class in the community, repeatedly referring to the biblical exhortation by the apostle John: "I have written unto you, young men, because ye are strong."[6] Young men were thought to be particularly exposed to the worst dangers of the new urban environment. As one Unitarian minister told his St. Louis audience, young men "are floating upon the surface of society, carried one way or the other by the currents of social influence, by the changing wind of good or ill success."[7] They needed to hear sound advice from moral guardians who served as surrogate parents. In contrast, young women were believed to be protected from the temptations of the world. Reading advice for them emphasized the tasks of self-discipline and moral education, which would prepare them for the duties of marriage and motherhood. Their future lives as wives and mothers were to be dedicated to the service of civic virtue, educating their sons, and influencing their husbands.[8]

Historians have recognized the difficulty of assessing to what degree advice on manners and morals was followed by the audience it targeted. Nonetheless, several scholars have taken for granted the success of those little manuals in shaping the attitudes and behavior of the first generation of young men in the industrial cities.[9] Yet the effect and popularity of conduct-of-life treatises are highly questionable. While William A. Alcott's *The Young Man's Guide,* originally published in 1833, ran through twenty-one editions by 1858, and the first edition of Daniel C. Eddy's *The Young Man's Friend* sold 10,000 copies in 1849, it is fair to say that most advice books did not quite sell like patent medicines. Only Lydia Sigourney's *Letters to Young Ladies* qualified as a "better seller" for the year 1833, with sales below the required number of 125,000 for best sellers.[10] Even the authors of advice books themselves were aware of the poor popularity of their production if compared with books of light reading. Alcott recalled a pseudo-autobiographical instance in *Familiar Letters to Young Men:* "Some six or seven months ago, I was stopping for a short time in one of the flourishing villages of New England, when two individuals came through the street selling books. One had such works as The Young Man's Guide, The Young Mother, Young Wife, &c. The other had books of a very different character—and among the rest, the catchpennies of the day, such as the cheaper lives of Scott, Taylor, the works of Eugene Sue, &c. The latter sold readily—the former hardly at all."[11] Whether real or fictional, the incident suggests that antebellum prescriptive literature shed more light on what its authors considered good behavior than on the actual behavior of American youth.

Certainly most conduct-of-life books were didactic and tedious. Yet they sometimes shared the same sensational undertones as the popular literature that they attacked. For instance, Henry Ward Beecher published in his 1846 *Lectures to Young Men* a lecture delivered on Christmas Eve—and much criticized—about the "Strange Woman," or licentiousness and prostitution. Beecher admitted that he did not alter the forms of expression peculiar to the pulpit into those better suited to a book. No doubt his gruesome rhetoric had a particular attraction for the reading public. One by one he describes five wards in the house of the "strange woman": pleasure, satiety, discovery, disease, and death. His gothic depiction of the repulsive fourth ward of "disease" is particularly graphic: "What is it to be put into a pit of snakes and slimy toads, and feel their cold coil or piercing fang, to the creeping of a whole body of vipers?—where every nerve is a viper, and every vein a viper, and every muscle a serpent; and the whole body, in all its parts, coils and twists upon itself in unimaginable anguish? . . . Look upon her fourth Ward—its vomited blood, its sores and fiery blotches, its prurient sweat, its dissolving ichor, and rotten bones! Stop, young man!"[12] But the reader was still to be taken to the threshold of the fifth and last ward, the ward of "death": "See the blood oozing from the wall, the fiery hands which pluck the wretches down, the light of hell gleaming through, and hear its roar as of a distant ocean chafed with storms. Will you sprinkle the wall with your blood?—will you feed those flames with your flesh?—will you add your voice to those thundering wails?—will you go down a prey through the fiery floor of the chamber of death?"[13]

Beecher then specifically warned against "a morbid imagination" (notwithstanding his own), evil companions, and, finally, evil books and pictures: "The Ten Plagues have visited our literature; water is turned to blood; frogs and lice creep and hop over our most familiar things,—the couch, the cradle, and the bread-trough; locusts, murrain, and fire, are smiting every green thing." Those horrendous images portrayed a literary threat that was omnipresent and omnipotent. "This black-lettered literature circulates in this town, floats in our stores, nestles in the shops, is fingered and read nightly, and hatches in the young mind broods of salacious thoughts."[14] For Beecher, the only salvation lay in plainly denouncing the impurity, not in clothing vice and disguising the horrible truth. His lectures and publications were most popular in part because of their sensational and lurid language. Whatever their effect on correcting behavior, they were primarily entertaining. Didactic manuals could thus become as popular as temperance novels, such as T. S. Arthur's bestseller, *Ten Nights in a Bar-Room;* the successful ones like Beecher's proved that their unavowed inclination for crude warnings against vice fared much better than a simple list of virtues.[15]

In any case, whether they aimed to scare—and titillate—their audience or chose to moralize in a straightforward fashion, writers of manuals attempted to define cultural norms for nineteenth-century youth. If it is impossible to measure how those norms were accepted, rejected, or modified by the actual readers, at least their prescriptions reveal the reformers' representations of popular reading and offer a filtered perspective on the nineteenth-century practice of reading. The learned men and women who undertook the role of moral guardian for urban youth recognized the prevalence of the new reading practices that they so deplored. They were not defining proper rules of behavior in a vacuum but reacting to what they regarded as reprehensible activities. If considered as a group in spite of their diverse opinions, reformers created a discourse on optimal reading that contrasted a "useful recreation" with idle and pleasurable reading. They described what and how the American people read and in so doing categorized the cultural consumption of their contemporaries. The issue, then, is less the effectiveness of the reformers' moral enterprise than the very emergence of a learned discourse that responded to the proliferation of printed materials and attempted to control popular reading.[16]

The fact that it was during the second quarter of the nineteenth century that the custodians of American culture condemned certain practices while legitimizing others is not just a coincidence. The changing attitudes towards amusement did not result from a simple liberalization of ideas or from changes in the ethnic composition of the American people. Admittedly, the new immigrants of the 1840s did bring new attitudes about leisure, and their practices of conviviality led to a sharp reaction among Sabbatarians by mid-century. But more important, the new social order dictated by industrialization and urbanization required an adjustment of the old values of work and play. The formation of a reformist and legitimizing discourse on leisure further stemmed from the changing attitudes of cultural authorities. In particular, the moral leadership shifted from religious guides to "managers of virtue" who provided moral support for industry and productivity. Americans indulging in "light reading" were not regarded merely as sinners who partook in condemned amusements, but rather as laboring men and women misusing leisure time that should be devoted to the re-creation of the labor force for improved industry.[17]

In the new social and economic context of industrial America, the activity of reading could no longer be considered simply as a means of social improvement. Proletarianization reigned, and, as Edward Pessen has convincingly demonstrated, social mobility became a myth in the so-called era of the common man.[18] The former function of reading as a necessity gave way to new uses of print as distraction and leisure activity. This became acceptable, provided that such an activity did not subvert the social and moral order. Nineteenth-century reformers understood that reading involved not just the words on a page but also the time and place of the act of reading. Thus they were far more concerned with the interaction between readers and texts than with a classification of reading matter by literary genre. Analysis of their specific advice on reading highlights the same precepts of discipline, industry, and self-improvement that characterized the broader ideological context.

Most advice books from the 1830s to the 1850s qualified moderate reading as good and a contribution to self-culture but argued that too much reading was bad. Reading in late hours and at night was vehemently denounced as self-destructive, being implicitly counterproductive for the next workday. In addition, solitary and secret reading after dark could be threatening to one's morality. Individual, attentive study of books was overwhelmingly recommended for the early hours of the day, before breakfast, with recurring reference to Benjamin Franklin. But "mere reading," that is to say, just for the pleasure of the moment, was criticized. A dictionary or a notebook might be a useful auxiliary because it would slow down the pace of reading and restrain the reader's involvement. Intensive reading of the same book was praised, in contrast to skimming many books for amusement. For T. S. Arthur, "extensive reading is all very good; but right thinking on what we read, even if the amount is small, is far better." Similarly, Lydia Maria Child concluded in *The Mother's*

Book that it was better to have a few good books than many middling ones.[19] The best way of avoiding the dangers of individual reading, however, remained the idealized image of collective reading. Reading aloud, in particular, seemed the sanctified protection against the dangers of solitary and escapist reading.

Antebellum reformers called for a return to the age of the spoken word and few books. In essence, they did not attack the availability of print but advised readers to reform their practices. As they were themselves writers of didactic fiction and contributors to popular magazines, they could not undermine their own use of the printed word. As the clergyman Henry Ware Jr. remarked in an 1846 lecture on the duties of young men, "However we may lament the vast proportion of worthless trash published and republished by the American press, we cannot deny that a large mass of valuable works also are continually brought before the public."[20] According to the Unitarian minister and writer of didactic fiction, good reading was at hand, and the responsibility of choice lay exclusively with the reader. In the age of abundance, reformers did not advocate the burning of all books but trumpeted discipline and selection as safeguards against excess. The cheapness of print, which added trashy books and periodicals to valuable publications, epitomized the dilemma of popularization in Jacksonian democracy. As William A. Alcott pointed out, both good and bad literature were accessible for a fair price: "That state of civilized society which brings upon us a flood of light papers and magazines, and a world of mawkish and sickly stuff, whose only recommendation is that it is new and cheap, brings us at the same time many highly valuable publications, both new and old, and at a greatly reduced price." The critics, Alcott ironically reminded his readers, should be grateful for the new opportunities of their time, that is, the existence of choice reading—both periodical and permanent— that was affordable.[21]

The question was whether or not the benefits of cheap reading matter could outweigh its pitfalls. For instance, newspaper reading was now an essential part of the American way of life and had to be reckoned with. Emerson would refer to it as the "second breakfast" of Americans. Well-selected newspapers might even be an appropriate incentive to reading for nonreaders and reluctant readers, who were advised to join a lyceum or debating society. A young man attending a lyceum would take part in a discussion and automatically be motivated to seek information in newspapers, and perhaps later in books of travels and stories. Thus acquaintance with a literate culture presupposed light reading as a source of delight and a necessary primary stage toward more serious reading.

Reformers recognized that the multiplicity and cheapness of periodical publications provided a source of entertaining knowledge accessible to all classes of the community. The press itself constituted a new and powerful monitor of manners and morals. Certainly excessive newspaper reading could be detrimental, but reformers trusted in the selection of a good newspaper with the assistance of friends. In any case, readers should avoid papers concerned solely with the details of human depravity, papers of "short and light" articles, and those that ridiculed the most sacred things.[22] Henry David Thoreau, in particular, expressed his disdain of news as gossip, writing in *Walden:* "If we read of one man robbed, or murdered, or killed by accident, or one house burned, or one vessel wrecked, or one steamboat blown up, or one cow run over on the Western Railroad, or one mad dog killed, or one lot of grasshoppers in the winter,—we never need read of another. One is enough."[23] For Thoreau, discrimination in newspaper reading was required: "If we will read newspapers, why not skip the gossip of Boston and take the best newspaper in the world at once?—not be sucking the pap of 'neutral family' papers, or browsing 'Olive-Branches' here in New England."[24]

Thoreau was not alone in believing that miscellaneous literature threatened the old authority of the word and debased the activity of reading. Antebellum custodians of culture considered discontinuous reading reprehensible. They criticized not only "light reading," that is, books, papers, and periodicals that amuse and enable the reader to "kill time" or "while" it away, but also reading "by snatches," for it might lead to a chain reaction. As Alcott warned his audience: "The more you read mere fragments, the more you are inclined to do so; and the more you will disrelish any and every other mode. And the more you spend your shreds of time in this way, on the plea that they are *mere* shreds, the shorter they seem to become. . . . This will probably explain the well-known fact that light reading, and reading little more than mere shreds—such as abound in the papers, especially the dailies—is perpetually increasing, so that no one can tell where it is likely to end."[25]

Such reading practices could ruin both the physical and mental health of the reader. Dr. Benjamin Rush had noted earlier the debilitating effect of reading magazines and miscellaneous literature; the frequent and rapid transition of the mind from one subject to another was thought to have a deteriorating effect on the brain. Rush observed that booksellers happened to suffer from such insanity: "The debilitating effects of these sudden transitions upon the mind, are sensibly felt after reading a volume of reviews or magazines. The brain in these cases is deprived of the benefit of habit, which prevents fatigue to a certain extent, from all the exercises of the body and mind, when they are confined to single objects."[26]

To the defenders of cultural orthodoxy, book reading was significantly better than newspaper and magazine reading, although reformers did not regard all books as equally valuable. Novel reading was rarely recommended, yet it was not totally forbidden. For instance, a careful selection of fictional works, along with biographies, could acquaint women readers with life. Such a view thus implicitly acknowledged the limitations of dry and serious literature. However, inexperienced readers, male and female, were told to avoid novels altogether, since they risked selecting the poisonous and obscene, most likely by Eugène Sue or Edward Bulwer-Lytton, instead of the better ones—by Walter Scott, for instance.[27]

Antebellum reformers still believed in the contribution of reading to self-improvement and to the betterment of the society as a whole. They carefully sought to teach respect for books, even in the form of basic advice similar to what William Alcott offered the readers of *The Young Man's Guide:*

> Never allow yourselves to use books for any other purpose but reading. I have seen people recline after dinner and at other times, with books under their heads for a pillow. Others will use them to cover a tumbler, bowl, or pitcher. Others again will raise the window, and set them under the sash to support it; and next, perhaps, the book is wet by a sudden shower of rain, or knocked out of the window, soiled or otherwise injured, or lost. I have seen people use large books, such as the family-bible, or encyclopedia, to raise a seat, especially for a child at table. Books should be kept in a dry, as well as clean place, for moisture greatly injures them.[28]

To be sure, advice on books and reading did not reckon solely with forbidding a wet finger or the habit of turning down corners of a book in dog's ears. In addition to civility, advice dealt more profoundly with the dissemination of a moral culture. Even though reformers gave such basic instructions as if they were entitled preservers of print culture who initiated the uncivilized into their high, written civilization, their discourse was not constructed in the wilderness. They mostly responded to changes in the written word and offered ways of countering the wide availability of cheap printed matter through reading exercises viewed as self-discipline. The antebellum threat did not come from illiteracy, but rather from a different print culture, one that was ephemeral, discontinuous, miscellaneous, and promiscuous.

From the reformers' point of view, reading matter represented "food for the mind." Since the Middle Ages, the Christian reader had been urged to meditate or ruminate on the Word of God: "Taste the goodness of your redeemer . . . chew the honeycomb of his words, suck their flavor," St. Anselm advised.[29] By the nineteenth century reading and the ingestion of words took on a particular significance. At a time when the movement for "body reform" blurred the distinction between physical and mental health, reading could affect both. Conduct-of-life books were therefore filled with food metaphors, some recalling religious reading advice of earlier times, others more specific to the age of dietary reform.[30] Excessive reading was often compared with luxurious food as a cause of weakness rather than strength. "Mere desultory and miscellaneous reading is more apt to be pernicious than useful. It is more likely to enervate than strengthen the mind," warned one reformer. The habit of young Americans "devouring books" and swallowing them whole was condemned. Good reading required that young men "read, mark, learn and inwardly digest."[31] Rev. William G. Eliot summed up what many contemporaries thought of as common sense: "Books are food to the mind. Well-selected books, like wholesome food, impart strength and vigor, and bring the mind to its full growth. But as all food is not wholesome, and we may use that which is poisonous or hurtful, so there is a great deal of reading which is poisonous and hurtful to the mind."[32] A few good books could offer wholesome food, but the public was more likely to favor a lighter fare of tales and romances. As Thoreau scorned, "This sort of gingerbread is baked daily and more sedulously than pure wheat or rye-and-Indian in almost every oven, and finds a surer market."[33]

Selection and moderation were key advice. Even a good novel might provide an "occasional refreshment," but not every day. As the radical abolitionist and conservative women's rights advocate Jane G. Swisshelm told girls, reading silly novels every day was not reading: "It was more like eating opium, or drinking brandy; for it is practiced just for excitement, and to kill time. Reading for amusement hours at a stretch, is like eating for half a day together."[34] Indeed, transgressive reading was often associated with drinking in the minds of antebellum teetotalers. For Henry Ware Jr., popular works and newspapers "offered at every corner like cheap spirits, are little else than poisonous stimulants, exciting the appetite, creating a craving for indulgence, and debilitating instead of nourishing the mind which resorts to them."[35] In sum, parsimony and restraint in reading were the motto of reformers, who shared similar views on the subjects of diet and sobriety. Omnivorous reading might result in the physical and mental destruction of the reader. "Much reading, but not so many books" was a new translation of the old maxim *non multa sed multum*. Habits of intensive reading inherited from an earlier age of scarcity threatened to disappear in the midst of the proliferation of print. For some middle-class reformers outraged by the abundance of "cheap and nasty" literature, the poor—still marginalized by the marketplace—might be the only reminders of a past when books were rare and better. For instance, James W. Alexander, a Presbyterian minister who wrote his first advice books under the pseudonym Charles Quill, remarked: "The poor man with few books is observed, even in our day, to peruse and reperuse until he has mastered their whole contents."[36]

In addition, ministers of a broad range of religious denominations agreed that books were second to virtue and religion, although the popularization of print was met with various degrees of opposition. The strongest suspicion of books came from the evangelical preacher Charles Grandison Finney, whose attacks on smoking, drinking, card playing, and theatergoing also included literature. "Let me visit your chamber, your parlor, or wherever you keep your books," Finney threatened. "What is here? Byron, Scott, Shakespeare, and a host of triflers and blasphemers of God." Evangelical piety thus rejected intellect and book reading. Spirituality was to come not from the "seminaries of learning," but rather from God's grace.[37]

Likewise, the Unitarian minister William G. Eliot claimed that "we can do without books; we cannot do without virtue and religion."[38] However, the Unitarian position on books and reading was slightly ambivalent. For William Ellery Channing, the champion of liberal Unitarianism, the religion of culture outlined in his treatise *Self-Culture* was moral, intellectual, and social, but also practical. Nature, revelation, the human soul, and human life were the means by which self-culture could be promoted, and they were accessible to all. Therefore, books were useful instruments as long as they did not absorb the reader, or create a "learned folly." The best books would be considered a good thing. "God be thanked for books," said Channing. "They are the voices of the distant and the dead, and make us heirs of the spiritual life of past ages." A good selection of books by real thinkers—the sacred writers, along with Milton, Shakespeare, and Franklin—and a reverential practice of reading could make this means of culture effectual.[39] For most Unitarians, however, books were not as central as the self in the culture of one's own spiritual nature and the self-forming power of the soul. The internal tension of Unitarian thought between flesh and spirit resulted in a dualist definition of self-culture. Moral culture meant development of the spirit, but also control of the flesh. Reading too reflected the dualism of flesh and spirit; when undisciplined, it offered a path not to spiritual growth, but to moral perdition.[40]

The rebellious Unitarian minister and preacher of radical individualism, Ralph Waldo Emerson, was an heir of Channing's self-culture. For Emerson, the book of Nature was seen as the ultimate redeemer in the age of print abundance. Book reading was not discarded at once, but integrated into a larger framework of "self-culture" and "self-examination." In his 1837 address, "The American Scholar," Emerson offered a severe critique of the rising market and the segmented society that produced bookworms instead of "Man Thinking." Ironically, Emerson benefited from the new commercial society, which allowed him to be a lyceum lecturer, that is, a secular preacher.[41] In his critique of the commodification of literature and the degradation of culture, the individualist Emerson shared a view of "genteel letters" with more moderate advocates of self-culture and self-discipline. Similarly, Henry David Thoreau longed for something other than a culture of books. The solitary writer by Walden Pond, who read but little, rhetorically asked: "Will you be a reader, a student merely, or a seer? Read your fate, see what is before you, and walk on into futurity."[42] For the transcendentalists, reading was only an auxiliary to the discovery of the self, and the essential reading matter was not in print but in each individual. "The dark walls of your mind are scrawled all over with facts, with thoughts," Emerson observed in one of his early lectures. "Bring a lanthorn and read the inscriptions."[43]

Along with ministers and writers, hygienists and health reformers were particularly worried about the mental and moral effect of reading. In particular, solitary abandonment in reading was associated with masturbation in the case of young men. Some critics of popular reading wrote extensively on such dangers. Rev. John Todd, a Congregationalist at war with Unitarians, attempted to bring back purity. In *The Student's Manual,* and more specifically in a section of the fourth chapter written in Latin and entitled "Beware of bad books," Todd argued that solitary reading of bad books led to masturbation. The independent and acquisitive act of reading would bring the young man rewards for life, if it did not transform into the debilitating act of onanism.[44] Similarly, William A. Alcott, the advocate of diet reform, warned young men against the moral and physical dangers of sitting up to read late at night. "If exciting books are read at all," said Alcott, "they should be read in the forenoon, and not in the evening."[45]

Indeed, as *Mental Health,* a later treatise by the physician Isaac Ray, testifies, popular reading was perceived through the lens of the masturbation phobia that developed in antebellum America and continued well into the Victorian era.[46] Instead of contributing to an ethic that encouraged production and reproduction, the pleasure of solitary reading ran the risk of unmanning the self-absorbed reader. Faced with a flood of cheap books and periodicals, moral reformers reaffirmed the education of character and downplayed the education afforded by books. The battle against omnivorous reading by men was also a reaction to the increasing feminization of American culture before the Civil War. While book reading was considered a feminine and passive occupation, character building was intrinsically manly. Only strenuous study and effort could redeem the danger of passivity embodied in the act of reading. Reading with a fixed purpose to remember and to profit from was seen as a mental health exercise, not an amusement. The mind was compared to muscles, whose strength and endurance were conditioned by continual exercise.[47]

Conduct-of-life books for young women also described good reading as a strong and manly exercise. While most reformers admitted that works of imagination usually predominated in the libraries of young women, they recommended a selection of history, biography, poetry, mental philosophy, and sacred literature along with, above all, the Bible. Usefulness instead of amusement was to direct the choice of books, but self-education did not necessarily require books. As William Eliot reminded his audience in *Lectures to Young Women*, "The highest education of the intellect is worthless, unless the moral nature is developed and manliness secured." For women, book culture was second to piety and the education of the heart. The habit of reading could not displace habits of prayer and thoughtfulness in duty.[48]

Writers of prescriptive literature for both young men and young women often gave both groups common advice on the practice of reading. The difference appeared more in the context of reading. While most lectures to young men first discussed self-education and self-improvement, and then transgressions, criminal behavior, and dangerous amusements, lectures to young women, in contrast, offered introductory chapters on home and duties before discussing female education and moral mission.[49] The education of women, although rated important, was not for the mere purpose of securing a good establishment in life but for her self-improvement. Eliot could not be more explicit: "So in woman's education, the attainment of knowledge and improvement of the manners, the cultivation of taste, the accomplishments of music, drawing, and dancing, need not be neglected, and ought not to be; but they must be made secondary and subordinate to moral culture. They should become the handmaids of religion and virtue; branches grafted into the healthy tree of home education."[50] Books educated the intellect, not the heart, and were marginal in female education. Even women writers of advice literature promoted a conservative view of female reading. They recommended useful books and devotional works for women's leisure. Self-improvement would make a woman of true intelligence, who would be a blessing at home, in her circle of friends, and in society.

The true sociability of reading, indeed, belonged to the family circle—that is, in complete opposition to newspaper reading in saloons. James W. Alexander, author of more than thirty volumes for the American Sunday School Union, seemed to advocate a return to a community of readers, where instruction and entertainment were intertwined and women were more likely to be listeners than silent readers. "Make the most of reading aloud," said Alexander in *The Working-Man,* describing home entertainment where the wife and daughters may read as well as sew.[51] Collective reading was a safeguard against solitary, depraved reading. Women were systematically portrayed in familial reading situations that had little in common with the images of reverie or contemplation to be found in giftbooks. Lydia Sigourney, "the Sweet Singer of Hartford," argued in *Letters to Young Ladies* that a taste for reading is peculiarly necessary for a woman: "She should render herself an entertaining and instructive fireside companion, by replenishing her treasury."[52] Sigourney advised young women to do a little reading aloud regularly and to memorize passages. The art of reading aloud was emphasized, even though women's reading was confined to the fireside and the domestic circle rather than invested into public speaking. Because reading was speaking the thoughts of others, a woman was regarded as an appropriate medium to transmit a literary message. It was important for her to read aloud, to speak the most naturally, like a conversation, to entertain her friends and family. Collective reading was then a decent substitute for dancing, and reading aloud was a cement of society. Such an idealized representation of a patriarchal and communitarian society of readers reveals the reformers' nostalgia for a past now displaced by the growing urban anonymity. William Alcott, for instance, seemed to mourn the bonds of a bygone society when he recalled "the practice of meeting one evening in the week to read the news together, and converse on the most interesting intelligence of the day."[53] In an age when popular reading of cheap books and periodicals made the fragmentation of the reading public salient and encouraged the privatization of reading, reformers longed for the return to an earlier community of readers.

The antebellum critique of bad reading habits went beyond preoccupations with morality and the family. It aligned itself with the new industrial discipline and the relation of play to work, at a time when the social environment was less favorable to social mobility simply through learning and reading. To be sure, the democratization of print made the cultivation of the mind possible for the common man. Much advice to young men continued to describe self-education as a path to social improvement: "It is to raise ourselves above mere servants and laborers into a position of influence and growing usefulness," William Eliot told his audience of young men. The acquisition of knowledge was no longer the prerogative of would-be gentlemen and merchants; the mechanic too should find time for reading and opportunity for self-improvement. "If he has the natural ability and will use the opportunities of improvement offered to him, he may rise to as great height as he can reasonably desire."[54]

Although the reformers' advice was fueled with optimism, the antebellum reality made reading less rewarding in a context of growing impoverishment, diminishing social mobility, and emerging class distinctions.[55] Reading alone was no longer a sufficient means of social improvement or a source of wealth. In addition, commitment to self-culture for the sole purpose of improving one's status was deemed hypocritical. Self-culture was now redefined in moral and elevating terms rather than blunt social benefit. Even though there was a consensus that serious study was more effective than dilettante reading, belief in the social power of learning was waning. "Self-education will not infallibly lift us into distinction; it will not infallibly give us wealth," Massachusetts educator William Parsons Atkinson told the Young Men's Christian Union of Boston in 1860.[56] Studious reading was not enough to ascend the social ladder, yet reading just for pleasure was not legitimate. Reformers were left with the task of arguing for the usefulness of reading, which, on the one hand, was challenged by the availability of leisure reading matter and, on the other, was constrained by the failure of social improvement. In their minds, the only convincing reason left for the usefulness of proper reading would then be its moral value.

The model of the learned mechanic embodied by Benjamin Franklin remained invaluable, but the new industrial order required some adjustments. By the nineteenth century, reformers carefully warned their audience against a strict imitation of Franklin's fondness for reading. Unlike Franklin, a would-be self-educated apprentice no longer had to choose a vegetarian diet in order to save money for books—which now were more affordable—and could therefore preserve his strength for work. As a Carey and Hart reprint of a publication by the Society for the Diffusion of Useful Knowledge indicated, reading was a pleasure, but working was a duty. Thus the pamphlet concluded, "Let every man who loves independence, avoid late hours, irregular living, and excess of reading as well as excess of any other kind."[57] Self-improvement now ranked second to work, even though Franklin's uses of print continued to represent a prototype of reading as a "useful recreation" and a source of pragmatic knowledge. In the end, the eighteenth-century printer was remembered not as a mere mechanic, fond of reading, but as an active and clever man of business.[58]

Self-culture à la Franklin was further praised for advocating little leisure. Workers would gain from emulating Franklin, who had been able to study in the midst of all his labors. Leisure in colonial Protestant America had been traditionally associated with idleness and the luxury of the few. Accordingly, the work ethic of early Americans left no possibility of recreation for the sake of mere pleasure. By the mid-nineteenth century, Franklin's belief that "Leisure is Time for doing something useful" was far from being outdated. Americans valued work as a dream of success; it was believed to be the highroad to independence, wealth, and status. At the same time, however, repose took on a new value in terms of the regeneration of the work force and its improved productivity in the industrial society.[59]

But the implications for self-education and the activity of reading did not draw a consensus. For many reformers, reading as Franklin did for improvement and useful knowledge was all very good and did not justify the grant of extra leisure time. "I know the objection which immediately arises," said William Eliot, "when any plan of self-education is proposed. It is the want of time. But, generally speaking, it would come nearer the truth to say 'want of inclination.' "[60] Antebellum reformers saw no contradiction in condemning the popular appetite for miscellaneous news and light reading while asserting the sanctity of learning "by stealth." They emphasized the joy and reward of husbanding odd moments, a definite advantage for men in straits. In *The Working-Man*, James W. Alexander, who hoped to discourage those doing "hand-work" from rising in the world, went on to underscore an odd dichotomy between manual and nonmanual work: "While the wealthy scholar often lounges away whole afternoons on the sofa of his library, unable to fix upon a topic of study, the poor fellow who hangs over a book-stall, or snatches a moment from his work, is enjoying a paradise of intellectual satisfaction." The mechanic of Jacksonian America, according to Alexander, should be content with his own station in life.[61] Indeed, moral reformers came to praise a program of long workdays, little leisure, and intense study. For Alcott, learning could result from "an old piece of newspaper, or a straggling leaf from some book, or an inscription on a monument, or the monument itself."[62] In any case, there was enough leisure time, reformers argued, in the evening, on the Sabbath, or during the intervals provided by the new machines in shops and factories. Just as low wages assured that wage earners needed to work six long days a week and had little time for dissipation, so the want of leisure was believed to guarantee a healthy appetite for knowledge. Yet to commend laborers for studying by stealth resulted in defending a cultural status quo in the face of print abundance.[63]

Those advocates of much work and few books were precisely the same critics who denigrated the popular newspapers and magazines that were tailored for a long working day and short leisure time. They sensed the potential subversiveness of a fragmented and ephemeral print culture and saw that the nonwork time of laboring men and women escaped their control. The worker-readers were getting piecemeal pleasure, while even these short moments of rest were supposed to help the regeneration of the work force. Defenders of moral culture reiterated endless exhortations for self-improvement, without sympathizing with the public demand for more leisure time. This resulted in part from the reformers' fear of excessive leisure and pleasure reading. They viewed recreation in continuity with work time, and as preparation for the next workday.

In contrast, workers defined their leisure time as nonwork time, squeezed between work hours. Also, recreational space sometimes coincided with the workplace—for instance, when apprentices went to the shop on Sunday to read newspapers and magazines. Of course, Sabbath reading was highly controversial, since pleasure reading on Sundays displaced Bible reading. By their own choice of reading matter, readers might celebrate or break the Sabbath. For Eliot, there was little comfort in the way young men practiced the Sabbath: "They rise very late; spend an unusual time over the newspaper; devote three or four hours to novel-reading, and two or three more, perhaps, after the dinner hour has been prolonged as much as possible, to an afternoon ride, in the progress of which it will be strange if something very much like dissipation does not occur."[64] While the

Sunday editions of newspapers were still irregular and constituted a major target for zealous Sabbatarians, the Saturday papers offered plenty of reading material, and the weekly repose was often devoted to entertaining reading at the expense of churchgoing.[65]

Not only did the pleasure of reading compete with religious duties, it also threatened to divert young workers from their commitment to labor organizations. As the apprentice cabinetmaker Edward J. Carpenter recalled in an entry of his journal, "There was an adjourned meeting of the 'rabble' (so called by the aristocrats) this evening, but I was so much engaged reading the 'game of life' that I have not been out the shop." The young apprentice kept the habit of reading papers and cheap books either in the evening or on Sunday. On that particular Tuesday evening in August 1844, Carpenter's class consciousness was somewhat weakened by his pleasure in reading Leith Ritchie's "The Game of Life," a story in *The Omnibus of Modern Romance (Six Inside)* (1844), which he had bought for 25 cents.[66]

It should come as no surprise that labor advocates did not acknowledge the popular taste for light literature. There was a fear in antebellum America that reading could be antisocial and lead to passivity. Pleasure reading might emasculate the worker, and labor advocates joined other moral reformers in their condemnation of dilettante reading. They too came to regard "good" reading as a "useful recreation." In a response to female readers who supposedly requested more anecdotes, stories, and light reading, the editor of *The Man,* George Henry Evans, advocated political and serious reading instead:

> We think it highly important that a different taste should be created, if possible. To those who can only afford to take *one* paper, it is highly necessary (though, unfortunately, it is not considered so,) that the paper they take should furnish them with correct *political* as well as other intelligence, for without it how can they be qualified to participate in the choice of public agents? . . . Is it not better, then, that we should devote a portion of our columns to the purpose of remedying the serious evil that we have pointed out, than that we should occupy them exclusively with "light reading?"[67]

Historians have recently argued that the American ten-hour workday movement evolved through the prism of republican ideology.

American workers chose more often to demand education than to contest the alienation of large-scale factories, increased use of machinery, and time-discipline. They came to regard long hours as a roadblock to their political participation. Apparently, a distinction emerged between working time and the time for civic duty, even before the differentiation between labor and leisure in industrial America.[68] In spite of their political exclusion, female workers also appropriated the discourse of improvement in their fight for a shorter working day. For example, in 1844 the *Working Man's Advocate* published a letter "in a female hand," signed "E.D.," in which the sender asked for more leisure time for working women. It is worth quoting at length:

> Men have began [*sic*] to awake to the necessity of cultivating the mind of woman, to see that she forms the common mind and teaches the young idea how to shoot, and that impressions received in the nursery are the strongest and most lasting. Ladies' books, magazines, and the like are daily published for the instruction of woman's mind; but what time has the widow who works from early morn until midnight for literary acquirements? If she could spend one hour over a passing newspaper, it would divert her thoughts from her own misfortune; but, alas! She can not afford a moment of time, and if, as is frequently the case, she can not obtain constant employ, what is she to do? what a temptation to vice of every kind! . . . But, where, alas! is the mechanic's widow to look for assistance or even friendship? For her there is no asylum but the grave.[69]

Whether the author of the letter sought improvement or pleasure, we cannot know. But in any case, she was aware of the legitimate argument in which she framed her aspirations. More often, however, calls by leaders such as Frances Wright or Robert Dale Owen for the improvement of working conditions and the education of workers may have been at odds with the workers' own perspective on leisure time for entertaining and escapist reading.[70] Hard work made play necessary, and workers clearly emphasized their need for light reading and amusement because of their exhaustion. In the Lowell mills, for instance, female factory operatives used the more militant publication *Voice of Industry* to repudiate the "Romance of Labor" of the *Lowell Offering* and voiced their discontent with the moral recreations. They acknowledged the presence of churches and ministers, the lectures of various kinds, and the libraries of well-selected books, which "continually invite to the soul-feast those who, tho' they hunger and thirst, cannot partake . . . simply from physical and mental exhaustion." After a thirteen-hour workday, the mill girls needed "amusement, relaxation, *rest,* and not mental exertion of any kind." They wanted "Jim Crow performances," that is, minstrel shows, and "the trashy and milk-and-water sentimentalities of *Lady's Book* and *Olive Branch*" rather than serious reading.[71]

While the workers called for either entertainment or shorter work hours, most reformers and labor advocates questioned the appropriateness of "light reading" after physically exhausting work. This was widely debated in antebellum prescriptive literature. Certainly, opinions differed over the rights of hardworking men and women to have access to light reading. For some, reading an interesting paper or book was an adequate amusement for the manual worker, because it required no bodily exertion and was better than drinking. Reading could transport the worker into a livelier and gayer world, and the next day he would still find himself with money in his pocket for his family and without a headache.[72] Yet most antebellum crusaders of good reading advocated mental work after manual work, while admitting that self-culture at night required strong resolution in those who had worked hard all day.[73]

By the antebellum period, the activity of reading had become a double-edged sword: it might be useful, but it could also be sidetracked. Because reading was less institutionalized than other cultural activities, it was accessible to all and was more difficult to control. The ubiquity and cheapness of new printed materials made reading potentially as transgressive an entertainment as other public amusements such as the theater, the ballroom or the saloon. To be sure, the new urban institutions such as lyceums, libraries, and mechanics' institutes promoted serious reading as a rational recreation.[74] But as Robert Gross has concluded in his analysis of the Concord Social Library in Massachusetts, a growing discrepancy between the goals of the promoters of reading and the taste of the reading public led to the collapse of the library, "a victim, in part, of the rage for light fiction that was sweeping through the town." Similarly, the unsuccessful experience of mechanics' libraries illustrates how the institutionalization of culture failed to respond to the popular audience.[75]

While managers of virtue attempted to curtail popular practices of reading in the name of democracy, the thirst of the reading public for light and ephemeral literature was satisfied outside institutional boundaries, and with the complicity of shrewd merchants of leisure such as James Gordon Bennett and Louis Godey. Reading was redefined by the public's patronage and shared with other public amusements the attraction of popular entertainment. Light reading of a magazine or a paper also provided the poor with affordable pleasure. Edward Carpenter, for instance, mentioned in his journal that he saved 25 cents by not attending a concert one evening. In contrast, he was often willing to spend 12½ cents or a quarter on books that occupied more than one evening.[76] In the eyes of both its consumers and its critics, pleasure reading belonged to a broader context of leisure activities.

A growing number of critics came to perceive the popular uses of print as reprehensible entertainment. Perhaps reading rooms were not in fact safe substitutes for places of "vicious resort" such as the theater, the gaming table, and the brothel. Some clergymen, including Baptist minister Daniel C. Eddy, continued to believe in books and habits of study as substitutes for vain amusements and called upon the literary lecture and the circulating library to provide innocent rather than sinful pleasures.[77] Yet the majority agreed with the Unitarian Henry Ware Jr. of Boston, who feared that the popular literature of the day led to the "effeminacy of the soul" instead of a "clear and strong mind" and believed that reading was therefore no different from indulging at the confectioner's or drinking at the tavern. Pleasure reading represented just another source of dissipation.[78] Although books had long been regarded as far more legitimate modes of instruction than the stage or the ballroom, in the pre–Civil War years both the theater and reproachable reading were condemned. Defenders of both reading and theatergoing were rare, although Unitarian minister Henry W. Bellows argued that the permissiveness in parlor and bedroom reading could justify claims for legitimate theater.[79] More commonly, however, at a time when industrialization transformed both work and play, reading was scrutinized along with other public and private recreations.

Since the 1970s, particularly with the work of Herbert Gutman, labor historians have broadened their study of working-class experience beyond the workplace and into the neighborhood and the community. More recently, nonwork time and space—in addition to work time and the workplace—have been the subject of new inquiries into class analysis, social control, and resistance. As the contested terrain between social groups, where *intra*-class and *inter*-class alliances were negotiated, leisure quickly became the new frontier for labor history.[80]

Social as well as cultural historians have increasingly explored the history of leisure in societies transformed by industrial capitalism. Traditional, preindustrial work in rural and self-sufficient societies was discontinuous, regulated not by the clock but by the task, and was performed collectively while workers sang or told stories. Work and play were intertwined, and there was no clear line where work ended and leisure began. The coming of large-scale machine-powered industry introduced work-discipline and the separation of work and leisure in both space and time; when irregular work rhythms gave way to work-discipline in factories, leisure emerged as a category separate from and subordinate to work.[81] Among targets for reform, employers and masters listed indolence in the workshop, lateness, and absenteeism, as well as late rising, attendance at weddings and funerals, the sociability of the tea table, and drinking—although the rituals of Saint Monday never persisted in early America in the same way as in Europe.[82] To be sure, the new time-discipline did not go uncontested, and the nineteenth century witnessed many acts of resistance to change. Nonetheless, while working men and women repeatedly challenged the new time values and struggled to control their own working lives, the ideology of "time-thrift" was persuasively internalized through the agency of moral rhetoric. Lessons of industry, frugality, order, and regularity were to be taught at school and at work. Evangelical religion allied with industrial capitalism to convert men and women to the new valuation of time, and to the belief that "time is money."[83]

Anglo-American historians of leisure have emphasized the dichotomy between preindustrial and industrial habits, while recognizing the persistence of traditional behavior intertwined with the more rational modes of industrial capitalism.[84] While documenting the moral power of middle-class promoters of improvement, some scholars underlined the working-class response to the new ideology of work and leisure. Resistance, accommodation, appropriation, and modification in popular recreations were strategies that revealed a "class expression." Following this line of argument, struggles over the control of leisure paralleled or even superseded struggles over the control of work. If on the British side the overpoliticization of leisure prompted Gareth Stedman Jones to call for a return to the workplace and a strong dependency of leisure on work, American scholars too began to reassess the framework of a history of leisure, underscoring in particular the similarities in class divergence or convergence in both the workplace and the place of leisure.[85]

Although nineteenth-century American workers inherited the values of leisurely artisanal work and were prompt to resist the new time-discipline and industrial morality, their conflicting responses reflected the internal divisions of their class into revivalists (or loyalists), traditionalists, and radicals.[86] Studies of leisure in primarily northeastern and midwestern cities also confirmed the class division along ethnic and religious lines that was characteristic of working-class struggles over the control of work.[87] For instance, Steven Ross argues in his study of nineteenth-century Cincinnati that formerly shared leisure pursuits divided between plebeian saloons and more respectable taverns. Similarly, Richard Stott has demonstrated that the antebellum working class of New York City was divided linguistically and ethnically. Such a division—for instance, between Irish and German—was reflected in "working-class institutions" such as boardinghouses, barrooms, fire companies, and theaters.[88]

However, the present study is concerned with a different perspective. Instead of asking whether debates over recreation have obliterated debates over production, it suggests that the public/private dichotomy poses problems in the history of leisure. Most studies that are concerned with working-class leisure have focused on recreational forms involving public space, such as the saloon, and public rituals, such as Fourth of July parades. Sports and fraternal lodges have also been examined as forms of recreation.[89] In addition to labor historians, cultural historians have explored public institutions of entertainment such as the theater, the lyceum, the museum, and the music hall.[90] Concepts of public and private have been intertwined in the class distinction between the private, refined amusements of the leisured classes and the public, rowdy amusements of the masses. Because the visibility of some forms of working-class recreation (e.g., saloon going and brawling on the street) aroused hostility among the middle and upper classes, historians have focused on public and visible recreations of the so-called dangerous classes. Yet the prescriptive literature of the antebellum era repeatedly indicates that private recreations such as reading were not exempt from criticism. Indeed, it was precisely the privacy of leisure reading that was under attack. The nature of the private sphere, whose existence had been fundamental to the creation of the young republic, is thus more complicated than it has appeared. If the history of the family has underlined the importance of nurturing and motherhood in the republican ideology, as well as the transforming power of women through the little commonwealth, the history of leisure reveals different aspects of the private sphere that further define leisure itself as a social construct.

The study of popular recreations as a separate entity has implicitly assumed the otherness of the working classes. We must ask if this reflects the contentious reality of nineteenth-century America, or merely the representation of working-class leisure by middle-class reformers. Private, individual leisure activities were no longer the prerogative of the well-to-do in antebellum America. Indeed, popular reading might subvert the values of the middle-class work ethic, while at the same time borrowing a legitimate discourse of improvement and self-culture to differentiate itself from reprehensible, "visible" popular recreations. Though a shift occurred in the early nineteenth century from a gospel of work—when preindustrial work was performed in leisurely rhythms—to a belief in rational recreation after exhaustive industrial labor, the middle-class values of the "duty of play" hardly applied for wage earners, and attacks continued on workers' wasted idleness.[91] What emerged in antebellum America were growing social distinctions regarding nonwork time, and the bifurcation between an increasingly leisured class and a "recreated" working class.

Yet by reiterating the primacy of the workplace over the amusement park, labor historians of leisure have implicitly borrowed the class boundary that nineteenth-century middle-class promoters of improvement underlined, that is, the function of leisure to recreate the labor force for improved efficiency. Leisured middle-class Americans, whose private amusements were confined to the fireside, attempted to control public recreations of the working class and promoted rational recreation. At the same time, they condemned the private amusements of working-class men and women that mimicked theirs. Indeed, while class-based saloon drinking compensated for the monotony of work-discipline and periodically threatened public order, reprehensible reading practices silently subverted the social order. The particular case of the controversial activity of reading may therefore offer a challenge to the overused dichotomy of, on the one hand, a popular-collective-public culture and, on the other, a learned-individual-private culture.[92]

What kept the popularity of private reading alongside public amusements was the attraction of printed materials. Newspapers, for instance, would not have drawn the same audience that attended the theater or the museum had they not formatted their news as public entertainment. Print certainly began to match other sources of pleasure. Newspapers served as an information platform for performances, lectures, exhibitions, and any kind of advertisement. At the same time, they staged the city life itself. They put on the page an urban theater, with new scenes and acts every day. Magazines too went hand in hand with public entertainments. They serialized dramas and plays that were also put on the stage. So when reformers condemned omnivorous reading along with public recreations, they censured various expressions of the same popular culture.

Nonetheless, their stand on books and reading was not an easy one. One needs to recall that the popular uses of print in Jacksonian America were in part legitimized by centuries of acclaim for the power of the printed word and precedence of reading over rowdy amusements. Because of the traditional aura of print, critics and readers, managers and workers all referred to reading as improvement and entertaining knowledge. Reading continued to be praised as a "useful recreation," but its recreational potentiality threatened its utilitarian value. Reformers, therefore, were rarely the advocates of unlimited reading in mid-Victorian America. Only publishers, the new patrons of commercial culture, responded favorably to the public demand for more printed matter that offered both pleasure and escape.

To be sure, antebellum ministers and reformers did not hold positions of consistent opposition to reading. They continued to praise books and reading when they addressed an audience of nonreaders. But when preaching to an audience of excessive readers, they vehemently condemned those reading habits. William Parsons Atkinson began his 1860 lecture on "Books and Reading" before the Young Men's Christian Union in Boston by listing three classes within the reading community: "First, people who, though knowing how to read, *neglect* books; next, people who, knowing how to read, but knowing nothing else, *abuse* books; and last, people who, knowing how to read, but knowing other things as well, *use* books."[93] While the last group of readers received only praise, the first two classes needed reform. There was a traditional way of dealing with people who neglected books, and any dislike of books could be corrected with diligence and time. Yet it was not the illiterate individual but the "abuser" of books, the omnivorous reader, the effeminate worker, who presented a threat to social cohesion and order. The excessive love of "cheap and light" reading matter had become a new vice, which in the pre–Civil War years could only be eradicated through habits of frugality and self-discipline.

As American society progressively accepted worldly amusements and blended its old work ethic with a new duty of play, the practice of reading became a borderline case. Serious reading as study and strenuous exercise was certainly praised and commended. But transgressive uses of print were censured along with the theater and the saloon. The private activity of reading potentially entailed greater dangers and vices than most public recreations and sports, and the traditional condemnation of specific literary genres was no longer a sufficient safeguard in the age of print abundance. Rather, a wide spectrum of custodians of culture joined in a crusade for good reading by way of both lectures and books. Their prescriptions flourished at a time when a ferment of reform touched all areas of human activity. This was also a period marked by the logic of industrial capitalism, which stripped reading of its power to offer social mobility and redefined it as either a source of moral uplift or a questionable leisure activity. Reading advisers called for the restoration of the public character of reading. Conservative reformers such as William Alcott and T. S. Arthur advocated a return to family reading and reading aloud as a way of preserving a traditional community of readers, whereas more liberal critics such as Channing and Emerson promoted a republic of "genteel letters." The latter believed in the moral influence of the cultivated class and envisioned a patrician leadership whose emulation would uplift the common man. Indeed, the boundless circulation of print in the Jacksonian era had provoked a cultural consolidation.[94]

The irony, of course, is that the reformers who joined in the jeremiad against deviant reading practices were themselves avid readers of books and periodicals. They sometimes conceded their private and voracious reading habits, as Lydia Maria Child wrote in a letter to her friend Marianne Silsbee: "I had read Jane Eyre before you had the kindness to send a copy. I was perfectly carried away with it. I sat up all night long to finish it."[95] Does this indicate that reformers were merely hypocritical arbiters of others' behavior? Or were they vehemently responding to changes in antebellum society while struggling with the contradictions embodied in their own culture? Whereas European societies saw state institutions and churches devise discourses on reading in the late nineteenth and twentieth centuries, American democratic society relied on middle-class crusaders who promoted self-discipline. The antebellum reformers who allied cultural elitism and norms of morality not only criticized the commodification of letters but overwhelmingly chose the printed word—and its commercial rewards—over the spoken word to rage against excessive reading. The singularity of both the form and the content of antebellum prescriptions for proper reading practices thus points far more to the historicity of the moment than to the utterance of traditional complaints about deviant behavior. The moral stewards, who were themselves readers, novelists, and pamphleteers—and therefore indispensable players in the carnivalesque market fair—had been prompted by the publishing outburst to denounce altogether "cheap and light" literature and the omnivorous behavior of the readers. Highbrow defenders such as Poe and Emerson did not fail to attack cheap papers, fashion magazines, and illustrated books equally. For them lowbrow publications were defined not merely by their economic value but also by their festive and spectacular outlook.

It is important to emphasize that those elegiac voices were not the only ones heard during the pre–Civil War decades. The traditional discourse of enlightenment and the emancipatory character of print continued to develop among free blacks, rebellious slaves, and antislavery activists. While Frederick Douglass's equation of freedom with literacy fueled both his personal resistance to oppression and his leadership in the fight against slavery, print also remained a major weapon for abolitionist crusaders who believed in moral suasion and who counted more than a handful of printers in their ranks. The history of what pitted the printed word against the "peculiar institution" during the first half of the nineteenth century would require an entire study in itself.[96] The subject of this book has been far less political, although it focuses on a period of contestation and growing polarities between high and low culture. The textual transformation at work during that ephemeral moment when the world of print turned upside down was pervasive enough to provoke fears of cultural erosion — and therefore a widespread condemnation. The result was not the eradication of the transgressive forms of print but a cultural alignment among Americans that lasted well beyond the mid-nineteenth century and is still echoed in more recent cultural wars.

Conclusion

This book set out to chronicle the circus atmosphere that pervaded most of American print culture in the pre–Civil War decades. It has described the playfulness and rowdiness of new printed artifacts that brought exuberance and theatricality to public culture and at the same time infused tactile pleasure in the private act of reading. By celebrating a bodily culture and deformity in either size or style, antebellum publishing innovations burlesqued American print culture. This was particularly evident in the fascination, or even saturation, with images. Already in the 1790s Parson Weems, the legendary book peddler and writer, had emphasized in letters to Philadelphia bookseller Mathew Carey the preference of his customers for illustrations. Cheap books should look "pretty" and contain "images."[1] Half a century later the public taste was amply satisfied with a proliferation of images.

Nonetheless, the carnival on the page that turned the world of print upside down during the second quarter of the nineteenth century was not a benign feast of words and images. It was rather a site for contest, and its historicity speaks to the ephemerality of that print upheaval. Some of the publications discussed in this study were short-lived commercial ventures, such as the mammoth weeklies, whereas others designed successful strategies to be imitated: the *New York Herald* was followed by the *New York Tribune,* a rival, Whig penny paper, and steel-engraved ladies à la *Godey's* appeared in a variety of magazines, including the literary *Graham's Magazine.* While the case studies examined recall the specificity of each publication, together they map out the scope and character of the new print culture. From the birth of the penny press in the mid-1830s to the economic depression and social unrest of 1857, popular reading matter crossed the boundaries of the legitimate print culture. A vernacular printed word that was cheap, sensational, and ephemeral mocked the long established authority of print. It offered an illustrated parody of reading for the enjoyment of the audiences it targeted. This festive print first emerged in the northeastern publishing centers of New York, Boston, and Philadelphia and was soon imitated across the nation.

The desecration of traditional print culture consisted not only in the popularization of specific literary genres but, more important, in the materiality of the new texts. Distinctive features of popular publications ranged from graphic descriptions of the human body in the daily press to images of women in giftbooks and magazines, from spectacles of the grotesque and the monstrous to collections of odds and ends and mélanges of texts and images, from orality in print through interviews and dialogues to silent contemplation of images. In the liminal zone of pleasure reading, past uses of print mixed with new needs for entertainment and sociability. Of course, as seen in Chapter 6, the public taste for lowbrow printed artifacts did not go unchallenged. Indeed, a highbrow critique attempted to curtail popular reading, which, unlike the traditional activity long encouraged by a Protestant and republican culture, had become controversial in the age of abundance and boundlessness. The reformers' elitist call for fasting and discipline in the midst of carnival was matched only by the contempt of European travelers, who did not fail to critique the outpouring of print in nineteenth-century America. While Charles Dickens ridiculed the Americans' addiction to reading newspapers in both *Martin Chuzzlewit* and his *American Notes,* Alexis de Tocqueville concluded that democracy introduced an industrial spirit into literature.[2]

Often accused of issuing "trash, corrupting literature" or scorned for their light, sentimental fare, the cheap publications and picture books were nonetheless hailed by others as harbingers of better days. Sarah Josepha Hale, for instance, spoke of periodicals as the "flying literature" of unforeseen times and the chief source of women's intellectual culture.[3] Perhaps the most eloquent defense of a democratic print culture was Walt Whitman's 1856 manifesto. In his "Letter to Ralph Waldo Emerson," Whitman was determined "to meet people and The States face to face, to confront them with an American rude tongue." In listing the literary means of the United States, Whitman wrote an ode to the constituent parts of the carnivalesque printed festival:

> The twelve thousand large and small shops for dispensing books and newspapers—the same number of public libraries, any one of which has all the reading wanted to equip a man or woman for American reading—the three thousand different newspapers, the nutriment of the imperfect ones coming in just as usefully as any—the story papers, various, full of strong-

flavored romances, widely circulated—the one cent and two-cent journals—the political ones, no matter what side—the weeklies in the country—the sporting and pictorial papers—the monthly magazines, with plentiful imported feed—the sentimental novels, numberless copies of them—the low-priced flaring tales, adventures, biographies—all are prophetic; all waft rapidly on. I see that they swell wide, for reasons. I am not troubled at the movement of them, but greatly pleased. I see plying shuttles, the active ephemeral myriads of books also, faithfully weaving the garments of a generation of men, and a generation of women, they do not perceive or know. What a progress popular reading and writing has made in fifty years! What a progress fifty years hence! The time is at hand when inherent literature will be a main part of These States, as general and real as steam-power, iron, corn, beef, fish.[4]

Although he later became disenchanted with the literary culture of his time, as *Democratic Vistas* testified in 1870, Whitman was first pleased by the flood of popular books and periodicals, for it announced even greater literary production. Whitman appreciated precisely what Emerson, in an elitist plea against the market economy of books, regarded as anathema. Americans, indeed, were also divided on the issue of whether the democratization of reading represented growth or decline. Their diatribes on the subject testify to the unstable cultural order that prevailed during the pivotal antebellum era.

The in-betweenness of antebellum America was further marked by the ambiguity of social categories. As this study has suggested, the ideological dichotomy between public man and private woman does not survive close examination. Nineteenth-century practices of reading blurred such a distinction. Women emerged in public print culture, even though they were portrayed in private settings. At the same time, male readers could be said to have retreated to a more private space for relishing their newspapers and magazines—but at the expense of more moral and useful undertakings. Authors of conduct-of-life books even characterized the transgressive activity of leisure reading as feminine and in sharp contrast with masculine character building through serious, useful, and frugal reading. Interestingly, the feminine activity of reading was associated with popular, commercial culture at the periphery of a core of masculine, genteel, legitimate culture. The moral reaction to the transformation of reading from duty to pleasure forced a process of cultural realignment, and by mid-century the liminal phase of American print culture gave way to the reaggregation phase and the consolidation of cultural order.

Finally, the history of antebellum carnivalesque print culture reveals the triumph of the market. Throughout this study of popular reading matter and reading practices, cultural values embodied in newspapers and magazines appeared intertwined with or opposed to their market value. Popularization was entangled in a process of commodification. The second quarter of the nineteenth century witnessed the coming together of commerce and culture. The present study primarily discussed the transformation and commercialization of American print culture from the standpoint of the consumers. Yet, even though readers had the power to communicate their needs and preferences, they were not in a position to make books. Indeed, the making of boldly different printed materials was due in large part to the art of aspiring entrepreneurs such as James Gordon Bennett, Park Benjamin, and Louis Godey. They represented a new class of merchants of pleasurable and popular reading that threatened the leadership of traditional custodians of culture.

In a sense, Mammon won over the moral crusade for proper reading. By the 1850s successful features of popular printed matter —such as illustrations and serialization—made their way into mainstream publishing, including biblical publications. But the antebellum formation of oppositional cultural spheres was by no means eradicated by the Civil War. Reading prescriptions such as Noah Porter's *Books and Reading; Or, What Books Shall I Read and How Shall I Read Them* continued to distinguish the good from the bad. Scholars of Victorian America have noted a late-nineteenth-century emphasis on cultural gentility, a plea for quality, and a fear of democratic mediocrity in the face of an expanding marketplace.[5] By the turn of the century, social strife accompanied an increased bifurcation between high culture and mass culture, and "the new cult of masculine writing," which was to mark the Progressive Era, was emerging. The reformist agenda of the muckrakers restored a public dimension to the role of print, in sharp contrast to the antebellum inversion of private and public. Even the control of bad reading habits relied not on self-discipline, as in earlier decades, but rather on legislation—beginning with the 1873 Comstock Act for the suppression of obscene literature.[6] In sum, although the popularization of reading matter and cultural disruption marked the antebellum era, to judge the print culture of that period as simply forecasting the late-nineteenth-century changes would be fallacious. With its ephemeral, yet exuberant publications, the pre–Civil War print culture had a character of its own.

Notes

INTRODUCTION

1. Alcott, *Young Woman's Guide*, 319.

2. Bakhtin, *Rabelais and His World*, 10.

3. Turner, *Ritual Process*, 112. The concept of liminality was first introduced by Arnold van Gennep (1909), who described three phases in all rites of passage: separation, margin or limen, and aggregation. Victor Turner has further analyzed the middle phase, or liminality. In the present case, the initial phase of separation might be represented by the religious press that initiated the popularization of print, as described in Chapter 1.

4. An interesting example of the use of both Bakhtin and Turner is presented in Rob Shields, " 'System of Pleasure.' "

5. Bakhtin, *Rabelais and His World*, 37–41.

6. LaCapra, "The Cheese and the Worms: The Cosmos of a Twentieth-Century Historian," in *History and Criticism*, 45–69, and "Bakhtin, Marxism, and the Carnivalesque," in *Rethinking Intellectual History*, 295, 304.

7. Stallybrass and White, *Politics and Poetics*, 6–15, 177–90.

8. Turner, *Ritual Process*, 95–96.

9. Turner expanded his analysis of liminality from an 1964 article in the *Proceedings of the American Ethnological Society* to the 1969 publication of *Ritual Process*, and then to the 1982 publication of *From Ritual to Theater: The Human Seriousness of Play* and the 1985 essays in *On the Edge of the Bush: Anthropology as Experience*.

10. See Vincent Crapanzano, "Liminal Recreations." The decline of Turner's influence was recently described in Donald Weber, "From Limen to Border."

11. Previous examples of the relevance of liminality for Jacksonian society can be found in the work of Carroll Smith-Rosenberg. See "Davy Crockett as Trickster: Pornography, Liminality, and Symbolic Inversion in Victorian America" in *Disorderly Conduct*, 90–108, and also her "Sex as Symbol in Victorian Purity."

12. Bynum, "Women's Stories, Women's Symbols."

13. Bakhtin, *Rabelais and His World*, 153–54.

14. Lears, *Fables of Abundance*, 9–10, 24.

15. For another example of the control and exploitation of a liminal zone by entrepreneurs, see Rob Shields's study of Brighton beach in " 'System of Pleasure.' "

16. The "pleasure zone" is borrowed from Shields's study of the beach at Brighton in ibid., 65–68. The concept of boundlessness comes from John Higham in his *From Boundlessness to Consolidation*.

17. *Clayton v. Stone*, 5 Fed. Cas. (No. 2872) 999 (Circuit Court, S.D. New

York, 1829); Ginsburg, "Tale of Two Copyrights," in Armbruster, *Publishing and Readership,* 109.

18. Examples of this argument can be found in Richard Brown's *Knowledge Is Power* and Richard John's *Spreading the News.*

19. The interesting argument of a fictive public is presented by Ronald Zboray. He suggests that the history of antebellum reading might be a history of misreadings and analyzes both the misconceptions authors or publishers had of their readers and the readers' own construction of meaning with the book newly produced. See *Fictive People,* 190–95.

20. See, for instance, Susan Davis, *Parades and Power,* for Philadelphia in the early republic; Wilentz, *Chants Democratic,* for antebellum New York City; and Mary Ryan's essay, "American Parade," for the transformation of parading from a civic ceremony to an ethnic festival through the examples of New York, San Francisco, and New Orleans from 1825 to 1880.

21. Waldstreicher, "Rites of Rebellion."

22. In contrast to the argument proposed here, literary scholars have attempted to reconstruct a nineteenth-century shared print culture. In their accounts, emphasis is on common literary texts that were available in various formats and arguably reached all levels of the social ladder. David Reynolds, in particular, argues that genres of popular literature traceable to circulating pamphlets and magazines were echoed in major literary works of the American Renaissance; see his *Beneath the American Renaissance.*

23. The field of research defined as the "history of the book" originated in France as *l'histoire du livre* and was carried on in the United States as "the social and cultural history of communication by print"; see Darnton, "What Is the History of Books?" The French history of the book began with Febvre and Martin, *Coming of the Book* (first published in French in 1958), and evolved in parallel with broader historiographical trends of the last three decades, from the quantitative history of book production and book circulation to the qualitative history of reading. See Chartier and Roche, "Le livre," and Chartier, "Du livre au lire."

24. Levine, *Highbrow/Lowbrow.*

25. For a history of reading that is based on personal documents, see Brown, *Knowledge Is Power.*

CHAPTER ONE

1. The gender specificity of reading aloud did not go unchallenged. Margaret Fuller, in particular, was critical of the passivity and submissiveness associated with reading aloud, which was sometimes compared to force feeding. See Gustafson, "Choosing a Medium," 44. Reading aloud remained a pleasurable habit of the upper-middle-class Hamiltons of Fort Wayne, Indiana. See Sicherman, "Sense and Sensibility," 206.

2. Leonard, "News at the Hearth," 380.

3. Francis Bennett Diary, June 26–July 2, 1854, American Antiquarian

Society, Worcester, Mass. Bennett's other reading habits are discussed in Chapter 3.

4. For the early republic, see Michael Warner, *Letters of the Republic*. For the late nineteenth century, see Richard Ohmann, "Where Did Mass Culture Come From?" and "Readers, Consumers: The Professional-Managerial Class," chap. 7 in *Selling Culture*.

5. Frank Luther Mott dates the first great incident in the history of cheap publishing around 1842–45, in particular with the weekly papers and their extras of pirated literature. See *Golden Multitudes*, 76–79.

6. Goodrich, *Recollections*, 386–88. See also Hall, "Uses of Literacy."

7. Fermer, *James Gordon Bennett*, 327; Saxton, *Rise and Fall*, 96. Patricia Anderson rates the circulation of the *London Journal* (1845–1906), a successor of the *Penny Magazine* of the 1830s, at 450,000 in 1855; see *Printed Image*, 3 n. 4.

8. Mackay, *Western World;* Trollope, *Domestic Manners*, 71–72, 247–49. Ronald Zboray discusses the high literacy rates and literacy-generating institutions such as the family, the church, the Sunday School, the academy, the common school, young men's associations, maternal associations, mechanics' institutes, libraries, and the lyceum in relation to novel reading; see his *Fictive People*, 96–109. Richard Brown notes the stability of literacy rates in "From Cohesion to Competition." Lee Soltow and Edward Stevens correlate literacy rates with economic development and urbanization; see *Rise of Literacy*, 50–56.

9. Goodrich, *Recollections*, 381–86.

10. Frederick F. Gleason, Boston publisher of fiction, coined the phrase "books for the million." Gordon Wood first introduced the idea of a "democratization of gentility"; see Joyce, *Printing and Society*, 304. The concept of "degentrification" is from the late Stephen Botein at the 1986 Summer Seminar in the History of the Book at the American Antiquarian Society.

11. Engelsing, *Bürger als Leser, Analphabetentum und Lektüre*, and "Perioden der Lesergeschichte."

12. For critiques of Engelsing's concepts of "intensive" and "extensive" reading, see Darnton, *Great Cat Massacre*, 249–52, and *Kiss of Lamourette;* Siegert, *Aufklärung und Volkslektüre*. In American history, David Hall has first used these concepts and then raised doubts about their applicability; see his "World of Print" and "History of the Book."

13. Davidson, *Revolution and the Word*, 73.

14. Gilmore, *Reading* and "Elementary Literacy."

15. Scott, "Popular Lecture."

16. One particular attempt to synthesize this period is Robert H. Wiebe's *Opening of American Society*. Even though Wiebe claims to analyze the period in its own terms, he in fact keeps an eye on the late-nineteenth-century segmentation of American culture.

17. Hall, "Uses of Literacy," and Brown, "From Cohesion to Competition." Brown also stresses the development of a "competitive information marketplace"; see his *Knowledge Is Power*, 268–96.

18. John Tebbel has again introduced the postbellum era as "the First Great Change in Magazines"; see *Magazine in America,* 57–72.

19. Williams, *Long Revolution,* ix–xiv.

20. Hall, "World of Print." For a comparison with early modern Europe, see David Cressy, "Literacy in Seventeenth-Century England" and *Literacy and the Social Order;* Lawrence Stone, "Literacy and Education"; Robert Mandrou, *De la culture populaire.*

21. Lockridge, *Literacy in Colonial New England.*

22. For critiques of Lockridge's argument, see Lawrence Cremin, "Reading, Writing and Literacy," and Hall, "Education and the Social Order" and "World of Print," 173. On women's literacy levels, see E. Jennifer Monaghan, "Literacy Instruction and Gender"; Joel Perlmann and Dennis Shirley, "When Did New England Women Acquire Literacy?"; Gloria L. Main, "Inquiry into When and Why Women Learned to Write." For a survey of literacy scholarship, see Carl F. Kaestle, "Studying the History of Literacy," in *Literacy in the United States,* 3–32.

23. Hall, "World of Print," 171–75, and his *Worlds of Wonder,* 21.

24. For instance, William J. Gilmore found an almost universal literacy among male Vermonters between 1760 and 1830; see his "Elementary Literacy." Perlman and Shirley observed a rise of women's literacy after 1765 yet minimized the impact of republican ideology; see "When Did New England Women Acquire Literacy?" On nineteenth-century literacy, see Lee Soltow and Edward Stevens, *Rise of Literacy,* and Harvey J. Graff, *Literacy Myth.* For a broad perspective, see Harvey J. Graff, *Legacies of Literacy.* For comparison with Britain, see David Vincent, *Literacy and Popular Culture.*

25. Bailyn, *Ideological Origins;* Bailyn and Hench, *The Press;* Levy, *Emergence of a Free Press.*

26. Warner, *Letters of the Republic,* 9, 31–33. See also his "Franklin and the Letters of the Republic" and "Textuality and Legitimacy."

27. Warner, *Letters of the Republic,* 39–40, 61–63. His argument of a link between the public sphere and literary culture comes from Jürgen Habermas's *Structural Transformation,* 1–26. In contrast to Warner, Jay Fliegelman has argued for a "dialectical relation between the authority of impersonality rooted in the discourse of descriptive science and the authority of sincerity rooted in the discourse of affective experience." See Fliegelman, *Declaring Independence,* 129.

28. Kerber, *Women of the Republic,* 233–64; see also Davidson, *Revolution and the Word.*

29. Brown, "From Cohesion to Competition," 304–5. Franklin's middling class of readers is discussed in Larzer Ziff, "Upon What Pretext."

30. Butler, *Awash in a Sea of Faith,* 277.

31. Nord, "Evangelical Origins," 2.

32. From Harry C. Stout and Nathan Hatch's essay, "The Religious Press in America," quoted in Hall and Hench, *Needs and Opportunities,* 108.

33. Hatch, *Democratization,* esp. 125–45. On the cultural significance of the rise of religious journalism, see Brumberg, *Mission for Life,* esp. 44–78; Nord,

"Evangelical Origins"; Michael H. Harris, " 'Spiritual Cakes Upon the Waters': The Church as a Disseminator of the Printed Word on the Ohio Valley Frontier to 1850," in Hackenberg, *Getting the Books Out*, 98–120. For the Methodists, see Walter Sutton, *Western Book Trade*, 150–65. For the evangelical print in Britain, see Altick, *English Common Reader*, 99–101.

34. From Gaylord P. Albaugh, "The Role of the Religious Press in the Development of American Christianity, 1730–1830," unpublished manuscript quoted in Hatch, *Democratization*, 142.

35. On the First Great Awakening, see Harry S. Stout, "Religion, Communications"; for the comparison with the Second Great Awakening, see Brown, "From Cohesion to Competition," 307.

36. A variety of antebellum religious dissent—from Mormonism to Spiritualism—made use of the printed word, even in the process of displacing the Scripture. The success of phrenology also testifies to the aura of the printed word and its link with most fads of antebellum America. See Stern, *Heads and Headlines*, xiv.

37. McGaw, *Most Wonderful Machine;* Saxton, "Problems of Class and Race"; Smith, *History of Papermaking.*

38. Ronald J. Zboray, "Antebellum Reading and the Ironies of Technological Innovation," in Davidson, *Reading in America*, 190–96, and Zboray, *Fictive People*, 133–35.

39. Charvat, *Literary Publishing*, esp. chap. 1; Clark and Wetherell, "Measure of Maturity."

40. The history of book production and book distribution in the United States has not been fully researched. See Gilreath, "American Book Distribution," and Zboray, "Transportation Revolution" and *Fictive People*. The pathbreaking work was Charvat, *Literary Publishing*. Some older studies include Tryon, "Publications of Ticknor and Fields in the South" and "Ticknor and Fields' Publications in the Old Northwest." The reference book for the transportation revolution is still Taylor, *Transportation Revolution.*

41. Tocqueville, *Democracy in America*, 2:121.

42. In the last twenty years American scholars have developed the field of the history of the book on "native grounds," while borrowing methodologies from both English bibliographers and French historians of publishing and reading. Yet the study of the cheapest forms of print has predominantly focused on the colonial period and the early republic. See, for instance, Williams, " 'Behold a Tragic Scene' "; Cohen, *Pillars of Salt;* Victor Neuburg, "Chapbooks in America," in Davidson, *Reading in America*, 81–113; and, for periodicals, Nord, "Republican Literature," and Charles E. Clark, *Public Prints.*

43. The majority of recent studies on nineteenth-century popular publications has been the work of literary scholars. See Denning, *Mechanic Accents;* Reynolds, *Beneath the American Renaissance;* Davidson, *Revolution and the Word;* Ellery Sedgwick, *Atlantic Monthly;* and Lund, *America's Continuing Story.* Historians are far from agreeing on their conceptualization of "mass." For Patricia Anderson, who describes an "early mass culture" in mid-nineteenth-century England, there is a "mass" market when a large number of people are con-

cerned and aware of it, even if the public is varied; see her *Printed Image,* introduction. By contrast, Richard Ohmann uses the concept of "mass culture" to describe a homogeneous, national audience in the late nineteenth century; see "Where Did Mass Culture Come From?"

44. Webster, *American Dictionary;* Cooper, *American Democrat.*

45. David Grimsted suggested the all-inclusive concept of "neglected culture" in order to avoid the elusiveness of "popular culture" and the theories of mass culture; see his "Books and Culture." For a nostalgic approach to popular culture, see Susan Davis, *Parades and Power.* The concept of cultural "reappropriation" is from Chartier, "Intellectual History," 30–38.

46. On the fiction of the "people," see Rodgers, *Contested Truths,* and Morgan, *Inventing the People,* esp. 263–87. Recent studies of nineteenth-century popular culture include Levine, *Highbrow/Lowbrow,* and Cmiel, *Democratic Eloquence.*

47. Edward Pessen, "Egalitarian Myth" and *Riches, Class, and Power.* Studies of the labor history of the antebellum period are numerous. Among the most recent are Paul Faler, *Mechanics and Manufacturers;* Bruce Laurie, *Working People of Philadelphia;* Sean Wilentz, *Chants Democratic;* Richard B. Stott, *Workers in the Metropolis.* On the tripartite division, see Blumin, *Emergence of the Middle Class.* The cultural bifurcation is discussed in Levine, *Highbrow/Lowbrow,* and Buckley, "To the Opera House." On religion, see Douglas, *Feminization,* and Moore, *Religious Outsiders.* For the evangelical crusade, see in particular Paul Johnson, *Shopkeepers' Millennium,* and Ryan, *Cradle of the Middle Class.*

48. In contrast to Schlesinger, *Age of Jackson,* see Saxton, *Rise and Fall,* and Rogin, *Fathers and Children.* Among historical syntheses, see Sellers, *Market Revolution,* and Harry Watson, *Liberty and Power.* For an earlier assessment of fragmentation and the lack of synthesis, see Formisano, "Toward a Reorientation of Jacksonian Politics," and Wilentz, "On Class and Politics." Works in political history include McCormick, *Party Period and Public Policy;* Silbey, *Partisan Imperative;* and Bridges, *City in the Republic.*

49. The quotation is from an 1836 letter of Margaret Browne to her friend Eliza Quincy, cited in Kerber, *Women of the Republic,* 237.

50. The argument of a shift from community to individualism is an extension of the "modernization theory." See Brown, "From Cohesion to Competition."

51. The concept of "textual classes" is from Jacques Dubois and Pascal Durand, "Literary Field and Classes of Texts."

52. Schiller has linked the penny press to the republican ideology and the rise of the middle class. In contrast, Saxton has underlined the symbiosis between what he describes as the "First Wave of the Penny Papers" and the workingmen's movement; see *Rise and Fall,* 96.

53. The concept of "literary field" is from Bourdieu, "Champ intellectuel." On the concept of "institution," see Hohendahl, *Building a National Literature* and *Institution of Criticism;* also Peter Bürger, "Institution Literatur." For an earlier theory of homologies between text and social class, see Goldmann, *Hidden God.*

54. The example of the Lowell mill girls' readership is further discussed in Chapter 5.

55. Tebbel, *Magazine in America,* 35–36; Endres, "Women's Press in the Civil War."

56. Artisan republicanism has represented a valuable alternative to Lockean liberalism for many historians, including labor historians. Pocock, *Machiavellian Moment.* For review essays, see Shalhope, "Toward a Republican Synthesis" and "Republicanism and Early American Historiography." See also Joyce Appleby, "Republicanism and Ideology" and "Republicanism in Old and New Contexts." The use of the republican paradigm in labor history is particularly exemplified by Wilentz, *Chants Democratic.*

57. For studies that see correspondence between popular texts and republican ideology: Michael Denning traces an artisan republican ideology in popular narrative in *Mechanic Accents,* and Dan Schiller discusses the revival of artisan republicanism in the new popular press in *Objectivity and the News,* 10, 17, 46. Also see Bruce Laurie, " 'Nothing on Compulsion' " and *Working People of Philadelphia,* where he uses the classification "loyalists," "traditionalists," and "radicals"; Paul Faler, "Cultural Aspects"; Sean Wilentz, "Artisan Republican Festivals" and *Chants Democratic.*

58. The theory of *Rezeptionsästhetik* originated around the Konstanz group. See Hans Robert Jauss, *Toward an Aesthetic of Reception* and *Aesthetic Experience;* Wolfgang Iser, *Act of Reading* and *Implied Reader.* For an overview, see Hohendahl, "Introduction to Reception Aesthetics." Among the prolific literature on reader-response criticism in the United States, see Suleiman and Crosman, *Reader in the Text;* Tompkins, *Reader-Response Criticism;* Fish, *Is There a Text in This Class?* The encounter between feminist and reader-response criticism produced important works. See Radway, *Reading the Romance,* and Flynn and Schweickart, *Gender and Reading.*

59. The return to historical readers has been advocated by Tony Bennett, "Texts, Readers, and Reading Formations." See also Mailloux, *Interpretive Conventions,* esp. 159–220, and Baym, *Novels, Readers, and Reviewers.*

60. Ginzburg, *The Cheese and the Worms.* On the playfulness and transgression of the activity of reading, see also Michel de Certeau, "Reading Is Poaching," in *Practice of Everyday Life,* 165–76, and Bakhtin, *Rabelais and His World.*

61. Michel Foucault advocated the study of discourses as practices; see *L'ordre du discours,* 54. The concept of *habitus* is from Pierre Bourdieu, "Genesis of the Concepts of *Habitus* and *Field*" and *Choses dites.* For a discussion of both Foucault and Bourdieu, see Certeau, *Practice of Everyday Life,* chap. 4.

62. The most obvious example was Timothy Shay Arthur, author of the sensational and bestselling *Ten Nights in a Barroom* as well as advice books for young men and young women.

63. Michael Gilmore, *American Romanticism,* 1–17; Teichgraeber, " 'A Yankee Diogenes' " and *Sublime Thoughts/Penny Wisdom,* 3–43.

64. Quoted in Charvat, *Profession of Authorship,* 266, 315.

65. Quoted in Tebbel, *Magazine in America,* 37.

66. Reynolds, *Beneath the American Renaissance.*

67. For the history of the perception of mass culture as feminine, see Huyssen, "Mass Culture as Woman."

68. Tocqueville, *Democracy in America,* 475.

69. Turner, *Ritual Process,* 94–95.

70. Bird, *Englishwoman,* 443.

71. Mott, *History of American Magazines,* 2:3.

CHAPTER TWO

A short version of this chapter was presented at the 1990 American Studies Association convention. I thank Janice Radway for her comments.

1. See the one-hundredth anniversary number of the *Sun,* September 2, 1933. See also O'Brien, *Story of the Sun.* Within two months the *Sun* had reached a circulation of 2,000; it allegedly reached 10,000 within one year and 30,000 in 1838. The newspaper became an institution. While in 1833 Ben Day served as publisher, editor, reporter, compositor, pressman, and mailing clerk, by 1844 the *Sun* employed eight editors and reporters, twenty compositors, sixteen pressmen, twelve folders and counters, one hundred carriers, and even one London correspondent.

2. *Herald,* May 6, 1835.

3. Studies of the *Herald* are numerous. Among those particularly helpful is Crouthamel, *Bennett's New York Herald.* On Bennett, see also Fermer, *James Gordon Bennett,* and Kluger, *The Paper.* Among older studies, Pray, *Memoirs of James Gordon Bennett;* Parton, "New York Herald"; and Hudson, *Journalism in the United States,* are still valuable. See also Hughes, *News and the Human Interest Story;* Carlson, *The Man Who Made News;* Seitz, *The James Gordon Bennetts.*

4. "Cheap Newspapers," in *Brother Jonathan,* May 9, 1840, 2, col. 3.

5. Ellard, *Newsboy,* 5–10. See also Brace, *Short Sermons,* and Hogeland, *Ten Years Among the Newsboys.*

6. *The Gift* (1843), 58–84; Seba Smith to Messrs. Carey and Hart, March 25, 1842, Edward Carey Gardiner Collection, Historical Society of Pennsylvania, Philadelphia. The same engraving was reused in *The Ruby* for 1850, with unsigned commentary entitled "The Newsboy"; see *The Ruby* (1850), 253–55.

7. William Wells Brown in *The Anglo-African,* August 8, 1863, as quoted in Sterling, *Speak Out in Thunder Tones,* 233.

8. On the tradition of almanacs, see Stowell, *Early American Almanacs,* and, in European history, Bollème, *Les almanachs populaires;* Spufford, *Small Books.*

9. A prejudice against pictures in dailies continued through the 1850s and into the Civil War. Not until the 1890s did American reporting value illustrations. See Leonard, *Power of the Press,* 101–2.

10. The French category of *occasionnels* is described by English and American bibliographers as broadsides, pamphlets, or miscellaneous literature. For an analysis of such printed matter, see Roger Chartier, "The Hanged Woman Miraculously Saved: An *occasionnel,*" in *The Culture of Print,* 59–91; on wood-

cut broadsheets and propaganda during the Reformation, see Scribner, *For the Sake of Simple Folk*, 1–13, 229–50.

11. Certeau, *Practice of Everyday Life*. On the opposition between individual and collective action, see Boltanski, Darré, and Schiltz, "La dénonciation." See also Foucault, *I, Pierre Rivière*.

12. As the linguist Tzvetan Todorov points out in his analysis of classical fiction, or the so-called representative texts, "Only by subjecting the text to a particular type of reading do we construct, from our reading, an imaginary universe." Diverse accounts of the same text describe "not the universe of the book itself, but this universe as it is transformed by the psyche of each individual reader." See Todorov, "Reading as Construction," 67, 72, 76.

13. The concept of "reading interludes" is from Prince, "Notes on the Text as Reader," 230.

14. *Herald*, September 10, 1835.

15. Crouthamel, "James Gordon Bennett" and *Bennett's New York Herald*, 28–31. Nineteenth-century newspapers used indifferently both names, Helen and Ellen, while scholars of the popular media have mostly used Ellen. Patricia Cline Cohen has restored the preference of the victim herself, that is, Helen. See her careful analysis of the gender character of the case in "Helen Jewett Murder" and "Mystery of Helen Jewett." The objectivity of the penny press is questioned in Tucher, *Froth and Scum*, 21–96.

16. The Robinson-Jewett case is analyzed as an eroticized murder narrative of the antebellum period in Cohen, "Mystery of Helen Jewett."

17. Gasffield, "To Speak and Act Bodily."

18. See Pray, *Memoirs of James Gordon Bennett*, 256–57; Schudson, *Discovering the News*, 52–53.

19. *Herald*, June 3, 1840, August 3, 1842. Crouthamel, *Bennett's New York Herald*, 37, 53–54. On Bennett's claims after the Moral War, see Hudson, *Journalism in the United States*, 453. A thorough treatment of the Moral War can be found in Hoover, *Park Benjamin*, 104–18. See also Seitz, *The James Gordon Bennetts*, and Mott, *American Journalism*, 235–37. To put the *Herald*'s revenue in perspective, one must note that it began with capital of $500. In comparison, Horace Greeley launched the *Tribune* with capital of $3,000 in 1841, and Henry J. Raymond started the *New York Times* in 1851 with $100,000.

20. Mott, *American Journalism*, 215–16, 304, 321, and his *News in America*.

21. Crouthamel, "Newspaper Revolution," 106, "James Gordon Bennett," and *Bennett's New York Herald*, esp. chaps. 2 and 3.

22. Schudson, *Discovering the News*, 31.

23. *Sun*, anniversary issue, September 2, 1933.

24. Schudson, *Discovering the News*, 60.

25. Pray, *Memoirs of James Gordon Bennett* (1855), quoted by Schudson, *Discovering the News*, 46.

26. Schiller, *Objectivity and the News*, 10. Schiller chose the case of the *National Police Gazette*, a weekly specializing in crime news.

27. Ibid., 17, 46. On artisan republicanism, see Wilentz, *Chants Democratic*.

On the working class in antebellum New York City, see also Stansell, *City of Women*, and Stott, *Workers in the Metropolis*.

28. Saxton, "Problems of Class and Race."

29. *Herald*, December 28, 1835.

30. Ibid., September 7, 1835.

31. Ibid., December 7, 1835.

32. Pred, *Urban Growth*, 23.

33. *Herald*, October 21, 1835.

34. The concept is from Benedict Anderson, *Imagined Communities*, 37–40. On earlier journalism, see Clark and Wetherell, "Measure of Maturity," and Bailyn and Hench, *The Press*.

35. As quoted by Benedict Anderson, *Imagined Communities*, 39. See also Eisenstein, "Some Conjectures."

36. *Herald*, May 6, 1835, as quoted in Crouthamel, *Bennett's New York Herald*, 22.

37. As quoted in Mott, *American Journalism*, 311.

38. *Herald*, October 2–3, 21–22, 24–26, 1839.

39. Ibid., December 4–5, 23–26, 1840.

40. For a comparative approach to nineteenth-century murders of consanguinity in France, see Guillais, *La chair de l'autre*, and Ariès and Duby, *History of Private Life*, vol. 4, *From the Fires of Revolution to the Great War*, ed. Michelle Perrot.

41. *Morning Herald,* January 15, 1840, 2. For the centrality of Shakespeare in antebellum culture, see Levine, "William Shakespeare" and *Highbrow/Lowbrow*.

42. *Herald*, August 31, 1835.

43. Darnton, "Writing News and Telling Stories." Lennard Davis, *Factual Fictions*, 42–70; Hunter, *Before Novels*, esp. chaps. 7 and 8.

44. Havens, *Diary of a Little Girl*, 47. See also McDade, *Annals of Murder*, 33. The case of Polly Bodine is discussed in the *Herald*, January 1–11, 21, June 27, 28, 1844, with numerous woodcuts, and in the *National Police Gazette*. Two pamphlets were published, one in Philadelphia in 1844 and the other in New York in 1846.

45. Tocqueville, *Democracy in America*, 2:121.

46. *Herald,* December 18–19, 1835.

47. Foster, *New York by Gas-Light;* McCabe, *Secrets of the Great City*. See also Browne, *Great Metropolis*. Analyses of urban descriptions in nineteenth-century fiction can be found in Blumin, "Explaining the New Metropolis"; Siegel, *Image of the American City;* Janis Stout, *Sodoms in Eden;* Spann, *New Metropolis*.

48. Poe, *Doings of Gotham*. See also Jacobs, *Poe*, and Linda Patterson Miller, "Poe on the Beat."

49. Sue, *Mysteries of Paris* (1843); Reynolds, *Mysteries of London* (1845); Lippard, *Quaker City* (1845); Buntline, *Mysteries and Miseries of New Orleans* (1851); Melville, *Pierre*. Reynolds proposes a different interpretation of this sensational literature in *Beneath the American Renaissance*. On Lippard, see Denning, *Mechanic Accents*. On Buntline, see Buckley, "To the Opera House."

50. See in particular Bosco, "Lectures at the Pillory," and Williams, "Puri-

tans and Pirates," " 'Behold a Tragic Scene,' " "Rogues, Rascals and Scoundrels," and "Doctor, Preacher, Soldier, Thief." See also Daniel Cohen, *Pillars of Salt*, "In Defense of the Gallows," and "A Fellowship of Thieves."

51. Crime literature of the eighteenth century included rogue narratives, which were still reprinted during the antebellum period; see Williams, "Rogues, Rascals, and Scoundrels." On the "cult of horror" in late-eighteenth-century murder narratives, see Halttunen, "Early American Murder Narratives" and "Humanitarianism."

52. Lane, "Urbanization and Criminal Violence." See also his *Policing the City* and *Violent Death in the City*. Several scholars have analyzed criminal history in relation to the growing control and institutionalization of the police in nineteenth-century American cities. See Monkkonen, *Police in Urban America;* David Johnson, *Policing the Urban Underground;* Wilbur Miller, *Cops and Bobbies;* Richardson, *New York Police;* Schneider, *Detroit and the Problem of Order*. A provocative account of a sensational murder case is offered in Kasserman's *Fall River Outrage*.

53. Papke, *Framing the Criminal*.

54. On the political implications of crime reporting, see Leonard, *Power of the Press,* esp. 137–65.

55. See Brodhead, "Sparing the Rod"; Halttunen, "Humanitarianism"; Laqueur, "Bodies, Details."

56. Poe's "The Mystery of Marie Rogêt" was first published in Snowden's *Ladies' Companion* for November and December 1842 and February 1843 (18: 15–20, 93–99, 162–67). Ingraham's *The Beautiful Cigar Girl* appeared in 1844. Also, the spiritualist Andrew Jackson Davis used the case of Mary Rogers in the description of the corpse of Mary Ruciel, or Molly Ruciel, in his *Tale of a Physician* (1869). On Poe's uses of the sensational press, see Walsh, *Poe the Detective;* Wimsatt, "Poe and the Mystery of Mary Rogers"; Reynolds, *Beneath the American Renaissance,* esp. 225–48; and David B. Davis, *Homicide in American Fiction,* esp. 262–65. On Ingraham, see Denning, *Mechanic Accents*. Srebnick makes the argument that while exposing the destroyed body of the female victim, the daily newspapers invented the Mary Rogers tragedy; see her "Death of Mary Rogers."

57. Details reappeared in the various versions of the murder mystery of Mary Rogers. In Charles Wallace's confession, a "curious satin cord" replaced what the *Herald* had described as the "fine lace trimming" around the neck of the victim. See *A Confession of the Awful and Bloody Transactions in the Life of Charles Wallace, the Fiend-Like Murderer of Miss Mary Rogers* (New Orleans: E. E. Barclay, 1851), engraving caption and page 9.

58. Poe, "The Mystery of Marie Rogêt," in *Collected Works,* 3:730.

59. "Examination of Dr. Cook: Excerpt from 'The Hoboken Tragedy': Murder of Miss Mary C. Rogers," *Herald,* August 17, 1841; reprinted in *Brother Jonathan,* August 21, 1841.

60. The case of Mary C. Rogers was discussed in the *Herald,* August 4, 9–14, 16–21, September 7, 17, 21, 24, 28, 1841. The September 17, 1841, issue featured a woodcut representing Mary Rogers's house.

61. Poe, "The Mystery of Marie Rogêt," in *Collected Works*, 3:730.

62. From *Trial, Confession, and Execution of Peter Robinson*, April 16, 1841. The *Herald* first mentioned the case in the December 10 and December 14, 1840, issues: "Another Mysterious Disappearance of a Banker" and "Search for a Banker." It later had an article on the trial and imprisonment of Robinson almost every day from March 18 to April 17, 1841, including "His Approaching Execution," "Life and Confession," "Last 24 Hours," and "Last Moments." The pamphlet form of "The Life and Confessions, and Execution of Peter Robinson" was announced in the April 19, 1841, issue. Other pamphlets include *Trial, Confession, and Execution of Robert M'Conaghy* (1841) and *A True Account of the Murder of Abraham Suydam* (1841). See also *Murder Did Pay*, 182. Poe's "The Tell-Tale Heart" was first published in *The United States Saturday Post* (Philadelphia), July 1842. On Poe's use of the Robinson case, see Reynolds, *Beneath the American Renaissance*, 232, 586n.

63. On the withdrawal of executions, see Foucault, *Discipline and Punish*. See also Rothman, *Discovery of the Asylum*.

64. *Herald*, January 10, 1844, December 10, 1840. On the popularity of Barnum's museum, see Harris, *Humbug*.

65. The same cut appeared in the *National Police Gazette*, March 13, 1847, and in the pamphlet form, *Wonderful Trial of Caroline Lohman, Alias Restell* (1847). See also Browder, *Wickedest Woman in New York*, and Keller, *Scandalous Lady*.

66. *New World*, March 20, 1841, 190.

67. On the new literary production, see Feltes, *Modes of Production*.

68. Altick, *Deadly Encounters*, 3–10.

69. Palmer, *Des petits journaux;* Seguin, *Nouvelles à sensation* and *Les canards illustrés;* Jean Watelet, "La presse illustrée," in Chartier and Martin, *Histoire de l'édition*, 3:329–41; Thiesse, *Le roman du quotidien*.

CHAPTER THREE

A first version of this chapter was presented at the 1989 meeting of the Society for the History of the Early American Republic. I owe special thanks to Mary Kupiec Cayton for her comments.

1. Barlow, "Letter to Elias Boudinot" (1783), as cited by William Charvat in his *Literary Publishing*, 63, 71.

2. Barnes, *Authors, Publishers*, 1–29.

3. On copyright, see Schreyer, "Copyright and Books"; Barnes, *Authors, Publishers*, 49–94.

4. For circulation figures, Barnes, *Authors, Publishers*, 10–12.

5. Engelsing, "Die Perioden der Lesergeschichte."

6. The concept of "consolidation" is from Higham, *From Boundlessness to Consolidation*. For a provocative study of the popularization of books in nineteenth-century France, see Bassy, "Le livre mis en pièce(s)."

7. See Hoover, *Park Benjamin*, esp. 119–47.

8. Mott, *History of American Magazines*, vol. 1; Noel, *Villains Galore;* Hart, *The*

Popular Book; Lehmann-Haupt, Wroth, and Silver, *The Book in America;* Charvat, *Literary Publishing.*

9. For the expansion of bibliography to cultural history, D. F. McKenzie's work has been most useful, particularly *Bibliography and the Sociology of Texts* and "Sociology of a Text." See also Tanselle, "Bibliography and Textual Study," 255. For the concept of *paratexte,* see Genette, *Seuils.* For a brief discussion of cheap format and cheap content, see Charvat, *Literary Publishing,* esp. 64.

10. Saxton, "Problems of Class and Race." See also Mott, *American Journalism.*

11. *New York Daily Sentinel,* November 13, 1832, 2.

12. Noel, *Villains Galore,* 15.

13. Henry J. Raymond to Rufus W. Griswold, July 20, 1839, Park Benjamin Papers, Rare Book and Manuscript Library, Butler Library, Columbia University, New York, N.Y.

14. The *Universal Yankee Nation—Mammoth Quarto,* January 1, 1842, 2.

15. For a discussion of P. T. Barnum, see Harris, *Humbug.*

16. Clark and Wetherell, "Measure of Maturity," 285; McGaw, *Most Wonderful Machine;* prices are cited in Saxton, "Problems of Class and Race."

17. Susan Davis, "Making Night Hideous" and *Parades and Power.*

18. Stott, *Workers in the Metropolis;* Gorn, *The Manly Art* and " 'Good-Bye Boys.' "

19. *Brother Jonathan,* October 8, 1842.

20. Hoggart, *Uses of Literacy,* 119.

21. "Lesson to Newspaper Borrowers," *Weekly Dispatch,* June 22, 1839, 3.

22. Zboray, *Fictive People.*

23. Christopher Clark, "Diary of an Apprentice Cabinetmaker"; Francis Bennett's diary, manuscript at the American Antiquarian Society, Worcester, Mass.

24. *Dwight's American Magazine, and Family Newspaper,* December 25, 1847, 827.

25. For a broader discussion of the reformers' discourse on popular practices of reading, see Chapter 6.

26. *Brother Jonathan,* advertisement, 1842.

27. The serialization of crime news is discussed in Chapter 2. On dime novels, see Denning, *Mechanic Accents,* and Noel, *Villains Galore.*

28. See Bourdieu, "Champ intellectuel" and *Choses dites.*

29. On the emergence of literary criticism in America, see Pritchard, *Literary Wise Men of Gotham;* Charvat, *Origins of American Critical Thought;* Baym, *Novels, Readers, and Reviewers.*

30. On the competition between New York and New England, see Perry Miller, *The Raven and the Whale.* It is worth noting that many New York literary men came from New England.

31. For a discussion of commodification and the role of the public, see Benjamin, "Author as Producer."

32. On earlier serialization, see Watt, *Rise of the Novel,* 42; Lennard Davis, *Factual Fictions,* 66, 102; Vann, *Victorian Novels,* 1; and Mayo, *English Novel.*

33. See Feltes, *Modes of Production;* Klancher, *Making of English Reading Audiences.*

34. For the distinction between ephemerality, continuity, and seriality in early journalism, see Lennard Davis, *Factual Fictions,* 71.

35. Naval tales included "The Nautilus: A Collection of Select Nautical Tales and Sea Sketches with an Authentic Narrative of the Mutiny of the Somers," edited by John K. Duer, U.S. Navy, *New World,* January 1843; "Gaspar; The Pirate of the Indian Seas. A Tale of the Ocean," *Brother Jonathan* 2, no. 2 (1842); and "The Captain's Wife," *Brother Jonathan* 2, no. 6 (1842). Historical romances included "The Chevalier; Or, the Twenty-Fourth of August, 1572," *New World,* August 20, 1842, and Rev. George Newenham Wright, "Life and Times of Louis Philippe, King of the French," *New World,* August 10, 1842.

36. "Letters of Mary, Queen of Scots," *New World,* December 1842; Edmund Flagg, "Francis of Valois, Or the Curse of St. Valliar. A Tale of the Middle Ages," *New World,* February 1843; John Yonge Akerman [Paul Pindar, pseud.], "The Adopted Son; A Legend of the Rebellion of Jack Cade," *Brother Jonathan* 2, no. 5 (1842). On the American craving for a medieval world in the nineteenth century, see Rosenthal and Szarmach, *Medievalism in American Culture,* 2–9. The romanticized Victorian vision of the medieval past, along with Gothic furniture and picturesque history, is discussed in Fleming, "Picturesque History," 1072.

37. *Brother Jonathan* (1843), advertisement on back cover of extra.

38. The circulation figures are from Barnes, *Authors, Publishers,* 11–12.

39. Ibid.

40. Eugène Sue's novels represented a particular target for moral critics of popular literature because the lurid descriptions of the dissoluteness of Parisian working classes seemed to overshadow the socialist message. For a virulent attack on both Bulwer-Lytton and Sue, see Beecher, *Lectures to Young Men,* 170–214, esp. 214n. For a broader discussion of Beecher's critique of popular reading, see Chapter 6.

41. *New World,* June 27, October 10, 1840; July 2, 1842; December 19, 1840; January 2, 1841.

42. On the career of Samuel French, see *Truly Yours,* 1. An early examination of the impact of print and the book as physical object on the stage can be found in Peters, *Congreve, the Drama, and the Printed Word,* 1–8.

43. On the importance of the theater in antebellum culture, see Grimsted, *Melodrama Unveiled,* and Levine, *Highbrow/Lowbrow.* For the popular practice of acting, see the diary of Thomas Chamberlain, manuscript in the New York Public Library. I am thankful to Richard B. Stott for the Chamberlain reference.

44. Eddy, *Young Man's Friend,* 94.

45. A post office order of April 1843 established higher rates on the extras, and the Postal Act of 1845 put an end to the convenient newspaper postage for large magazines. In addition, rates for magazines depended on the weight rather than the distance. Lower book rates were also introduced by the Postal Act, therefore encouraging legitimate publishers to compete with the cheap

reprinters as long as the books remained unbound. See Mott, *History of American Magazines*, 1:361; Barnes, *Authors, Publishers*, 1–29.

46. Noel, *Villains Galore*, 17.

CHAPTER FOUR

An earlier version of this chapter was presented at the 1990 Berkshire Conference on Women. I thank Joy Kasson and Sherry Sullivan for their comments.

1. Ralph Thompson indicated that "before the gift book fashion spent itself, over a thousand different volumes more or less similarly conceived were issued in the United States." See his *American Literary Annuals*, 11. By the mid-1840s, about sixty giftbooks were published each year; see Pearson, "Lilies and Languors," 43.

2. One giftbook was specifically titled *Leaflets of Memory*. It was published in Philadelphia from 1845 to 1855.

3. Goodrich, *Recollections*, 2:260.

4. The position of nineteenth-century writers was ambiguous. They often partook of the profitable business of the new literary annuals, while criticizing their sentimentalism. See Pearson, "Lilies and Languors"; Booth, "Taste in the Annuals"; Winslow, "Books for the Lady Reader." A general antisentimental critique can be found in Douglas, *Feminization*.

5. Poe, *The Letters* (1948), cited in Gürtler, *Englischen literarischen Taschenbücher*, 69.

6. Emerson, April 1852, in *Emerson in His Journals*, 433.

7. Cressy, "Books as Totems," 93. See also Natalie Zemon Davis, "The Sacred and the Body Social."

8. See Baudrillard, *Le système des objets*.

9. The poem was reprinted in *The Garland* (1830) and *The Forget-Me-Not* (1855).

10. Appadurai, "Commodities and the Politics of Value."

11. The first annual to appear in England, in November 1822, was Rudolf Ackermann's *Forget me not, a Christmas and New Year's Present for 1823*. See Hunnisett, *Steel-Engraved Book Illustration*, 139–40. One of the first American annuals combined the old genre of almanac with the new genre of literary anthology; see *The Souvenir, or Picturesque Pocket Diary for 1826, with an Almanack, Ruled Pages for Memoranda, Literary Selections, and a Variety of Useful Information* (Philadelphia: A. R. Poole, 1826).

12. Gifts of printed books in early modern Europe recalled the gift of illuminated manuscripts in the Middle Ages. With the coming of print, however, patterns of gifts were diversified and multiplied. See Natalie Zemon Davis, "Beyond the Market," 82. The custom of offering books as New Year's gifts persisted in England well into the sixteenth century. See H. S. Bennett, *English Books and Readers*, 49. On the meaning of giving in Elizabethan court culture, see Montrose, "Gifts and Reasons." The motives for reciprocal giving did not exclude profit and cash value, but they were disguised under formal rites and

customs. The symbolic value of the act of giving overshadowed the material value of the gift.

13. *The Gift* by Mauss was first published in 1925. According to Pierre Bourdieu, "Practice never ceases to conform to economic calculation even when it gives every appearance of disinterestedness by departing from the logic of interested calculation (in the narrow sense) and playing for stakes that are non-material and not easily quantified." See *Outline of a Theory of Practice*, 177.

14. Quoted in Winslow, "Books for the Lady Reader," 94.

15. Leslie, *Behaviour Book*, 180–81.

16. Eliza Leslie, "The Souvenir," *The Pearl; Or, Affection's Gift* (1830), 106–23; also in *Affection's Gift* (1832).

17. Warner, *Wide, Wide World*, 29–42. George P. Putnam published Warner's novel in 1850 under the pseudonym of Elizabeth Wetherell. It subsequently went through thirteen editions in the United States and several in England.

18. For a wide-ranging discussion of the material dimension of religious life in America, see McDannell, *Material Christianity*, esp. chap. 1.

19. Winslow, "Books for the Lady Reader," 94. To be found in the bookcase were first Shakespeare, Milton, and Bunyan's *Pilgrim's Progress*, and on the secular shelves, Scott, Dickens, and Bulwer-Lytton. Irving and Cooper were among the few Americans who appeared next to the English writers.

20. From Mark Twain, *Life on the Mississippi*, as quoted in Bode, *Anatomy of American Popular Culture*, 52–53. The first half of *Life on the Mississippi* was originally published in 1875 as "Old Times on the Mississippi," a series of articles for the *Atlantic Monthly*. Twain wrote the second half in 1882.

21. Halttunen, *Confidence Men and Painted Women*, 59–60. The concept of "cultural podium" is from Sklar, *Catharine Beecher*, 137. See also Grier, "Imagining the Parlor," and Blumin, *Emergence of the Middle Class*, 184–85.

22. Thorstein Veblen argued in *Theory of the Leisure Class* (1899) that the consumption of goods served not to satisfy needs but to maintain social prestige. For Veblen, social amenities served only as disguise. For a critique of Veblen, see Adorno, "Veblen's Attack on Culture," and Lears, "Beyond Veblen."

23. *Young Lady's Friend*, 258–61. Antebellum advice literature often discussed the great uses of reading and "reading societies" or "reading parties" as substitutes for dancing and gossiping.

24. "Annuals," in *The Laurel Wreath* (1846), 9–13.

25. Harris, *Artist in American Society*, 146–51, 364–65.

26. Apostolos-Cappadona, *The Spirit and the Vision*, 42–49. On the nineteenth-century clergy's views of the visual arts, see also Dillenberger, *Visual Arts and Christianity*, 39–56.

27. Thoreau, journal entry for October 3, 1859, in *Writings of Thoreau*, cited by Harris, *Artist in American Society*, 181.

28. Apostolos-Cappadona, *The Spirit and the Vision*, 80–82.

29. Wolf, *Romantic Re-Vision*, 3; Joy Kasson, *Artistic Voyagers*, 47.

30. David Miller, "Washington Allston," 52.

31. The source is C. Edwards Lester, *The Artists of America: A Series of Bio-*

graphical Sketches of American Artists (New York: Baker and Scribner, 1846), as cited by Lovejoy, "American Painting," 356.

32. Hannah Flagg Gould's early contributions to magazines and annuals were assembled for the publication of *Poems* (1832). Her other works on religious subjects and child life include *The Golden Vase: A Gift for the Young* (Boston: B. B. Mussey, 1843) and *The Mother's Dream and Other Poems* (Boston: Crosby, Nichols, 1853).

33. The biblical quotation appears as the last two verses in Gould, "The Mother's Jewel," in *The Token* (1837), 146. On the sacred quality of home and family life in nineteenth-century America, see McDannell, *Christian Home*, 20–51.

34. The Italian master Raphael influenced more than one American painter of the nineteenth century, including Benjamin West and Washington Allston. On the frequent display of the Madonna in both Protestant and Catholic homes of the nineteenth century, see McDannell, *Christian Home*, 154. Paintings of the Immaculate Conception by Spanish baroque artist Bartolomé Esteban Murillo also inspired American artists and engravers. See, for instance, *The Christian Mother*, in *Godey's Lady's Book*, August 1850, 67, after Murillo's *Madonna and Child*.

35. Thomson, "Childhood," *The Gift* (1840), 37.

36. On the importance of death in the culture of antebellum America, see Saum, "Death in the Popular Mind"; Douglas, "Heaven Our Home"; Vinovskis, "Angels' Heads and Weeping Willows"; Hoffert, "'A Very Peculiar Sorrow.'"

37. Cranch, "Beatrice," *The Gift* (1844), 148.

38. Wolf, *Romantic Re-Vision*, 71.

39. Elizabeth Garrity Ellis, "'Intellectual and Moral Made Visible,'" 63.

40. On the tradition of the sister arts that was revived by Allston, see Eager, "Washington Allston's *The Sisters*," and David Miller, "Washington Allston."

41. "Dante's Beatrice," *The Token* (1836), 105–12. When Allston's painting was first exhibited in 1827 at the Boston Athenaeum, and again during the 1839 retrospective, Elizabeth Peabody wrote that it was the very Beatrice of Dante. See her *Remarks on Allston's Paintings* (1839), as cited by Ellis, "'Intellectual and Moral Made Visible,'" 65–67. Another Beatrice, with the veil of a nun and a cross, appeared in *The Ruby* for 1850, after a painting by Thomas Sully, which had previously been engraved as *Isabella* for *The Gift* (1840).

42. Henry James wrote of the mid-nineteenth century that "it was still the age in which an image had, before anything else, to tell a story." See his *William Wetmore Story*, 2:76, as cited by Joy Kasson, *Marble Queens and Captives*, 2.

43. Kasson, *Marble Queens and Captives*, 243.

44. For the parallel between Shelley and Hawthorne, see Robert L. White, "'Rappaccini's Daughter.'" Shelley's reading of the "Guido portrait" has been analyzed by Young-Ok An, "Beatrice's Gaze Revisited," 27–31. According to Stuart Curran, as cited by Young-Ok An, Melville too was haunted by "the sweetest, most touching, but most awful of all feminine heads" (ibid., 61 n. 4).

45. Bensick, *La Nouvelle Beatrice*, 87–92, 117–24. Carol Marie Bensick also traces the historical details of "Rappaccini's Daughter" to the *Autobiography of Benvenuto Cellini* (1500–1571), which was translated in 1828. For different readings of Hawthorne's tale, see Evans, "Allegory and Incest in 'Rappaccini's Daughter,'" and Morton Ross, "What Happens in 'Rappaccini's Daughter.'" Hawthorne's tale first appeared in John L. O'Sullivan's *Democratic Review* in 1844 and was republished in his collection *Mosses from an Old Manse* (New York: Wiley and Putnam, 1846). See "Notes on the Texts" in Hawthorne, *Tales and Sketches*, 1492.

46. Another appearance of Beatrice was in Shakespeare's *Much Ado about Nothing;* this character was often cited by women authors of the nineteenth century for her representation of female intelligence. See in particular [Anna] Jameson, *Characteristics of Women, Moral, Poetical, and Historical by Mrs. Jameson* (Boston: Ticknor and Fields, 1859), 99–110. Visual representations of Shakespeare's Beatrice were for the most part portraits of actresses. Examples include a Longacre engraving, *Miss Kelly as Beatrice* (ca. 1826), from a painting by John Neagle, and *Fanny Kemble as Beatrice* (1833), a portrait by Thomas Sully.

47. These remarks are based on a study of both subjects and style of engravings in a wide range of giftbooks from 1826 to 1855, in particular *The Atlantic Souvenir, The Christian Keepsake, The Gem, The Gift, The Iris, The Parlour Scrap Book,* and *The Token.*

48. This conclusion results from a comparison with the Longacre collection of prints held at the Library Company of Philadelphia. Moreover, giftbooks featured very few male portraits, with the exception of *The Christian Keepsake,* which published some portraits of ministers.

49. On the mid-nineteenth-century contempt for portraiture as a craft, see Hennessey, *American Portrait*, 6.

50. Lovejoy, "American Painting," 360.

51. Monroe H. Fabian estimates the number of Sully's portraits to be more than 2,000, out of 2,600 paintings. See Fabian, *Mr. Sully, Portrait Painter*, 10.

52. Several group portraits of "sisters" were engraved by Sartain. For instance, see *The Christian Keepsake* (1847), *Christmas Blossoms* (1850), and *Leaflets of Memory* (1852).

53. Allston's paintings are particularly relevant for an interpretation of the sister arts tradition. See Eager, "Washington Allston's *The Sisters.*"

54. Lydia Maria Child's "The Valentine," in *The Atlantic Souvenir* (1828), 3–4, was subsequently collected in Child's *The Coronal: A Collection of Miscellaneous Pieces, Written at Various Times* (Boston: Carter and Hendee, 1832). The engraving reappeared as an illustration for *The Common-Place Book of Romantic Tales* (New York: Charles Wells, 1831).

55. Margaret Fuller, "A Record of Impressions," *Dial* 1, no. 1 (July 1840): 73–84; Oliver Wendell Holmes, "The Allston Exhibition," *North American Review* 50 (April 1840): 358–81. On the 1839 retrospective, see Ellis, "'Intellectual and Moral Made Visible,'" and Apostolos-Cappadona, *The Spirit and the Vision*, 82–85.

56. Child, "The Valentine," 3–4.

57. On the relation of a portrait to its beholder, see Marin, "Toward a Theory of Reading."

58. My data cover the annual publication of *The Atlantic Souvenir* from 1826 to 1832 and *The Gift* from 1836 to 1845 — except 1839 and 1841. The cost books of Carey and Hart are held in the Edward Carey Gardiner Collection at the Historical Society of Pennsylvania, Philadelphia. The cost books of Carey and Lea have been partially published in Lea and Febiger, *Cost Book of Carey and Lea*.

59. The average 6 percent for *The Gift* was calculated on the basis of cost description for 1836, 1837, 1838, 1840, 1842, and 1843. If one excludes 1836 (with $200, or 2.6 percent, just for Leslie's editing), the average for contributions reaches 6.7 percent. I have not included the data for 1844 ($670.50) and 1845 ($722), since the total costs for these years do not mention binding cost. The 1826 edition of *The Atlantic Souvenir* cost $2,600, including $470 to authors, for 2,000 annuals. But the production of 10,500 annuals in 1831 and 10,000 in 1832 amounted respectively to $12,609 and $12,443, including $500 and $535 to contributors. While payments to writers represented 18 percent of the total cost in 1826, almost equivalent payments in 1831 and 1832 comprised only 4 percent of the total cost.

60. Ralph Thompson noted the unusual generosity of *The Gift* toward writers in *American Literary Annuals,* 13.

61. In the case of new editions in 12mo or octavo, binding would make almost 60 percent of the cost.

62. The item cost for *The Gift* was between $1.25 and $2.00 for the first edition, and up to $3.60 for an octavo. The item cost for *The Atlantic Souvenir* was about $1.18.

63. Prices appeared in an advertisement in the *Morning Herald,* December 23, 1839, 4. Goodrich also noted the high price of giftbooks: "Four thousand volumes of one annual, at the price of $12 each, have been sold in a single season. Not five hundred would have been sold in the same space of time, twenty years ago." See his *Recollections,* 260. In the case of *The Atlantic Souvenir,* the wholesale value was $1.66 average per item from 1826 to 1832, but Carey and Lea reached a ceiling of about 10,000 by 1830. Publication of *The Atlantic Souvenir* ceased in 1836, when it was incorporated into *The Token,* published by Goodrich in Boston, although the data do not suggest that *The Atlantic Souvenir* was no longer profitable. See Thompson, *American Literary Annuals,* 11. In the discussion of production limits, one also needs to take into account the high storage costs at the time, as well as the seasonal character of the giftbook sales.

64. In the case of *The Gift,* the cost of engravings remained relatively stable from 1836 to 1845. On the other hand, the cost of binding for each book moved from 40 cents to about 90 cents apiece, while the number of volumes reached a peak in 1840 with 7,500 books and decreased to 3,500 by 1845 (Carey and Hart Record Books, Edward Carey Gardiner Collection, Historical Society of Pennsylvania). For the study of bindings, see Edwin Wolf, *From Gothic Windows to Peacocks.*

65. For the link between modern consumer behavior and a Protestant, pietistic tradition of romantic feeling, see Colin Campbell's analysis of an alter-

native to Weber's theory of Protestant asceticism in *The Romantic Ethic and the Spirit of Modern Consumerism,* esp. part 1. Lori Merish also offers a case study of the "civilizing" power of artifacts and the feminization of American consumerism in " 'The Hand of Refined Taste.' "

66. Flaubert, *Madame Bovary,* 42–43.

67. The editor, Francis Herbert, explained that *The Talisman* was produced "with some attention to the forms and ceremonies with which charms and spells are usually compounded in the East. . . . The book was printed with virgin types; the typesetters were all born under the planet Mercury. . . . The paper was sized with strict observation of the planetary hour." *The Talisman* (1828), iii–x. On the New York publication, see Thompson, *American Literary Annuals,* 56–64. Another "magical" publication was *The Amulet* (1846).

68. David Cressy describes the Bible as "a sacred *object,* something like a totem or fetish fraught with ancestral, religious, and communal meaning," in "Books as Totems," 94–98. See also Fabre, "Le livre et sa magie."

69. On the Marxian theory of commodity fetishism, see Karl Marx, *Capital,* chap. 1; Lukacs, "Phenomenon of Reification"; Benjamin, "Work of Art"; Adorno, "On the Fetish-Character."

70. Joy Kasson's remarks were made in the context of a session on giftbooks at the 1990 Berkshire Conference on Women.

71. Mezzotint and chromolithography made steel engravings appear old-fashioned. See Marzio, *Democratic Art.* On photography, see Trachtenberg, *Reading American Photographs.*

CHAPTER FIVE

1. The *Louisville Varieties,* as quoted in Mott, *History of American Magazines,* 1:594.

2. For a brilliant analysis of turn-of-the-century magazines, see Garvey, *Adman in the Parlor.*

3. Lawrence Martin, "Genesis of *Godey's,*" 52.

4. The major reference remains Mott, *History of American Magazines,* 1:580–94. In passing, Ann Douglas mentions fashion plates à la Godey in most magazines of the period; see *Feminization,* 229. Recent works on Sarah Josepha Hale and Godey's magazine include Winkler, "Influence of Godey's *Lady's Book,*" and Zophy, "For the Improvement of My Sex." See also Glenda Gates Riley, "The Subtle Subversion: Changes in the Traditional Image of the American Woman," *The Historian* 32 (1970): 210–27; Finley, *The Lady's of Godey's;* Entrikin, *Sarah Josepha Hale.*

In " 'Reign of Brute Force,' " Laura McCall provides a content analysis of the magazine based on coding sheets for 234 female characters from 120 stories. An expanded version of her analysis appears in her "Symmetrical Minds." For McCall, nineteenth-century magazines were neither visual nor frivolous; see " 'Reign of Brute Force,' " 224 n. 15.

On the question of sentimental literature, see Baym, *Woman's Fiction;* Kelley,

Private Women, Public Stage; Matthews, *"Just a Housewife,"* 42–44; Sklar, *Catharine Beecher.*

5. Bertha Monica Stearns acknowledges the popularity of *Godey's* in all regions, including the South. It seemed to fit Louis Godey's self-definition as "The Book of the nation." See Stearns, "Southern Magazines for Ladies," 70.

6. Douglas, *Feminization;* Horkheimer and Adorno, "Culture Industry." For the tenets of the nineteenth-century opposition to popular women novelists, see Henry Nash Smith, "Scribbling Women," and Frederick, "Hawthorne's Scribbling Women."

7. On fiction writers and their women readers, see Tompkins, *Sensational Designs;* Kelley, *Private Women* and "Sentimentalists"; Baym, *Woman's Fiction* and *Novels, Readers, and Reviewers;* Davidson, *Revolution and the Word.*

8. Studies of the death of Little Eva include Ann Douglas, "The Legacy of American Victorianism: The Meaning of Little Eva," in *Feminization,* 3–12, and Jane Tompkins, "Sentimental Power: *Uncle Tom's Cabin* and the Politics of Literary History," in *Sensational Designs,* 122–46.

9. Here I am applying to print culture the concept of a separate sphere, which was part of the ideology of domesticity in nineteenth-century America. A true woman was to provide moral influence in the private space of the home, while the public sphere and the immoral marketplace remained the province of men. An ideology of subservience and domesticity was deeply intertwined with the separation of public and private spheres, male and female worlds. The concept of "feminization" is from Barbara Welter, "The Feminization of American Religion, 1800–1860," in *Dimity Convictions,* 83–102. Similarly, Ann Douglas describes the "feminization" of American culture in the period between 1820 and 1875, when "American culture seemed bent on establishing a perpetual Mother's Day," in *Feminization,* 6–13.

10. Bertha Monica Stearns describes several predecessors to *Godey's,* in the tradition of the British *Lady's Magazine.* See "Early New England Magazines"; "Before *Godey's*"; "Early Philadelphia Magazines"; "New England Magazines." See also Lawrence Martin, "Genesis of *Godey's.*" On English ladies' magazines, see Adburgham, *Women in Print,* and Shevelow, *Women and Print Culture.*

11. Stearns, "Early Philadelphia Magazines," 480, 488, 490. It is important to note, however, that other periodicals besides ladies' magazines also featured fashion plates. For instance, the *Port Folio* published in Philadelphia contained a fashion plate as early as 1809. See "Nineteenth-Century American Color Plate Books" (American Print Conference, Winterthur, Del., 1982), as cited in Abraham, "The Library of Lady Jean Skipwith," 314n.

12. For instance, *The Casket,* a magazine founded in 1826 and later incorporated in *Graham's American Monthly Magazine of Literature, Art and Fashion,* had its first fashion plate in the 1831 issue.

13. Lawrence Martin, "Genesis of *Godey's,*" 56.

14. The long history of illustrations in print includes successive phases from the production of images for the poor and illiterate to images for refined taste. Crude and exquisite qualities of images came to reflect the social strata of the public. Nineteenth-century illustrations particularly denoted the

emergence of the middle classes both in Europe and in America. The technique of steel engraving was perfected in 1818 and proved adaptable to the industrialization of printing. See Gordon Ray, *The Illustrator and the Book;* Hunnisett, *Steel-Engraved Book Illustration;* Melot, *L'Illustration*, 130. See also Febvre and Martin, *Coming of the Book.*

15. For a discussion of the social meaning of fashion in nineteenth-century America, see Halttunen, *Confidence Men and Painted Women.* Halttunen analyzes the antebellum shift from romantic dress to sentimental dress and the ideal of simplicity. She examines the antebellum social conventions of dress and the acceptance of fashion as a necessary evil in a society established on the promise of social mobility. While Halttunen regards the representation of fashion in *Godey's Lady's Book* as evidence of changes in dress and its social meaning, the present chapter considers the historical specificity of visual texts in women's magazines.

16. For a provocative discussion of composite text and the interactions between image and text, see Mitchell, *Iconology* and "Visible Language," and three articles by Louis Marin: "Mimésis et description," "On Reading Pictures," and "Toward a Theory of Reading." See also Schapiro, *Words and Pictures.*

17. This was also true of the English ladies' magazines of the 1790s. See Adburgham, *Women in Print*, 206.

18. The concept of "residual culture" is from Raymond Williams, "Base and Superstructure."

19. See, for example, back covers of *Godey's Lady's Book* for 1853.

20. Tebbel, *American Magazine*, 50.

21. Grimsted, *Melodrama Unveiled*, 43.

22. Adburgham, *Women in Print*, 205.

23. *Godey's Lady's Book*, August 1839, 95.

24. Ibid., May 1839, 239. See also Kunciov, *Mr. Godey's Ladies*, 2. The shift from an auratic art to a postauratic art occurred with the advent of photography in the late nineteenth century. See Benjamin, "Work of Art."

25. Back-cover advertisement, *Godey's Lady's Book*, September 1851; Mott, *History of American Magazines*, 1:593.

26. Cott, *Bonds of Womanhood*, 115.

27. Chapman, *American Drawing-Book*, 8; "Our Artists," *Harper's New Monthly Magazine* 28 (1864): 242.

28. The concept of "civilization of the hand" is from Barthes, "Image, raison, déraison."

29. Welter, "Cult of True Womanhood." For the question of leisure and conspicuous consumption, see Thorstein Veblen, *Theory of the Leisure Class* (1899).

30. Marin, "Toward a Theory of Reading," 301.

31. Barbara Welter argues that "women in the first half of the nineteenth century took Christianity and molded it to their image and likeness" (*Dimity Convictions*, 102). The concept of "tongue snatcher" is from Claudine Herrmann, *Tongue Snatchers.*

32. *Godey's Lady's Book*, April 1852, 298.

33. Halttunen, *Confidence Men and Painted Women*, 157.

34. Before theater staging became widespread, books of theater proved a success in eighteenth-century Europe. See Baumgart, "Der Leser als Zuschauer."

35. *Godey's Lady's Book*, February 1852, 170.

36. Cott, *Bonds of Womanhood;* Smith-Rosenberg, "Female World."

37. Mary H. Blewett's study *Men, Women, and Work* discusses how working women defended their rights as domestic mothers and daughters. Their consciousness as workers in production was intertwined and in conflict with the family values of artisan culture. See also her article "Women Shoeworkers." Christine Stansell also analyzes the support for an ideology of domesticity among New York City working men, who wanted to protect their wives and daughters from a system of exploitation that they themselves were enduring; see her *City of Women*. Class distinction among antebellum women is the subject of Lerner's "The Lady and the Mill Girl."

38. *Voice of Industry*, December 3, 1847, cited in Foner, *Factory Girls*, 93.

39. On antebellum women's associations, see in particular Cott, *Bonds of Womanhood;* Ryan, *Cradle of the Middle Class;* Epstein, *Politics of Domesticity*.

40. Lawrence Martin, "Genesis of *Godey's*," 65.

41. For a broader discussion of antebellum prescriptions of ascetic reading and a critique of pleasurable reading, see Chapter 6.

42. *Godey's Lady's Book*, September 1851, 187.

43. See Tebbel, *American Magazine*, 50.

44. See also Harris, *Artist in American Society*, 148. A Philadelphia Unitarian minister, the Rev. William H. Furness, provides a good example of the new trust in the power of art; see *An Address Delivered Before the Art-Union of Philadelphia*.

45. For a discussion of the clergy's attitudes toward the visual arts, see Dillenberger, *Visual Arts and Christianity*, and Apostolos-Cappadona, *The Spirit and the Vision*, esp. chap. 2.

46. Welter, *Dimity Convictions;* Douglas, *Feminization;* Hoffert, " 'A Very Peculiar Sorrow' " and *Private Matters*.

47. Alice B. Neal, "The Coquette," *Godey's Lady's Book*, March 1851. The engraving was by W. E. Tucker from an original drawing made expressly for *Godey's* by John Gilbert of London. "The Constant" refers to the antithetical story of a good wife and mother, also by Alice B. Neal, published with a plate in ibid., January 1851.

48. Ibid., February 1845, 49, 60; Sarah J. Hale, "New Year at Home," ibid., January 1840, 1–4.

49. Clerical disestablishment and the competition between ministers and women writers is the subject of Douglas's *Feminization*.

50. On the depiction of cottages, see Neville Thompson, "Tools of Persuasion." On furnishing designs and needlework, see Winkler, "Influence of Godey's."

51. *Godey's Lady's Book*, August 1845, 84.

52. Sarah J. Hale had also accepted the publication of fashion plates in

her *Ladies' Magazine* as a means of exhibiting the domestic life. See Lawrence Martin, "Genesis of *Godey's*," 55–56.

53. *Godey's Lady's Book*, February 1840, 96.

54. For the importance of objects, see McDannell, *Christian Home;* Jaffee, "One of the Primitive Sort"; Saisselin, *The Bourgeois and the Bibelot.*

55. Colleen McDannell argues that Catholic women of Philadelphia read *Godey's* because there was no Catholic journal available. See *Christian Home,* 55, 103.

56. On lavish illustration of Bibles in the nineteenth century, McDannell argues that "family Bibles became so lavish and encyclopedic that they functioned more like religious furniture than biblical texts." See *Material Christianity,* 15.

57. Emerson's journal entry cited by Matthiessen, *American Renaissance,* 51. The reference to elephants is from Emerson, April 1852, in *Emerson in His Journals,* 433.

CHAPTER SIX

Brief versions of this chapter were presented at the 1990 convention of the American Historical Association and the 1991 convention of the Organization of American Historians. I am thankful to Peter G. Buckley, Elliott J. Gorn, and Sally Foreman Griffith for their useful comments.

1. *Atlantic Monthly,* January 1858, 343–53.

2. Emerson, "The American Scholar," in *Collected Works,* 1:56.

3. For instance, Rev. Daniel C. Eddy discussed books in two separate chapters on "innocent amusements" and "dangerous amusements." See *Young Man's Friend,* 93, 110.

4. See Hall, "Uses of Literacy," in *Worlds of Wonder,* 21–70.

5. Hawes, *Lectures Addressed to the Young Men,* 5.

6. From 1 John 2:14, as cited in Eliot, "Introductory Lecture," *Lectures to Young Men,* 5; Hawes, "Lecture 1: Claims of Society on Young Men," *Lectures Addressed to the Young Men,* 1; and in epigram of Eddy, *Young Man's Friend.*

7. See Eliot, *Lectures to Young Men,* 5–9.

8. For instance, see Eliot's appeal in his *Lectures to Young Women.* On the republican ideology of motherhood, see Kerber, "Republican Mother"; Lewis, "Republican Wife"; and Ryan, *Cradle of the Middle Class.*

9. Kett, *Rites of Passage,* 95. On the emergence of advice literature for youth, see also Demos and Demos, "Adolescence in Historical Perspective"; Rorabaugh, *Craft Apprentice,* 158–66; Horlick, *Country Boys;* Bode, *Anatomy of American Popular Culture,* esp. chap. 9, "Manuals for All Things," 119–31; Schlesinger, *Learning How to Behave.* On social etiquette, see John Kasson, *Rudeness and Civility;* Halttunen, *Confidence Men and Painted Women;* Bobbitt, *Bibliography of Etiquette Books.*

10. Mott, *Golden Multitudes,* 318.

11. Alcott, *Familiar Letters to Young Men,* 81–82.

12. Beecher, *Lectures to Young Men,* 205.

13. Ibid., 207.

14. Ibid., 211.

15. Clifford Clark, "Changing Nature of Protestantism" and *Henry Ward Beecher,* 57–59; McLoughlin, *Meaning of Henry Ward Beecher;* and Bode, *Anatomy of American Popular Culture,* 126.

16. My discussion of norms of behavior has been influenced by European studies, in particular Elias, *The Civilizing Process, Power and Civility,* and *Court Society.* See also Roger Chartier, "Distinction et divulgation: la civilité et ses livres," in *Lectures et lecteurs,* 45–86; Revel, "Uses of Civility," 167–205.

17. Daniel Rodgers discusses the shift from an old work ethic to a new "duty of play" in his *Work Ethic,* esp. chap. 4, "Play, Repose, and Plenty." Rodgers qualifies the liberal reformers' attitudes on leisure as zigzag thinking. On liberal ministers, see also Douglas, *Feminization,* esp. chap. 4, "The Loss of Theology," and Scott, *From Office to Profession.* A discussion of reform and social order appears in Paul Johnson, *Shopkeepers' Millennium.* For an influential work on changing interaction between rulers and ruled in a different historical context, see Veyne, "Foucault révolutionne l'histoire."

18. Pessen, "Egalitarian Myth."

19. Arthur, *Advice to Young Ladies,* 64; Child, *Mother's Book,* 86–89. See also Alcott, *Young Man's Guide,* 189, and *Familiar Letters,* 75–77; Atkinson, *Books and Reading,* 42–48.

20. Ware, "Duties of Young Men," 218. Among the well-known writers of moralistic fiction were T. S. Arthur, author of *Ten Nights in a Bar-Room,* and the so-called scribbling women: Sarah J. Hale, Lydia Maria Child, Catharine Sedgwick, and Lydia H. Sigourney. Henry Ward Beecher was also the author of the popular novel *Norwood,* serialized in the *New York Ledger* in 1867.

21. Lawrence Cremin introduced the term "dilemmas of popularization" in *American Education,* 2:298–334. Alcott, *Familiar Letters,* 84–85.

22. Alcott, *Young Man's Guide,* 188, 205–7.

23. Thoreau, *Walden,* 138.

24. Ibid., 155.

25. Alcott, *Familiar Letters,* 78–81.

26. Rush, *Medical Inquiries and Observations,* 35.

27. For attacks on Bulwer-Lytton and novels of the French School, see Beecher, *Lectures to Young Men,* 210–14. A condemnation of Sue's *Wandering Jew* is found in Eddy, *Young Man's Friend,* 110.

28. Alcott, *Young Man's Guide,* 212–13.

29. From M. T. Clanchy, *From Memory to Written Record,* 216–17, quoted in Hall, "Uses of Literacy," 29.

30. For the importance of physiology in antebellum reform, see Nissenbaum, *Sex, Diet, and Debility,* and Whorton, *Crusaders for Fitness.* For general background, see Walters, *American Reformers* and *Primers for Prudery.* On the political consequences of the metaphor that equates the reading process with food consumption in mass culture, see Radway, "Reading Is Not Eating" and *Reading the Romance.*

31. Burnap, *Lectures to Young Men,* 19; Alcott, *Familiar Letters,* 75–77.

32. Eliot, *Lectures to Young Men,* 72.

33. Thoreau, *Walden,* 151.

34. Eliot, *Lectures to Young Men,* 75; Swisshelm, *Letters to Country Girls,* 151.

35. Ware, "Duties of Young Men," 217.

36. Alexander, *Working-Man,* 97.

37. Charles Grandison Finney, *Lectures on Revivals of Religion,* as quoted in Hofstadter, *Anti-Intellectualism,* 92–95. On Finney, see Cross, *Burned-Over District,* and Timothy L. Smith, *Revivalism and Social Reform.*

38. Eliot, *Lectures to Young Women,* 119.

39. Channing, *Self-Culture,* 33, 39–41.

40. For Channing's and Ware's views on self-culture, see Robinson, *Apostle of Culture,* 11–29. For a broader discussion of self-culture and American Unitarianism, see also Wright, *American Unitarianism,* and Howe, *Unitarian Conscience,* 174–204.

41. Emerson, "The American Scholar," in *Collected Works,* 1:52–70. On Emerson as lecturer, see Cayton, *Emerson's Emergence,* esp. 148–50.

42. Thoreau, *Walden,* 156.

43. Ralph Waldo Emerson, *Early Lectures,* ed. Whicher et al., 2:251, quoted in Joseph Ellis, *After the Revolution,* 221. See also Ziff, "Upon What Pretext," 314.

44. Todd, *Student's Manual,* esp. chap. 4. Todd's *Student's Manual* had run into seven editions in two years and by 1854 was in the twenty-fourth edition. It was probably the most outspoken in its genre. Todd was also the author of *Index Rerum, Young Man's Guide,* and *Moral Influences.* For a discussion of Todd in a context of masturbation phobia and spermatic economy, see Barker-Benfield, *Horrors of the Half-Known Life,* 135–226.

45. Alcott, *Familiar Letters,* 75–77. Alcott returned to sexual reform in *The Young Husband* and *The Physiology of Marriage.* On sexuality see also Rosenberg, "Sexuality, Class and Role," and Nissenbaum, *Sex, Diet, and Debility.*

46. Isaac Ray, *Mental Hygiene,* 56–58, 233–77.

47. Eliot, *Lectures to Young Women,* 119; Sigourney, *Letters to Young Ladies,* 133–51. See Douglas, *Feminization.*

48. Eliot, *Lectures to Young Women,* 119–22.

49. Among others, William G. Eliot, T. S. Arthur, and William A. Alcott presented advice books to both young men and young women.

50. Eliot, *Lectures to Young Women,* 125–27.

51. Alexander, *Working-Man,* 81–82.

52. Sigourney, *Letters to Young Ladies,* 134.

53. Alcott, *Young Man's Guide,* 178–79. A provocative study of representations of reading was offered by Chartier, "Figures of the 'Other': Peasant Reading in the Age of the Enlightenment," in *Cultural History,* 151–71.

54. Eliot, *Lectures to Young Men,* 43–44, 49–51. For the effect of reading and learning on social mobility, see also Arthur, *Advice to Young Men.*

55. Pessen, "Egalitarian Myth."

56. Atkinson, *Books and Reading,* 56–58. See also Channing, *Self-Culture,* 71–76.

57. *Cottage Evenings,* 131–34.

58. Ibid., 139–40. On Franklin's model of useful knowledge, see also Alcott, *Young Man's Guide,* 191.

59. Franklin, "The Way to Wealth," 170. The best cultural history of the transformation of work remains Rodgers, *Work Ethic,* 10–13. On the liberalization of play, see Moore, "Learning to Play." For background, see Dulles, *History of Recreation,* and Wilmeth, *Variety Entertainment.*

60. Eliot, *Lectures to Young Men,* 39.

61. Alexander, *Working-Man,* 83–84. For a discussion of Alexander's social views, see Blumin, *Emergence of the Middle Class,* 130–33.

62. Alcott, *Young Man's Guide,* 193–94.

63. On the association of work, play, and morality, see Rodgers, *Work Ethic,* esp. chap. 4.

64. Eliot, *Lectures to Young Men,* 64–65. See also Chamlee, "Sabbath Crusade," and Beecher, *Libraries and Public Reading Rooms.*

65. Despite unsuccessful attempts in 1835 and 1838, the *Herald* did not have a regular Sunday edition until 1841. According to Mott, by 1860 the *Sunday Herald* had topped the daily issue by 10,000 copies; see *American Journalism,* 318. But only in the 1880s did the Sunday editions of newspapers succeed in competing with magazines; see Tebbel, *The Magazine in America.*

66. Entry for Tuesday, August 20, 1844, Edward Jenner Carpenter Journal, 1844–45, American Antiquarian Society, Worcester, Mass. See also Christopher Clark, "Diary of an Apprentice Cabinetmaker," 353.

67. *The Man,* April 3, 1834, 146.

68. Roediger, "Movement for a Shorter Working Day," 20–21. On the struggles for a shorter working day, see also Commons et al., *Documentary History,* and Montgomery, *Beyond Equality.* On labor advocates, see Pessen, *Most Uncommon Jacksonians.*

69. *Working Man's Advocate,* April 6, 1844, 2.

70. Wright, *Address to Young Mechanics.*

71. *Voice of Industry,* December 3, 1847, cited in Foner, *Factory Girls,* 93. See also Zonderman, *Aspirations and Anxieties.*

72. Sir J. Herschell, "Pleasures of Reading," *Dwight's American Magazine,* June 12, 1847, 378. For a discussion of novels acceptable after hard work, see Atkinson, *Books and Reading,* 19–20.

73. See Eliot, *Lectures to Young Men,* 49–51.

74. On the lyceum, see Scott, "Print and the Public Lecture System" and "Popular Lecture"; Bode, *American Lyceum.* On libraries, see Kaser, *Book for a Sixpence;* Garrison, *Apostles of Culture;* Robert Williams, "Public Library."

75. Gross, "Much Instruction," 177. On mechanics' libraries, see Rorabough, *Craft Apprentice,* 158.

76. Christopher Clark, "Diary of an Apprentice Cabinetmaker," esp. entry for Tuesday, August 6, 1844.

77. Eddy, *Young Man's Friend,* 88. For earlier encouragement for reading, see Hawes, *Lectures Addressed to the Young Men,* 58–60.

78. Ware, "Duties of Young Men," 217.

79. *The Theatre,* 5. Bellows, *Public Amusements,* 40. For a recent discussion of ministers' views of the theater, see Moore, "Religion, Secularization."

80. In the 1960s and 1970s historians moved away from the institutional and economic perspective of John R. Commons and the Wisconsin School. Among the major works of the new labor history, see Brody, *Steelworkers in America;* Montgomery, *Beyond Equality* and "Shuttle and the Cross"; Gutman, *Work, Culture and Society.* For the English inspiration of the new social history, see Thompson, *Making of the English Working Class,* and Hobsbawm, *Primitive Rebels.* More recently, the history of leisure has served to explain distinctive features of American working-class development, such as the absence of socialism and the weakness of American working-class consciousness. See Rosenzweig, *Eight Hours for What We Will,* 2.

81. The characterization of work and leisure in preindustrial and industrial societies was initiated in 1963 by Thompson, *Making of the English Working Class,* followed by the 1964 Past and Present Conference in London, in particular with a paper by Thomas, "Work and Leisure in Pre-Industrial Society." Thompson, "Time, Work-Discipline," published in 1967, had a major impact on American historiography.

82. Thompson, "Time, Work-Discipline," 74, 83. The practice of Saint Monday continued well into the nineteenth century, revealing a deeply established custom of devoting Monday to friendship and conviviality rather than work. Short workdays on Monday and even Tuesday, when workers were drinking their earnings from the previous week, were followed by long hours from Wednesday to Saturday. If Sunday was reserved for family, Monday was for friends. See Reid, "Decline of Saint-Monday." For the scarce reference to Saint Monday in America, see Brody, "Time and Work," 13.

83. For the internalization of discipline, see Thompson, *Making of the English Working Class,* esp. chaps. 11 and 12 on the Methodists, and his "Time, Work-Discipline," 95. See also Rodgers, *Work Ethic.*

84. A strong emphasis on the dichotomy is to be found in Malcolmson, *Popular Recreations.* See also Golby and Purdue, *Civilisation of the Crowd.* For the argument of continuity, see Cunningham, *Leisure in the Industrial Revolution.* Peter Bailey discusses change and resistance to change in a context of "social control" in his *Leisure and Class,* 47–67.

85. For a review of the "class expression" argument, see Yeo and Yeo, "Ways of Seeing." For a critique of the overpoliticization of leisure, see Gareth Stedman Jones, "Class Expression Versus Social Control? A Critique of Recent Trends in the Social History of 'Leisure,'" in *Languages of Class,* 76–89.

86. See Laurie, "'Nothing on Compulsion'"; Faler, "Cultural Aspects"; Rodgers, *Work Ethic,* esp. 15–19; Dodd, "Working Classes." See also Wilentz, "Artisan Republican Festivals" and *Chants Democratic.*

87. For the importance of ethnicity and religion in the composition of the American working class, see Gutman, *Work, Culture and Society.* For the study of play and leisure in the South, Breen, "Horses and Gentlemen"; Gorn, "'Gouge and Bite'"; Isaac, *Transformation of Virginia;* and Click, *Spirit of the Times.*

88. Steven J. Ross, *Workers on the Edge,* 164; Stott, *Workers in the Metropolis,*

esp. chap. 8. Recreational patterns in postbellum America reflected a greater division within the working classes, and even class convergence between part of the working class and the middle-class reformers of a given community. The case of Albany is analyzed in Greenberg, *Worker and Community*. For Lynn and Fall River in Massachusetts, see Cumbler, *Working-Class Community*.

89. For a provocative treatment of public recreations, see Rosenzweig, *Eight Hours for What We Will*. Rosenzweig used Raymond Williams's distinction between an "alternative culture"—separate and distinct from the dominant society—and "oppositional"—a direct challenge to that society—to describe the working-class recreational patterns in Worcester, Massachusetts, from 1870 to 1920. See Raymond Williams, "Base and Superstructure," 11. Studies of late-nineteenth-century leisure include Couvares, "Triumph of Commerce" and *Remaking of Pittsburgh*. For women's leisure, see Peiss, *Cheap Amusements*, and Loomis, "Piety and Play."

90. Levine, *Highbrow/Lowbrow*; Buckley, "To the Opera House"; Scott, "Print and the Public Lecture System" and "Popular Lecture and the Creation of a Public"; Harris, *Humbug*; Erenberg, *Steppin' Out*. For a recent review, see Moore, "Religion, Secularization" and "Learning to Play."

91. Rodgers, *Work Ethic*, 98–109. On the successive waves of reform, see Hardy and Ingham, "Games, Structures, and Agency," and Boyer, *Urban Masses*.

92. An engaging discussion has been initiated by French historiography of private life and the ongoing debate over the validity of distinguishing between high culture and popular culture. See the multivolume study edited by Ariès and Duby, *History of Private Life*. For a discussion of popular culture and culture as appropriation, see Chartier, *Cultural Uses of Print* and "Intellectual History."

93. Atkinson, *Books and Reading*, 5. In New England, the reading community included the whole native-born community.

94. For a patrician view of culture, see also Joseph Ellis, *After the Revolution*. For the Unitarian faith in elevating literature, see Howe, *Unitarian Conscience*. The concept of a boundless culture is from Higham, *From Boundlessness to Consolidation*.

95. Lydia Maria Child to Marianne Silsbee, New York, April 17, 1848, cited in Child, *Lydia Maria Child: Selected Letters*, 238.

96. Works in that direction include Dana Nelson Salvino, "The Word in Black and White," in Davidson, *Reading in America*, 140–56. On literacy's link with freedom, see Cornelius, *"When I Can Read My Title Clear."* Incidentally, the debate over proper reading was not limited to the white community. As scattered evidence indicates, periodicals such as *The Colored American* and New York's *Freedom's Journal*, which targeted an African American audience in northern cities, advocated habits of good and useful reading similar to white prescriptive literature.

CONCLUSION

1. Cited in Hall, "Books and Reading," 365.
2. Tocqueville, *Democracy in America*, 475.

3. *Godey's Lady's Book,* December 1857, 557.

4. Whitman, "Letter to Ralph Waldo Emerson" (1856), 2019.

5. See Hall, "Victorian Connection"; Stevenson, *Scholarly Means,* 128–30; Bledstein, *Culture of Professionalism,* 77–79.

6. Wilson, *Labor of Words,* xiv; Stevenson, *Victorian Homefront,* 30–47; Boyer, *Urban Masses.*

Selected Bibliography

PRIMARY SOURCES

Manuscripts

Cambridge, Mass.
  Houghton Library, Harvard University
  Bulwer-Lytton, Edward. Promptbooks.
New York, N.Y.
  New York Public Library
  Chamberlain, Thomas. Diary, 1835–53.
  Rare Book and Manuscript Library, Butler Library, Columbia University
  Benjamin, Park. Papers, 1645–1925.
  Harper and Brothers. Records, 1817–1929.
Philadelphia, Pa.
  Historical Society of Pennsylvania
    Autograph Collection of Simon Gratz
    Dreer Autograph Collection
      American Prose Writers
      Painters and Engravers
    Edward Carey Gardiner Collection
      Henry C. Baird Papers
      Carey and Hart and Carey and Lea, Publishers
        Correspondence, 1830–50
        Record Books, 1830–86
      Edward L. Carey Section
    Sartain Family Collection, 1771–1929
    Society Collection, 1760–1935
      Cheney, John. Letters.
      Godey, Louis A. Letters.
  Library Company of Philadelphia
    Longacre, James Barton. Papers, 1806–69.
Worcester, Mass.
  American Antiquarian Society
    Beekley, N. Diary, 1849.
    Bennett, Francis, Jr. Diary, 1852–54.
    Carpenter, Edward Jenner. Journal, 1844–45.
    Clapp, David. Journal, 1820–24.
    Edes, Sarah Louisa. Diaries, 1852–53.
    Forbes, Susan E. P. Brown. Diaries, 1841–1908.
    Thurston, Brown. Journal, 1834–50.
    White, Mary Avery. Diary, 1836–61.

Newspapers, Periodicals, and Annuals

Affection's Gift. New York, 1832.

The Amulet. Boston, 1846.

The Atlantic Souvenir. Philadelphia, 1826–32.

Brother Jonathan. New York, 1840–43.

The Catholic Keepsake. Philadelphia, 1845.

The Christian Keepsake. Philadelphia, 1838–49.

The Christian Keepsake. New York, 1856.

Constellation. New York, 1859.

Dwight's American Magazine, and Family Newspaper. New York, 1847.

Forget-me-not. London, 1823.

The Forget-me-not. New York, 1855.

Frank Leslie's Illustrated Newspaper. New York, 1855.

The Garland. New York, 1830.

The Gem. Philadelphia, 1840–55.

The Gift. Philadelphia, 1836–45.

The Gift of Friendship. Philadelphia, 1848–55.

Gleason's Pictorial Drawing Room Companion. Boston, 1851–54.

Godey's Lady's Book. Philadelphia, 1830–58.

Harper's Illuminated and New Pictorial Bible. New York, 1843–46.

Illustrated News. New York, 1853.

The Iris. Philadelphia, 1851–53.

The Laurel Wreath. Hartford, 1845–46.

Leaflets of Memory. Philadelphia, 1845–55.

The Man. New York, 1834–35.

New World. New York, 1840–45.

New York Herald. 1835–55.

New York Sun. 1833.

The Parlour Scrap Book. Philadelphia, 1836–37.

The Pearl. Philadelphia, 1829–40.

The Religious Souvenir. Philadelphia, 1833–46.

The Rose of Sharon. Boston, 1840–57.

The Snow Flake. Philadelphia, 1849–55.

The Souvenir. Philadelphia, 1826.

The Talisman. New York, 1828–30.

The Token. Boston, 1828–41.

Universal Yankee Nation. Boston, 1841.

The Violet. Philadelphia, 1837–42.

Voice of Industry. Boston, 1845–47.

Working Man's Advocate. New York, 1834–44.

Books and Pamphlets

Alcott, William A. *Familiar Letters to Young Men on Various Subjects. Designed as a Companion to the Young Man's Guide.* Buffalo: George H. Derby, 1850.

———. *The Physiology of Marriage.* Boston: John P. Jewett, 1860.

———. *Tea and Coffee: Their Physical, Intellectual, and Moral Effects on the Human System.* New York: Fowlers and Wells, 1836.

———. *Use of Tobacco.* Boston: G. W. Light, 1844.

———. *Vegetable Diet: As Sanctioned By Medical Men, and By Experience in All Ages.* Boston: Marsh, Capen and Lyon, 1838.

———. *The Young Husband, or Duties of the Man in the Marriage Relation.* Boston: George W. Light, 1839.

———. *The Young Man's Guide.* Boston: Lilly, Wait, Colman, and Holden, 1834.

———. *The Young Woman's Guide to Excellence.* 1840. Boston: Waite, Peirce, 1845.

Alexander, James Waddel [Charles Quill, pseud.]. *The American Mechanic and Working-Man.* 2 vols. New York, 1847.

———. *The Working-Man.* 1839. Philadelphia: Perkins and Purves, 1843.

Arthur, Timothy Shay. *Advice to Young Ladies on their Duties and Conduct in Life.* 1847. Boston: Phillips, Samson, 1849.

———. *Advice to Young Men on their Duties and Conduct in Life.* Boston: N. C. Barton, 1849.

———. *Ten Nights in a Bar-Room, and What I Saw There.* 1854. Reprint, edited by Donald A. Koch, Cambridge, Mass.: Belknap Press of Harvard University Press, 1964.

Atkinson, William Parsons. *Books and Reading: A Lecture.* Boston: Crosby, Nichols, Lee, 1860.

Beecher, Henry Ward. *Lectures to Young Men, on Various Important Subjects.* Salem, Mass.: John P. Jewett, 1846.

———. *Libraries and Public Reading Rooms: Should They Be Opened on Sunday?* New York, 1872.

Bellows, Henry W. *The Relation of Public Amusements to Public Morality, Especially of the Theatre to the Highest Interests of Humanity. An Address, Delivered at the Academy of Music, New York, before "The American Dramatic Fund Society," for the Benefit of the Fund.* New York: C. S. Francis, 1857.

Bird, Isabella Lucy. *The Englishwoman in America.* Madison: University of Wisconsin Press, 1966.

Brace, Charles Loring. *Short Sermons to News Boys: With a History of the Formation of the News Boys' Lodging-House.* New York: Charles Scribner, 1866.

Browne, Junius Henry. *The Great Metropolis: A Mirror of New York.* Hartford, Conn., 1869.

Buntline, Ned [Edward Zane Carroll Judson]. *The Mysteries and Miseries of New Orleans.* New York: Akarman and Ormsby, 1851.

———. *The Mysteries and Miseries of New York.* New York: Berford, 1848.

Burnap, George W. *Lectures to Young Men, On the Cultivation of the Mind, the Formation of Character, and the Conduct of Life: Delivered in Masonic Hall, Baltimore.* Baltimore: John Murphy, 1840.

Channing, William E. *Self-Culture. An Address Introductory to the Franklin Lec-*

tures. Delivered at Boston, September 1838. Boston: Dutton and Wentworth, 1838.

Chapman, J. G. *The American Drawing-Book: A Manual for the Amateur, and Basis of Study for the Professional Artist.* New York: J. S. Redfield, 1847.

Child, Lydia Maria. *Lydia Maria Child: Selected Letters, 1817–1880.* Edited by Milton Meltzer and Patricia G. Holland. Amherst: University of Massachusetts Press, 1982.

———. *The Mother's Book.* New York: C. S. Francis, 1846.

Cooper, James Fenimore. *The American Democrat; Or, Hints on the Social and Civic Relations of the United States of America.* With an introduction by H. L. Mencken and an introductory note by Robert E. Spiller. New York: Vintage Books, 1956.

———. *Home as Found.* Philadelphia: Lea and Blanchard, 1838.

Cottage Evenings. Under the Superintendence of the Society for the Diffusion of Useful Knowledge: The Working-Man's Companion. 1st American ed. Philadelphia: Carey and Hart; Boston: Carter, Hendee and Babcock, 1831.

Cummins, Maria Susanna. *The Lamplighter.* Edited by Nina Baym. New Brunswick, N.J.: Rutgers University Press, 1988.

The Daughter's Own Book; Or, Practical Hints from a Father to his Daughter. Boston: Lilly, Wait, Colman, and Holden, 1833.

Davis, Andrew Jackson. *Tale of a Physician; Or, the Seeds and Fruits of Crime.* Boston: William White, 1869.

Eddy, Daniel C. *The Young Man's Friend; Containing Admonitions for the Erring, Counsel for the Tempted, Hope for the Fallen. Designed for the Young Man, the Husband, and the Father.* 1849. Boston: G. W. Cottrell, 1866.

Eliot, William G. *Lectures to Young Men.* 1853. Boston: American Unitarian Association, 1869.

———. *Lectures to Young Women.* 1853. Boston: American Unitarian Association, 1869.

Ellard, John. *The Newsboy.* Philadelphia: William S. and Alfred Martien, 1860.

Emerson, Ralph Waldo. *The Collected Works of Ralph Waldo Emerson.* 4 vols. Edited by Robert E. Spiller, Alfred R. Ferguson, Joseph Slater, and Jean Ferguson Carr. Cambridge, Mass.: Harvard University Press, 1971.

———. *The Conduct of Life.* Boston: Ticknor and Fields, 1861.

———. *Emerson in His Journals.* Edited by Joel Porte. Cambridge, Mass.: Belknap Press of Harvard University Press, 1982.

Farrar, Mrs. John. *The Young Lady's Friend. By a Lady.* Boston: American Stationers' Company, 1837.

Fergurson, Anna. *The Young Lady; Or Guide to Knowledge, Virtue, and Happiness.* Nashua, N.H.: J. M. Fletcher, 1850.

Finney, Charles Grandison. *Lectures on Revivals of Religion.* Cambridge, Mass.: Belknap Press of Harvard University Press, 1960.

Flaubert, Gustave. *Madame Bovary.* Translated by Francis Steegmuller. New York: Random House, 1957.

Foster, George G. *New York by Gas-Light: With Here and There a Streak of Sunshine.* New York, 1850.

Franklin, Benjamin. "The Way to Wealth." 1758. In *Autobiography, and Other Writings,* edited by Russel B. Nye, 168–76. Boston: Houghton Mifflin, 1958.

Fuller, Margaret. *Woman in the Nineteenth Century and Kindred Papers Relating to the Sphere, Condition and Duties, of Woman.* Boston: John P. Jewett, 1855.

Furness, William H. *An Address Delivered Before the Art-Union of Philadelphia in the Academy of Fine Arts.* Philadelphia: Griggs and Adams, 1848.

Goodrich, Samuel Griswold. *Recollections of a Lifetime, Or Men and Things I Have Seen: In a Series of Familiar Letters to a Friend, Historical, Biographical, Anecdotical, and Descriptive.* 2 vols. New York: Miller, Orton, 1857.

Hale, Sarah J. *Manners; or, Happy Homes and Good Society All the Year Round.* Boston: J. E. Tilton, 1868.

Havens, Catherine Elizabeth. *Diary of a Little Girl in Old New York.* New York: H. C. Brown, 1919.

Hawes, Joel. *Lectures Addressed to the Young Men of Hartford and New-Haven, and Published at Their United Request.* Hartford, Conn.: Oliver D. Cooke, 1828.

Hawthorne, Nathaniel. *Tales and Sketches: Including Twice-Told Tales, Mosses from an Old Manse, and the Snow-Image.* New York: Library of America, 1982.

Hogeland, Col. Alexander. *Ten Years Among the Newsboys. Dedicated to the Newsboys of the United States.* Louisville, Ky., 1882.

Hudson, Frederic. *Journalism in the United States from 1690 to 1872.* New York: Harper and Brothers, 1873.

Ingraham, Joseph Holt. *The Beautiful Cigar Girl; Or, the Mysteries of Broadway.* New York, 1844.

Lea and Febiger. *The Cost Book of Carey and Lea, 1825–1838.* Edited by David Kaser. Philadelphia: University of Pennsylvania Press, 1963.

Leslie, Eliza. *The Behaviour Book: A Manual for Ladies.* 3d ed. Philadelphia: Willis P. Hazard, 1853.

Lippard, George. *The Quaker City; Or, the Monks of Monk Hall. A Romance of Philadelphia Life, Mystery and Crime.* Philadelphia: T. B. Peterson and Brothers, 1845. Reprint, as *The Monks of Monk Hall,* edited by Leslie A. Fiedler, New York: Odyssey, 1970.

McCabe, James Dabney, Jr. [Edward Winslow Martin, pseud.]. *The Secrets of the Great City: A Work Descriptive of the Virtues and Vices, the Mysteries, Miseries, and Crimes of New York City.* Philadelphia: Jones Brothers, 1868.

Mackay, Alexander. *The Western World, or Travels in the United States in 1846–47.* New York, 1850.

Melville, Herman. *Pierre; Or, the Ambiguities.* Edited by Harrison Hayford and Hershel Parker. Evanston, Ill.: Northwestern University Press, 1971.

Ménétra, Jacques Louis. *Journal of my Life.* Edited by Daniel Roche. Translated by Arthur Goldhammer. New York: Columbia University Press, 1986.

Neal, John. *Brother Jonathan; Or, the New Englander.* 3 vols. Edinburgh: W. Blackwood, 1825.

Parton, James. "The New York Herald." *North American Review* 102 (April 1866): 373–419.

Poe, Edgar Allan. *Collected Works of Edgar Allan Poe*. Vol. 3, *Tales and Sketches, 1843–1849*. Edited by Thomas Ollive Mabbott. Cambridge, Mass.: Belknap Press of Harvard University Press, 1978.

———. *Doings of Gotham: As Described in a Series of Letters to the Editors of the Columbia Spy*. Edited by Jacob E. Spannuth, with comments by Thomas Ollive Mabbott. Pottsville, Pa.: J. E. Spannuth, 1929.

Porter, Noah. *Books and Reading; Or, What Books Shall I Read and How Shall I Read Them*. New York: Charles Scribner, 1871.

Pray, Isaac C. *Memoirs of James Gordon Bennett and His Times*. New York: Stringer and Townsend, 1855.

Ray, Isaac. *Mental Hygiene*. 1863. Reprint, New York: Halner, 1968.

Reynolds, George William MacArthur. *The Mysteries of London*. London, 1845.

Rush, Benjamin. *Medical Inquiries and Observations, Upon the Diseases of the Mind*. Philadelphia: Kimber and Richardson, 1812.

Sedgwick, Catharine Maria. *Means and Ends: Or, Self-Training*. Boston: Marsh, Capen, Lyon, and Webb, 1840.

Sigourney, Lydia H. *Letters to Young Ladies*. New York: Harper and Brothers, 1838.

———. *Whisper to a Bride*. Hartford: H. S. Parsons, 1850.

Sue, Eugène. *The Mysteries of Paris, Being the Last and Concluding Chapters of the Story Just Received from Paris and Wholly Omitted in Harpers' Edition*. New World, November 14, 1843. New York: J. Winchester, 1843.

———. *The Mysteries of Paris. A Novel*. Translated by Charles H. Town. New York: Harper and Brothers, 1843.

———. *The Mysteries of Paris. A Romance of the Rich and Poor*. Translated by Henry C. Deming. New World Extra Series. New York: J. Winchester, 1844.

———. *The Wandering Jew*. Translated by Henry William Herbert. New York: New World Press, 1844.

———. *The Wandering Jew*. New York: Harper and Brothers, 1844–45.

Swisshelm, Jane G. *Letters to Country Girls*. New York, 1853.

The Theatre; A Voice to the Friends of Morality in Large Towns and Cities, Remonstrating Against Its Patronage. New York: J. S. Redfield, 1849.

Thoreau, Henry David. *Walden and Civil Disobedience*. New York: Penguin Books, 1986.

Tocqueville, Alexis de. *Democracy in America*. 2 vols. in 1. New York: Vintage Books, 1945.

Todd, John. *Index Rerum or Index of Subjects: Intended as a Manual, to Aid the Student and the Professional Man, in Preparing Himself for Usefulness, With an Introduction, Illustrating Its Utility and Method of Use*. Northampton, Mass.: J. H. Butler, 1834.

———. *Moral Influences, Dangers, and Duties Connected With Great Cities*. Northampton, Mass.: J. H. Butler, 1841.

———. *The Student's Manual; Designed, By Specific Directions, to Aid In Forming*

and Strengthening the Intellectual and Moral Character and Habits of the Student.
Northampton, Mass.: J. H. Butler; Boston: W. Peirce, 1835.

———. *Young Man's Guide: Hints Addressed to the Young Men of the United States.*
1844. Northampton, Mass.: Hokins, Bridgman, 1856.

*Trial, Confession, and Execution of Peter Robinson for the Murder of Abraham
Suydam, Esq., of New Brunswick, N.J.* New York, 1841.

*Trial, Confession, and Execution of Robert M'Conaghy, for the Murder of Six of His
Relatives, Mrs. Brown and her Five Children. To Which is Added the Confession
of Peter Robinson, the Murderer of Mr. Suydam, of New Brunswick, on the 3d
December, 1840, And Was Hung at New Brunswick, N.J., on Friday, April 16th,
1841.* Philadelphia, 1841.

Trollope, Frances. *Domestic Manners of Americans.* Edited by Donald Smalley.
New York: Knopf, 1949.

*A True Account of the Murder of Abraham Suydam, Late of New Brunswick, Together
With an Accurate Outline of the Testimony, Elicited on the Examination of
Witnesses.* New Brunswick, 1841.

Ware, Henry, Jr. "The Duties of Young Men in Respect to the Dangers of the
Country." In *The Works of Henry Ware, Jr., D.D.,* 2:203–25. Boston: James
Munroe, 1846.

Warner, Susan [Elizabeth Wetherell, pseud.]. *The Wide, Wide World.* New
York: Putnam, 1851.

Waterbury, Jared Bell. *Considerations for Young Men.* New York: American
Tract Society, 1851.

Webster, Noah. *American Dictionary of the English Language.* 2 vols. New York:
S. Converse, 1828.

Whitman, Walt. "Letter to Ralph Waldo Emerson." 1856. In *The Norton
Anthology of American Literature,* edited by Nina Baym et al., 1:2017–24.
New York: W. W. Norton, 1989.

Wonderful Trial of Caroline Lohman, Alias Restell. New York, 1847.

Wright, Frances. *An Address to Young Mechanics as Delivered at a Meeting in the
Hall of Science, June 13, 1830.* New York, 1830.

SECONDARY SOURCES

Abraham, Mildred K. "The Library of Lady Jean Skipwith: A Book Collection from the Age of Jefferson." *Virginia Magazine of History and Biography*
91, no. 3 (1983): 296–347.

Adburgham, Alison. *Women in Print: Writing Women and Women's Magazines
from the Restoration to the Accession of Victoria.* London: Allen and Unwin,
1972.

Adorno, Theodor W. "On the Fetish-Character in Music and the Regression
of Listening." In *The Essential Frankfurt School Reader,* edited by Andrew
Arato and Eike Gebhardt, 270–99. New York: Continuum, 1987.

———. "Veblen's Attack on Culture." In *Prisms,* translated by Samuel and
Shierry Weber, 73–94. Cambridge, Mass.: MIT Press, 1981.

Agnew, Jean-Christophe. *Worlds Apart: The Market and the Theater in Anglo-*

American Thought, 1550–1750. New York: Cambridge University Press, 1986.

Alexander, Ruth M. " 'We Are Engaged as a Band of Sisters': Class and Domesticity in the Washington Temperance Movement, 1840–1850." *Journal of American History* 75, no. 3 (December 1988): 763–85.

Altick, Richard D. *Deadly Encounters: Two Victorian Sensations.* Philadelphia: University of Pennsylvania Press, 1986.

————. *The English Common Reader: A Social History of the Mass Reading Public, 1800–1900.* Chicago: University of Chicago Press, 1957.

An, Young-Ok. "Beatrice's Gaze Revisited: Anatomizing *The Cenci.*" *Criticism* 38, no. 1 (Winter 1996): 27–68.

Anderson, Benedict. *Imagined Communities: Reflections on the Origin and Spread of Nationalism.* London: Verso, 1983.

Anderson, Patricia. *The Printed Image and the Transformation of Popular Culture, 1790–1860.* New York: Oxford University Press, 1991.

Apostolos-Cappadona, Diane. *The Spirit and the Vision: The Influence of Christian Romanticism on the Development of Nineteenth-Century American Art.* Atlanta, Ga.: Scholars Press, 1995.

Appadurai, Arjun. "Commodities and the Politics of Value." In *The Social Life of Things: Commodities in Cultural Perspective,* edited by Arjun Appadurai, 3–63. New York: Cambridge University Press, 1986.

Appleby, Joyce. "Republicanism and Ideology." *American Quarterly* 37, no. 4 (Fall 1985): 461–73.

————. "Republicanism in Old and New Contexts." *William and Mary Quarterly* 43 (January 1986): 20–34.

Ariès, Philippe, and Georges Duby, eds. *A History of Private Life.* 4 vols. Cambridge, Mass.: Belknap Press of Harvard University Press, 1987–90.

Bailey, Peter. *Leisure and Class in Victorian England: Rational Recreation and the Contest for Control, 1830–1885.* London: Routledge and K. Paul; Buffalo: University of Toronto Press, 1978.

Bailyn, Bernard. *The Ideological Origins of the American Revolution.* Cambridge, Mass.: Belknap Press of Harvard University Press, 1967.

Bailyn, Bernard, and John Hench, eds. *The Press and the American Revolution.* Worcester, Mass.: American Antiquarian Society, 1980.

Bakhtin, Mikhail. *Rabelais and His World.* Translated by Helene Iswolsky. Cambridge, Mass.: MIT Press, 1968.

Banning, Lance. "Jeffersonian Ideology Revisited: Liberalism and Classical Ideas in the New Republic." *William and Mary Quarterly* 43 (January 1986): 3–19.

Barker-Benfield, G. J. *The Horrors of the Half-Known Life: Male Attitudes toward Women and Sexuality in Nineteenth-Century America.* New York: Harper and Row, 1976.

Barnes, James J. *Authors, Publishers and Politicians: The Quest for an Anglo-American Copyright Agreement, 1815–1854.* Columbus: Ohio State University Press, 1974.

Barthes, Roland. "Image, raison, déraison." In *L'Univers de l'Encyclopédie,* edited by Roland Barthes, Robert Mauzi, and Jean-Pierre Seguin. Paris: Les Libraires Associés, 1964.

Bassy, Alain-Marie. "Le livre mis en pièce(s). Pensées détachées sur le livre romantique." *Romantisme* 43 (1984): 19–27.

Baudrillard, Jean. *Le système des objets.* Paris: Gallimard, 1968.

Baumgart, Wolfgang. "Der Leser als Zuschauer: Zu Chodowieckis Stichen zur Minna von Barnhelm." In *Die Buchillustration im 18. Jahrhundert,* 13–25. Heidelberg: Winter, 1980.

Baym, Nina. *Novels, Readers, and Reviewers: Responses to Fiction in Antebellum America.* Ithaca, N.Y.: Cornell University Press, 1984.

————. *Woman's Fiction: A Guide to Novels by and about Women in America, 1820–1870.* Ithaca, N.Y.: Cornell University Press, 1978.

Benjamin, Walter. "The Author as Producer." In *The Essential Frankfurt School Reader,* edited by Andrew Arato and Eike Gebhardt, 254–69. New York: Continuum, 1982.

————. "The Work of Art in the Age of Mechanical Reproduction." In *Illuminations,* edited by Hannah Arendt, 217–51. New York: Schocken Books, 1969.

Bennett, H. S. *English Books and Readers, 1475 to 1557: Being a Study in the History of the Book Trade from Caxton to the Incorporation of the Stationers' Company.* Cambridge: Cambridge University Press, 1952.

Bennett, Tony. "Texts, Readers, and Reading Formations." *The Bulleting of the Midwest Modern Language Association* 16, no. 1 (Spring 1983): 3–17.

Bensick, Carol Marie. *La Nouvelle Beatrice: Renaissance and Romance in "Rappaccini's Daughter."* New Brunswick, N.J.: Rutgers University Press, 1985.

Birkerts, Sven. *The Gutenberg Elegies: The Fate of Reading in an Electronic Age.* Boston: Faber and Faber, 1994.

Bledstein, Burton J. *The Culture of Professionalism: The Middle Class and the Development of Higher Education in America.* New York: Norton, 1976.

Blewett, Mary H. *Men, Women, and Work: Class, Gender, and Protest in the New England Shoe Industry, 1780–1910.* Urbana: University of Illinois Press, 1988.

————. "The Sexual Division of Labor and the Artisan Tradition in Early Industrial Capitalism: The Case of New England Shoemaking, 1780–1860." In *"To Toil the Livelong Day": America's Women at Work, 1780–1980,* edited by Carol Groneman and Mary Beth Norton, 35–46. Ithaca, N.Y.: Cornell University Press, 1987.

————. "Women Shoeworkers and Domestic Ideology: Rural Outwork in Early Nineteenth-Century Essex County." *New England Quarterly* 60 (1987): 403–28.

Bloch, Ruth H. "American Feminine Ideals in Transition: The Rise of the Moral Mother, 1785–1815." *Feminist Studies* 4 (June 1978): 100–126.

Blumin, Stuart M. *The Emergence of the Middle Class: Social Experience in the American City, 1760–1900.* New York: Cambridge University Press, 1989.

————. "Explaining the New Metropolis: Perception, Depiction, and Analysis in Mid-Nineteenth-Century New York City." *Journal of Urban History* 11 (1984): 9–38.

Bobbitt, Mary Reed. *A Bibliography of Etiquette Books Published in America before 1900.* New York: New York Public Library, 1947.

Bode, Carl. *The American Lyceum: Town Meeting of the Mind.* Carbondale: Southern Illinois University Press, 1968.

———. *The Anatomy of American Popular Culture, 1840–1861.* Berkeley: University of California Press, 1959.

Bollème, Geneviève. *Les almanachs populaires aux XVIIe et XVIIIe siècles. Essai d'histoire sociale.* Paris: Mouton, 1969.

Bollème, Geneviève, Jean Ehrard, François Furet, Daniel Roche, and Jacques Roger. *Livre et Société dans la France du XVIIIe siècle.* 2 vols. Paris: Mouton, 1965.

Boltanski, Luc, Yann Darré, and Marie-Ange Schiltz. "La dénonciation." *Actes de la Recherche en Sciences Sociales* 51 (March 1984): 3–40.

Booth, Bradford A. "Taste in the Annuals." *American Literature* 14, no. 3 (November 1942): 299–302.

Bosco, Ronald A. "Lectures at the Pillory: The Early American Execution Sermon." *American Quarterly* 30 (1978): 156–76.

Bourdieu, Pierre. "Champ intellectuel et projet créateur." *Les Temps Modernes* 246 (November 1966): 865–906.

———. *Choses dites.* Paris: Minuit, 1987.

———. *Distinction: A Social Critique of the Judgment of Taste.* Translated by Richard Nice. Cambridge, Mass.: Harvard University Press, 1984.

———. "The Genesis of the Concepts of *Habitus* and *Field*." Translated by Channa Newman. *Sociocriticism* 1, no. 2 (December 1985): 11–24.

———. "Le marché des biens symboliques." *L'Année Sociologique* 22 (1971): 49–126.

———. *Outline of a Theory of Practice.* New York: Cambridge University Press, 1977.

———. "La production de la croyance: contribution à une économie des biens symboliques." *Actes de la Recherche en Sciences Sociales* 13 (February 1977): 3–43.

Boyer, Paul. *Urban Masses and Moral Order in America, 1820–1920.* Cambridge, Mass.: Harvard University Press, 1978.

Breen, T. H. "Horses and Gentlemen: The Cultural Significance of Gambling among the Gentry of Virginia." *William and Mary Quarterly* 34 (1977): 256–57.

Brewer, John, and Roy Porter, eds. *Consumption and the World of Goods.* New York: Routledge, 1993.

Bridges, Amy. *A City in the Republic: Antebellum New York and the Origin of Machine Politics.* New York: Cambridge University Press, 1984.

Brodhead, Richard H. *Cultures of Letters: Scenes of Reading and Writing in Nineteenth-Century America.* Chicago: University of Chicago Press, 1993.

———. *The School of Hawthorne.* New York: Oxford University Press, 1986.

———. "Sparing the Rod: Discipline and Fiction in Antebellum America." *Representations* 21 (Winter 1988): 67–96.

Brody, David. "The Old Labor History and the New: In Search of an American Working Class." *Labor History* 20 (1979): 111–26.

———. *Steelworkers in America: The Nonunion Era.* Cambridge, Mass.: Harvard University Press, 1960.

———. "Time and Work during Early American Industrialism." In *In Labor's Cause: Main Themes on the History of the American Worker,* 3–42. New York: Oxford University Press, 1993.

Browder, Clifford. *The Wickedest Woman in New York: Madame Restell, the Abortionist.* Hamden, Conn.: Archon Books, 1988.

Brown, Richard D. "From Cohesion to Competition." Afterword to *Printing and Society in Early America,* edited by William L. Joyce, David D. Hall, Richard D. Brown, and John B. Hench, 300–309. Worcester, Mass.: American Antiquarian Society, 1983.

———. *Knowledge Is Power: The Diffusion of Information in Early America, 1700–1865.* New York: Oxford University Press, 1989.

———. *Modernization: The Transformation of American Life, 1600–1865.* New York: Hill and Wang, 1976.

Brumberg, Joan Jacobs. *Mission for Life: The Story of the Family of Adoniram Judson, the Dramatic Events of the First American Foreign Mission, and the Course of Evangelical Religion in the Nineteenth Century.* New York: Free Press, 1980.

Buckley, Peter George. "To the Opera House: Culture and Society in New York City, 1820–1860." Ph.D. diss., State University of New York at Stony Brook, 1984.

Buell, Lawrence. *New England Literary Culture from Revolution through Renaissance.* New York: Cambridge University Press, 1986.

Bürger, Peter. "Institution Literatur und Modernisierungsprozeß." In *Zum Funktionswandel der Literatur,* edited by Peter Bürger, 9–32. Frankfurt am Main: Suhrkamp, 1983.

———. "Literarischer Markt und autonomer Kunstbegriff." In *Zur Dichotomisierung von hoher und niederer Literatur,* edited by Christa Bürger, Peter Bürger, and Jochen Schulte-Sasse. Frankfurt am Main: Suhrkamp, 1982.

Butler, Jon. *Awash in a Sea of Faith: Christianizing the American People.* Cambridge, Mass.: Harvard University Press, 1990.

Bynum, Caroline Walker. "Women's Stories, Women's Symbols: A Critique of Victor Turner's Theory of Liminality." In *Fragmentation and Redemption: Essays on Gender and the Human Body in Medieval Religion,* 27–51. New York: Zone Books, 1991.

Carlson, Oliver. *The Man Who Made News, James Gordon Bennett.* New York: Duell, Sloan and Pearce, 1942.

Carpenter, Kenneth E., ed. *Books and Society in History: Papers of the Association of College and Research Libraries, Rare Books and Manuscripts Preconference, 24–28 June, 1980, Boston, Massachusetts.* New York: R. R. Bowker, 1983.

Cayton, Mary Kupiec. *Emerson's Emergence: Self and Society in the Transformation of New England, 1800–1845.* Chapel Hill: University of North Carolina Press, 1989.

Certeau, Michel de. *The Practice of Everyday Life.* Translated by Steven Rendall. Berkeley: University of California Press, 1984.

Chamlee, Roy Zebulon, Jr. "The Sabbath Crusade, 1810–1920." Ph.D. diss., George Washington University, 1968.

Chartier, Roger. *Cultural History: Between Practices and Representations.* Translated by Lydia G. Cochrane. Ithaca, N.Y.: Cornell University Press, 1988.

———. *The Cultural Uses of Print in Early Modern France.* Translated by Lydia G. Cochrane. Princeton, N.J.: Princeton University Press, 1987.

———. "Intellectual History or Sociocultural History? The French Trajectories." In *Modern European Intellectual History: Reappraisals and New Perspectives,* edited by Dominick LaCapra and Steven L. Kaplan, 13–46. Ithaca, N.Y.: Cornell University Press, 1982.

———. *Lectures et lecteurs dans la France d'Ancien Régime.* Paris: Seuil, 1987.

———. "Du livre au lire." In *Pratiques de la lecture,* edited by Roger Chartier, 61–82. Marseille: Rivages, 1985.

———, ed. *The Culture of Print: Power and the Uses of Print in Early Modern Europe.* Translated by Lydia G. Cochrane. Cambridge, Eng.: Priority Press, 1989.

Chartier, Roger, and Henri-Jean Martin, eds. *Histoire de l'édition.* Vol. 3, *Le temps des éditeurs. Du Romantisme à la Belle Epoque.* Paris: Promodis, 1985.

Chartier, Roger, and Daniel Roche. "Le livre: un changement de perspective." In *Faire de l'histoire,* edited by Jacques Le Goff and Pierre Nora, 3:156–84. Paris: Gallimard, 1974.

Charvat, William. *Literary Publishing in America, 1790–1850.* Philadelphia: University of Pennsylvania Press, 1959.

———. *The Origins of American Critical Thought, 1810–1835.* Philadelphia: University of Pennsylvania Press, 1936.

———. *The Profession of Authorship in America, 1800–1870.* Edited by Matthew J. Bruccoli. Columbus: Ohio State University Press, 1968.

Chrisman, Miriam Usher. *Lay Culture, Learned Culture: Books and Social Change in Strasbourg, 1490–1599.* New Haven: Yale University Press, 1982.

Clark, Charles E. *The Public Prints: The Newspaper in Anglo-American Culture, 1665–1740.* New York: Oxford University Press, 1994.

Clark, Charles E., and Charles Wetherell. "The Measure of Maturity: The *Pennsylvania Gazette,* 1728–1765." *William and Mary Quarterly* 46, no. 2 (April 1989): 279–303.

Clark, Christopher. "The Diary of an Apprentice Cabinetmaker: Edward Jenner Carpenter's Journal, 1844–45." *Proceedings of the American Antiquarian Society* 98 (October 1988): 303–94.

Clark, Clifford E. "The Changing Nature of Protestantism in Mid-Nineteenth-Century America: Henry Ward Beecher's Seven Lectures to Young Men." *Journal of American History* 57, no. 4 (March 1977): 832–46.

———. *Henry Ward Beecher: Spokesman for a Middle-Class America*. Urbana: University of Illinois Press, 1978.

Clawson, Mary Ann. *Constructing Brotherhood: Class, Gender, and Fraternalism.* Princeton, N.J.: Princeton University Press, 1989.

Click, Patricia C. *The Spirit of the Times: Amusements in Nineteenth-Century Baltimore, Norfolk, and Richmond.* Charlottesville: University Press of Virginia, 1989.

Cmiel, Kenneth. *Democratic Eloquence: The Fight over Popular Speech in Nineteenth-Century America.* New York: William Morrow, 1990.

Cohen, Daniel A. "A Fellowship of Thieves: Property Criminals in Eighteenth-Century Massachusetts." *Journal of Social History* 22, no. 1 (1988): 65–92.

———. "In Defense of the Gallows: Justifications of Capital Punishment in New England Sermons, 1674–1825." *American Quarterly* 40, no. 2 (June 1988): 147–64.

———. *Pillars of Salt, Monuments of Grace: New England Crime Literature and the Origins of American Popular Culture.* New York: Oxford University Press, 1993.

Cohen, Patricia Cline. "The Helen Jewett Murder: Violence, Gender, and Sexual Licentiousness in Antebellum America." *NWSA Journal* 2, no. 3 (Summer 1990): 374–89.

———. "The Mystery of Helen Jewett: Romantic Fiction and the Eroticization of Violence." *Legal Studies Forum* 17, no. 2 (1993): 133–45.

Commons, John R., Ulrich B. Phillips, Eugene A. Gilmore, Helen L. Sumner, and John B. Andrews, eds. *A Documentary History of American Industrial Society.* New York: Russell and Russell, 1958.

Cornelius, Janet Duitsman. *"When I Can Read My Title Clear": Literacy, Slavery, and Religion in the Antebellum South.* Columbia: University of South Carolina Press, 1991.

Cott, Nancy F. *The Bonds of Womanhood: "Woman's Sphere" in New England, 1780–1835.* New Haven: Yale University Press, 1977.

Couvares, Francis G. *The Remaking of Pittsburgh: Class and Culture in an Industrializing City, 1877–1919.* Albany: State University of New York Press, 1984.

———. "The Triumph of Commerce: Class Culture and Mass Culture in Pittsburgh." In *Working-Class America: Essays on Labor, Community, and American Society,* edited by Michael H. Frisch and Daniel J. Walkowitz, 123–52. Urbana: University of Illinois Press, 1983.

Crapanzano, Vincent. "Liminal Recreations." *Times Literary Supplement,* April 27, 1984, 473.

Cremin, Lawrence. *American Education: The National Experience, 1783–1876.* Vol. 2. New York: Harper and Row, 1980.

———. "Reading, Writing and Literacy." *Review of Education* 1 (November 1975): 517–21.

Cressy, David. "Books as Totems in Seventeenth-Century England and New England." *Journal of Library History* 21, no. 1 (Winter 1986): 92–106.

———. *Literacy and the Social Order: Reading and Writing in Tudor and Stuart England*. Cambridge: Cambridge University Press, 1980.

———. "Literacy in Seventeenth-Century England: More Evidence." *Journal of Interdisciplinary History* 8, no. 1 (Summer 1977): 141–50.

Cross, Whitney R. *The Burned-Over District: The Social and Intellectual History of Enthusiastic Religion in Western New York, 1800–1850*. Ithaca, N.Y.: Cornell University Press, 1950.

Crouthamel, James L. *Bennett's New York Herald and the Rise of the Popular Press*. Syracuse, N.Y.: Syracuse University Press, 1989.

———. "James Gordon Bennett, the *New York Herald,* and the Development of Newspaper Sensationalism." *New York History* 54 (July 1973): 294–316.

———. "The Newspaper Revolution in New York, 1830–1860." *New York History* 45 (April 1964): 91–113.

Crowley, John Edward. *This Sheba, Self: The Conceptualization of Economic Life in Eighteenth-Century America*. Baltimore: Johns Hopkins University Press, 1974.

Cumbler, John T. *Working-Class Community in Industrial America: Work, Leisure and Struggle in Two Industrial Cities, 1880–1930*. Westport, Conn.: Greenwood Press, 1979.

Cunningham, Hugh. *Leisure in the Industrial Revolution, c. 1780–c. 1880*. New York: St. Martin's Press, 1980.

Darnton, Robert. *The Business of Enlightenment: A Publishing History of the "Encyclopédie," 1775–1800*. Cambridge, Mass.: Harvard University Press, 1979.

———. *The Great Cat Massacre and Other Episodes in French Cultural History*. New York: Basic Books, 1984.

———. *The Kiss of Lamourette: Reflections in Cultural History*. New York: Norton, 1990.

———. *The Literary Underground of the Old Regime*. Cambridge, Mass.: Harvard University Press, 1982.

———. "What Is the History of Books?" *Daedalus* 111, no. 3 (Summer 1982): 65–93.

———. "Writing News and Telling Stories." *Daedalus* 104, no. 2 (1975): 175–94.

Davidson, Cathy N. *Revolution and the Word: The Rise of the Novel in America*. New York: Oxford University Press, 1986.

———, ed. *Reading in America: Literature and Social History*. Baltimore: Johns Hopkins University Press, 1989.

Davis, David Brion. *Homicide in American Fiction, 1798–1860*. Ithaca, N.Y.: Cornell University Press, 1957.

Davis, Lennard J. *Factual Fictions: The Origins of the English Novel*. New York: Columbia University Press, 1983.

Davis, Natalie Zemon. "Beyond the Market: Books as Gifts in Sixteenth-Century France." *Transactions of the Royal Historical Society* 33 (1983): 69–88.

———. "The Sacred and the Body Social in Sixteenth-Century Lyon." *Past and Present,* no. 90 (February 1981): 40–70.

Davis, Susan G. "'Making Night Hideous': Christmas Revelry and Public Order in Nineteenth-Century Philadelphia." *American Quarterly* 34 (Summer 1982): 185–99.

———. *Parades and Power: Street Theater in Nineteenth-Century Philadelphia.* Philadelphia: Temple University Press, 1986.

Dawley, Alan. *Class and Community: The Industrial Revolution in Lynn.* Cambridge, Mass.: Harvard University Press, 1976.

Dawley, Alan, and Paul Faler. "Working-Class Culture and Politics in the Industrial Revolution: Sources of Loyalism and Rebellion." *Journal of Social History* 9 (Summer 1976): 466–80.

Demos, John, and Virginia Demos. "Adolescence in Historical Perspective." *Journal of Marriage and the Family* 31 (November 1969): 632–38.

Denning, Michael. *Mechanic Accents: Dime Novels and Working-Class Culture in America.* New York: Verso, 1987.

Dethlefsen, Edwin, and James Deetz. "Death's Heads, Cherubs, and Willow Trees." In *Passing: The Vision of Death,* edited by Charles O. Jackson, 48–59. Westport, Conn.: Greenwood Press, 1977.

Dillenberger, John. *The Visual Arts and Christianity in America: The Colonial Period through the Nineteenth Century.* Chico, Calif.: Scholars Press, 1984.

Dodd, Jill Siegel. "The Working Classes and the Temperance Movement in Antebellum Boston." *Labor History* 19 (Fall 1978): 510–31.

Douglas, Ann. *The Feminization of American Culture.* New York: Knopf, 1977.

———. "Heaven Our Home: Consolation Literature in the Northern United States, 1830–1880." In *Death in America,* edited by David E. Stannard, 49–68. Philadelphia: University of Pennsylvania Press, 1975.

Dublin, Thomas, ed. *Farm to Factory: Women's Letters, 1830–1860.* New York: Columbia University Press, 1981.

Dubois, Jacques, and Pascal Durand. "Literary Field and Classes of Texts." In *Literature and Social Practice,* edited by Philippe Desan, Priscilla Parkhurst Ferguson, and Wendy Griswold, 137–53. Chicago: University of Chicago Press, 1988.

Dulles, Foster Rhea. *A History of Recreation: America Learns to Play.* New York: Appleton-Century-Crofts, 1965.

Eager, Gerald. "Washington Allston's *The Sisters:* Poetry, Painting, and Friendship." *Word and Image* 6, no. 4 (October–December 1990): 298–307.

Eisenstein, Elizabeth L. *The Printing Press as an Agent of Change: Communications and Cultural Transformations in Early Modern Europe.* 2 vols. New York: Cambridge University Press, 1979.

———. "Some Conjectures about the Impact of Printing on Western Society and Thought." *Journal of Modern History* 40, no. 1 (March 1968): 42.

Elias, Norbert. *The Civilizing Process: The History of Manners.* Translated by Edmund Jephcott. New York: Urizen Books, 1978.

———. *Court Society*. Translated by Edmund Jephcott. New York: Pantheon Books, 1983.

———. *Power and Civility*. Translated by Edmund Jephcott. New York: Pantheon Books, 1982.

Ellis, Elizabeth Garrity. "The 'Intellectual and Moral Made Visible': The 1839 Washington Allston Exhibition and Unitarian Taste in Boston." *Prospects* 10 (1985): 39–76.

Ellis, Joseph J. *After the Revolution: Profiles of Early American Culture*. New York: W. W. Norton, 1979.

Endres, Kathleen L. "The Women's Press in the Civil War: A Portrait of Patriotism, Propaganda, and Prodding." *Civil War History* 30, no. 1 (March 1984): 31–53.

Engelsing, Rolf. *Analphabetentum und Lektüre: Zur Sozialgeschichte des Lesers in Deutschland zwischen feudaler und industrieller Gesellschaft*. Stuttgart: J. B. Metzler, 1973.

———. *Der Bürger als Leser: Lesegeschichte in Deutschland, 1500 bis 1800*. Stuttgart: Metzler, 1974.

———. "Die Perioden der Lesergeschichte in der Neuzeit." In *Zur Sozialgeschichte deutscher Mittel- und Unterschichten*, 112–54. Göttingen: Vandenhoeck and Ruprecht, 1973.

Entrikin, Isabelle Webb. *Sarah Josepha Hale and Godey's Lady's Book*. Lancaster, Pa.: Lancaster Press, 1946.

Epstein, Barbara Leslie. *The Politics of Domesticity: Women, Evangelism, and Temperance in Nineteenth-Century America*. Middletown, Conn.: Wesleyan University Press, 1981.

Erenberg, Lewis A. *Steppin' Out: New York Nightlife and the Transformation of American Culture, 1890–1930*. Westport, Conn.: Greenwood Press, 1981.

Evans, Oliver. "Allegory and Incest in 'Rappaccini's Daughter.'" *Nineteenth Century Fiction* 19 (1964): 185–95.

Fabian, Monroe H. *Mr. Sully, Portrait Painter: The Works of Thomas Sully (1783–1872)*. Washington, D.C.: Published for the National Portrait Gallery by the Smithsonian Institution, 1983.

Fabre, Daniel "Le livre et sa magie: les liseurs dans les sociétés pyrénéennes aux XIXème et XXème siècles." In *Pratiques de la lecture*, edited by Roger Chartier, 181–206. Marseille: Rivages, 1985.

Faler, Paul. "Cultural Aspects of the Industrial Revolution: Lynn, Massachusetts, Shoemakers and Industrial Morality, 1820–1860." *Labor History* 15 (1974): 367–94.

———. *Mechanics and Manufacturers in the Early Industrial Revolution: Lynn, Massachusetts, 1780–1860*. Albany: State University of New York Press, 1981.

Farge, Arlette. *La vie fragile: Violence, pouvoirs et solidarités à Paris au XVIIIème siècle*. Paris: Hachette, 1986.

———, ed. *Vivre dans la rue à Paris au XVIIIème siècle*. Paris: Gallimard/Julliard, 1979.

Farrell, James J. *Inventing the American Way of Death, 1830–1920*. Philadelphia: Temple University Press, 1980.

Faxon, Frederick W. *Literary Annuals and Gift Books*. London: Private Libraries Association, 1973.

Febvre, Lucien, and Henri-Jean Martin. *The Coming of the Book: The Impact of Printing, 1450–1800*. Translated by David Gerard. London: N.L.B., 1976.

Feltes, N. N. *Modes of Production of Victorian Novels*. Chicago: University of Chicago Press, 1986.

Fermer, Douglas. *James Gordon Bennett and the New York Herald: A Study of Editorial Opinion in the Civil War Era, 1854–1867*. New York: St. Martin's Press, 1986.

Fiering, Norman. "The Transatlantic Republic of Letters: A Note on the Circulation of Learned Periodicals." *William and Mary Quarterly*, 3d ser., no. 33 (1976): 642–60.

Finley, Ruth E. *The Lady's of Godey's: Sarah Josepha Hale*. Philadelphia: Lippincott, 1931.

Fish, Stanley. *Is There a Text in This Class?: The Authority of Interpretive Communities*. Cambridge, Mass.: Harvard University Press, 1980.

Fleming, Robin. "Picturesque History and the Medieval in Nineteenth-Century America." *American Historical Review* 100, no. 4 (October 1995): 1061–94.

Fliegelman, Jay. *Declaring Independence: Jefferson, Natural Language and the Culture of Performance*. Stanford: Stanford University Press, 1993.

Flynn, Elizabeth A., and Patrocinio P. Schweickart, eds. *Gender and Reading: Essays on Readers, Texts, and Contexts*. Baltimore: Johns Hopkins University Press, 1986.

Foner, Philip S., ed. *The Factory Girls: A Collection of Writings on Life and Struggles in the New England Factories of the 1840s*. Urbana: University of Illinois Press, 1977.

Formisano, Ronald P. "Toward a Reorientation of Jacksonian Politics: A Review of the Literature, 1959–1975." *Journal of American History* 63 (1976): 42–65.

Foucault, Michel. *Discipline and Punish: The Birth of the Prison*. Translated by Alan Sheridan. New York: Pantheon Books, 1977.

———. *L'ordre du discours*. Paris: Gallimard, 1971.

———, ed. *I, Pierre Rivière, Having Slaughtered My Mother, My Sister, and My Brother . . . : A Case of Parricide in the Nineteenth Century*. Translated by Frank Jellinek. New York: Pantheon Books, 1975.

Fox, Richard Wightman, and T. J. Jackson Lears. *The Culture of Consumption: Critical Essays in American History, 1880–1980*. New York: Pantheon Books, 1983.

Frederick, John T. "Hawthorne's Scribbling Women." *New England Quarterly* 48 (1975): 231–40.

Garrison, Dee. *Apostles of Culture: The Public Librarian and American Society, 1876–1920*. New York: Free Press, 1979.

Garvey, Ellen Gruber. *The Adman in the Parlor: Magazines and the Gendering of Consumer Culture, 1880s to 1910s.* New York: Oxford University Press, 1996.

Gasffield, Gary D. " 'To Speak and Act Bodily in the Cause of God': Profession and Practice in American Journalism, 1815–1845." *Journal of Popular Culture* 15, no. 2 (1981): 3–23.

Geertz, Clifford. "Ideology as a Cultural System." In *The Interpretation of Cultures.* New York: Basic Books, 1973.

Genette, Gérard. *Seuils.* Paris: Seuil, 1987.

Gilje, Paul A. *The Road to Mobocracy: Popular Disorder in New York City, 1763–1834.* Chapel Hill: University of North Carolina Press, 1987.

Gilkeson, John S., Jr. *Middle-Class Providence, 1820–1940.* Princeton, N.J.: Princeton University Press, 1986.

Gilmore, Michael T. *American Romanticism and the Marketplace.* Chicago: University of Chicago Press, 1985.

Gilmore, William J. "Elementary Literacy on the Eve of the Industrial Revolution: Trends in Rural New England, 1760–1830." *Proceedings of the American Antiquarian Society* 92, no. 1 (1982): 87–178.

———. *Reading Becomes a "Necessity of Life": Material and Cultural Life in Rural New England, 1760–1830.* Knoxville: University of Tennessee Press, 1988.

Gilreath, James. "American Book Distribution." *Proceedings of the American Antiquarian Society* 95, no. 2 (1985): 501–83.

Ginsburg, Jane C. "A Tale of Two Copyrights: Literary Property in Revolutionary France and America." In *Publishing and Readership in Revolutionary France and America,* edited by Carol Armbruster, 95–114. Westport, Conn.: Greenwood Press, 1993.

Ginzburg, Carlo. *The Cheese and the Worms: The Cosmos of a Sixteenth-Century Miller.* Translated by John and Anne Tedeschi. Baltimore: Johns Hopkins University Press, 1980.

Golby, J. M., and A. W. Purdue. *The Civilisation of the Crowd: Popular Culture in England, 1750–1900.* New York: Schocken Books, 1985.

Goldmann, Lucien. *The Hidden God: A Study of Tragic Vision in the Pensées of Pascal and the Tragedies of Racine.* Translated by Philip Thody. New York: Humanities Press, 1964.

Gorn, Elliott J. " 'Good-Bye Boys, I Die a True American': Homicide, Nativism, and Working-Class Culture in Antebellum New York City." *Journal of American History* 74 (1987): 388–410.

———. " 'Gouge and Bite, Pull Hair and Scratch': The Social Significance of Fighting in the Southern Backcountry." *American Historical Review* 90, no. 1 (February 1985): 18–43.

———. *The Manly Art: Bare-Knuckle Prize Fighting in America.* Ithaca, N.Y.: Cornell University Press, 1986.

Graff, Harvey J. *The Legacies of Literacy: Continuities and Contradictions in Western Culture and Society.* Bloomington: Indiana University Press, 1987.

———. *The Literacy Myth: Literacy and Social Structure in the Nineteenth-Century City.* New York: Academic Press, 1979.

Greenberg, Brian. *Worker and Community: Response to Industrialization in a*

Nineteenth-Century American City, Albany, New York, 1850–1884. Albany: State University of New York Press, 1985.

Grier, Katherine C. "Imagining the Parlor, 1830–1880." In *Perspectives on American Furniture,* edited by Gerald W. R. Ward, 205–39. New York: W. W. Norton, 1988.

Griffin, Clifford S. *Their Brothers' Keepers: Moral Stewardship in the United States, 1800–1865.* New Brunswick, N.J.: Rutgers University Press, 1960.

Grimsted, David. "Books and Culture: Canned, Canonized, and Neglected." *Proceedings of the American Antiquarian Society* 94, no. 2 (1984): 297–335.

———. *Melodrama Unveiled: American Theater and Culture, 1800–1850.* Berkeley: University of California Press, 1987.

Gross, Robert A. "Much Instruction from Little Reading: Books and Libraries in Thoreau's Concord." *Proceedings of the American Antiquarian Society* 97, no. 1 (1987): 128–88.

Guillais, Joëlle. *La chair de l'autre: le crime passionnel au XIXe siècle.* Paris: O. Orban, 1986.

Gürtler, Marie-Louise. *Die englischen literarischen Taschenbücher im 19. Jahrhundert.* Binningen: Buchdr. Wirz, 1961.

Gustafson, Sandra M. "Choosing a Medium: Margaret Fuller and the Forms of Sentiment." *American Quarterly* 47, no. 1 (March 1995): 34–65.

Gutman, Herbert G. *Power and Culture: Essays on the American Working Class.* Edited by Ira Berlin. New York: Pantheon Books, 1987.

———. *Work, Culture and Society in Industrializing America: Essays in American Working-Class and Social History.* New York: Knopf, 1976.

Habermas, Jurgen. *The Structural Transformation of the Public Sphere: An Inquiry into a Category of Bourgeois Society.* Translated by Thomas Burger, with the assistance of Frederick Lawrence. Cambridge, Mass.: MIT Press, 1989.

Hackenberg, Michael. *Getting the Books Out: Papers of the Chicago Conference on the Book in Nineteenth-Century America.* Washington, D.C.: Library of Congress, 1987.

Hall, David D. "Books and Reading in Eighteenth-Century America." In *Of Consuming Interests: The Style of Life in the Eighteenth Century,* edited by Cary Carson, Ronald Hoffman, and Peter J. Albert. Charlottesville: University Press of Virginia, 1994.

———. "Education and the Social Order in Colonial America." *Reviews in American History* 3 (June 1975): 178–83.

———. "The History of the Book: New Questions? New Answers?" *Journal of Library History* 21, no. 1 (Winter 1986): 32.

———. "The Uses of Literacy in New England, 1600–1850." Introduction to *Printing and Society in Early America,* edited by William L. Joyce, David D. Hall, Richard D. Brown, and John B. Hench, 1–47. Worcester, Mass., American Antiquarian Society, 1983.

———. "The Victorian Connection." In *Victorian America,* edited by Daniel Walker Howe, 81–94. Philadelphia: University of Pennsylvania Press, 1976.

———. "The World of Print and Collective Mentality in Seventeenth-

Century New England." In *New Directions in American Intellectual History*, edited by John Higham and Paul K. Conkin, 166–80. Baltimore: Johns Hopkins University Press, 1979.

———. *Worlds of Wonder, Days of Judgment: Popular Religious Belief in Early New England*. New York: Knopf, 1989.

Hall, David D., and John B. Hench, eds. *Needs and Opportunities in the History of the Book: America, 1639–1876*. Worcester, Mass.: American Antiquarian Society, 1987.

Halttunen, Karen. *Confidence Men and Painted Women: A Study of Middle-Class Culture in America, 1830–1870*. New Haven: Yale University Press, 1982.

———. "Early American Murder Narratives: The Birth of Horror." In *The Power of Culture*, edited by Richard Wightman Fox and T. J. Jackson Lears, 67–101. Chicago: University of Chicago Press, 1993.

———. "Humanitarianism and the Pornography of Pain in Anglo-American Culture." *American Historical Review* 100, no. 2 (April 1995): 303–34.

Hamilton, Milton W. *The Country Printer: New York State, 1785–1930*. New York: Columbia University Press, 1936.

Hardy, Stephen, and Alan G. Ingham. "Games, Structures, and Agency: Historians on the American Play Movement." *Journal of Social History* 17 (Winter 1983): 285–301.

Harris, Neil. *The Artist in American Society: The Formative Years, 1790–1860*. Chicago: University of Chicago Press, 1982.

———. *Humbug: The Art of P. T. Barnum*. Chicago: University of Chicago Press, 1973.

Harrison, Brian. "Religion and Recreation in Nineteenth-Century England." *Past and Present*, no. 38 (December 1967): 98–125.

Harrison, Brian, and E. J. Hobsbawm. "Work and Leisure in Industrial Society." *Past and Present*, no. 30 (April 1965): 96–102.

Hart, James D. *The Popular Book: A History of America's Literary Taste*. New York: Oxford University Press, 1950.

Hatch, Nathan O. *The Democratization of American Christianity*. New Haven: Yale University Press, 1989.

Hennessey, William J. *The American Portrait: From the Death of Stuart to the Rise of Sargent*. Worcester, Mass.: Worcester Art Museum, 1973.

Henretta, James. "Families and Farms: Mentalité in Pre-Industrial America." *William and Mary Quarterly* 35 (January 1978): 3–32.

Hermann, Claudine. *The Tongue Snatchers*. Translated by Nancy Kline. Lincoln: University of Nebraska Press, 1989.

Hexter, J. H. "Republic, Virtue, Liberty, and the Political Universe of J. G. A. Pocock." In *On Historians: Reappraisals of Some of the Makers of Modern History*, edited by J. H. Hexter, 255–303. Cambridge, Mass.: Harvard University Press, 1979.

Higham, John. *From Boundlessness to Consolidation: The Transformation of American Culture, 1848–1860*. Ann Arbor, Mich.: Clements Library, 1969.

Hobsbawm, Eric J. *Primitive Rebels: Studies in Archaic Forms of Social Move-*

ments in the Nineteenth and Twentieth Centuries. Manchester: Manchester University Press, 1959.

Hoffert, Sylvia D. *Private Matters: American Attitudes toward Childbearing and Infant Nurture in the Urban North, 1800–1860.* Urbana: University of Illinois Press, 1989.

———. "'A Very Peculiar Sorrow': Attitudes toward Infant Death in the Urban Northeast, 1800–1860." *American Quarterly* 39 (1987): 601–16.

Hofstadter, Richard. *Anti-Intellectualism in American Life.* New York: Random House, 1962.

Hoggart, Richard. *The Uses of Literacy: Changing Patterns in English Mass Culture.* Boston: Beacon Press, 1957.

Hohendahl, Peter Uwe. *Building a National Literature: The Case of Germany, 1830–1870.* Translated by Renate Baron Franciscono. Ithaca, N.Y.: Cornell University Press, 1989.

———. *The Institution of Criticism.* Ithaca, N.Y.: Cornell University Press, 1982.

———. "Introduction to Reception Aesthetics." *New German Critique* 10 (Winter 1977): 29–64.

Hoover, Merle M. *Park Benjamin: Poet and Editor.* New York: Columbia University Press, 1948.

Horkheimer, Max, and Theodor W. Adorno. "The Culture Industry: Enlightenment as Mass Deception." In *Dialectic of the Enlightenment,* translated by John Cumming, 120–67. New York: Herder and Herder, 1972.

Horlick, Allan. *Country Boys and Merchant Princes: The Social Control of Young Men in New York.* Lewisburg, Pa.: Bucknell University Press, 1975.

Howe, Daniel W. *The Unitarian Conscience: Harvard Moral Philosophy, 1805–1861.* Cambridge, Mass.: Harvard University Press, 1970.

Hughes, Helen MacGill. *News and the Human Interest Story.* Chicago: University of Chicago Press, 1940.

Hunnisett, Basil. *Steel-Engraved Book Illustration in England.* London: Scolar Press, 1980.

Hunt, Lynn, ed. *The New Cultural History.* Berkeley: University of California Press, 1989.

Hunter, J. Paul. *Before Novels: The Cultural Contexts of Eighteenth-Century English Fiction.* New York: W. W. Norton, 1990.

Huyssen, Andreas. "Mass Culture as Woman: Modernism's Other." In *Studies in Entertainment: Critical Approaches to Mass Culture,* edited by Tania Modleski, 188–207. Bloomington: Indiana University Press, 1986.

Isaac, Rhys. *The Transformation of Virginia, 1740–1790.* Chapel Hill: University of North Carolina Press, 1982.

Iser, Wolfgang. *The Act of Reading: A Theory of Aesthetic Response.* Baltimore: Johns Hopkins University Press, 1978.

———. *The Implied Reader: Patterns of Communication in Prose Fiction from Bunyan to Beckett.* Baltimore: Johns Hopkins University Press, 1974.

Jacobs, Robert D. *Poe: Journalist and Critic.* Baton Rouge: Louisiana State University Press, 1969.

Jaffee, David. "One of the Primitive Sort: Portrait Makers of the Rural North, 1760–1860." In *The Countryside in the Age of Capitalist Transformation: Essays in the Social History of Rural America,* edited by Steven Hahn and Jonathan Prude, 103–38. Chapel Hill: University of North Carolina Press, 1985.

Jauss, Hans Robert. *Aesthetic Experience and Literary Hermeneutics.* Translated by Michael Shaw. Minneapolis: University of Minnesota Press, 1982.

———. *Toward an Aesthetic of Reception.* Translated by Timothy Bahti, with an introduction by Paul de Man. Minneapolis: University of Minnesota Press, 1982.

John, Richard R. *Spreading the News: The American Postal System from Franklin to Morse.* Cambridge, Mass.: Harvard University Press, 1995.

Johnson, David R. *Policing the Urban Underground: The Impact of Crime on the Development of the American Police, 1800–1887.* Philadelphia: Temple University Press, 1979.

Johnson, Paul E. *A Shopkeepers' Millennium: Society and Revivals in Rochester, New York, 1815–1837.* New York: Hill and Wang, 1978.

Jones, Gareth Stedman. *Languages of Class: Studies in English Working Class History, 1832–1982.* Cambridge: Cambridge University Press, 1983.

Joyce, William L., David D. Hall, Richard D. Brown, and John B. Hench, eds. *Printing and Society in Early America.* Worcester, Mass.: American Antiquarian Society, 1983.

Kaestle, Carl F. *Pillars of the Republic: Common Schools and American Society, 1780–1860.* New York: Hill and Wang, 1983.

———, ed. *Literacy in the United States: Readers and Reading since 1880.* New Haven: Yale University Press, 1991.

Kaser, David. *A Book for a Sixpence: The Circulating Library in America.* Pittsburgh: Beta Phi Mu, 1980.

———. *Messrs. Carey and Lea of Philadelphia: A Study in the History of the Booktrade.* Philadelphia: University of Pennsylvania Press, 1957.

Kasserman, David Richard. *Fall River Outrage: Life, Murder, and Justice in Early Industrial New England.* Philadelphia: University of Pennsylvania Press, 1986.

Kasson, John F. *Rudeness and Civility: Manners in Nineteenth-Century Urban America.* New York: Hill and Wang, 1990.

Kasson, Joy S. *Artistic Voyagers: Europe and the American Imagination in the Works of Irving, Allston, Cole, Cooper and Hawthorne.* Westport, Conn.: Greenwood Press, 1982.

———. *Marble Queens and Captives: Women in Nineteenth-Century American Sculpture.* New Haven: Yale University Press, 1990.

Katznelson, Ira, and Aristide R. Zolberg, eds. *Working-Class Formation: Nineteenth-Century Patterns in Western Europe and the United States.* Princeton, N.J.: Princeton University Press, 1986.

Keller, Allan. *Scandalous Lady: The Life and Times of Madame Restell, New York's Most Notorious Abortionist.* New York: Atheneum, 1981.

Kelley, Mary. *Private Woman, Public Stage: Literary Domesticity in Nineteenth-Century America.* New York: Oxford University Press, 1984.

———. "The Sentimentalists: Promise and Betrayal in the Home." *Signs* 4 (Spring 1979): 434–46.

Kerber, Linda K. "The Republican Ideology of the Revolutionary Generation." *American Quarterly* 37, no. 4 (Fall 1985): 474–95.

———. "The Republican Mother: Women and the Enlightenment—An American Perspective." *American Quarterly* 28 (Summer 1976): 187–205.

———. "Separate Spheres, Female Worlds, Woman's Place: The Rhetoric of Women's History." *Journal of American History* (June 1988): 9–39.

———. *Women of the Republic: Intellect and Ideology in Revolutionary America.* Chapel Hill: University of North Carolina Press, 1980.

Kett, Joseph F. *Rites of Passage: Adolescence in America from 1790 to the Present.* New York: Basic Books, 1977.

Kirkham, E. Bruce, and John W. Fink. *Indices to American Literary Annuals and Gift Books, 1825–1865.* New Haven, Conn.: Research Publications, 1975.

Klancher, Jon P. *The Making of English Reading Audiences, 1790–1832.* Madison: University of Wisconsin Press, 1987.

Kluger, Richard. *The Paper: The Life and Death of the New York Herald Tribune.* New York: Knopf, 1986.

Kramnick, Isaac. "Republican Revisionism Revisited." *American Historical Review* 87 (June 1982): 629–64.

Kunciov, Robert, ed. *Mr. Godey's Ladies: Being a Mosaic of Fashions and Fancies.* New York: Bonanza Books, 1971.

LaCapra, Dominick. *History and Criticism.* Ithaca, N.Y.: Cornell University Press, 1985.

———. *Rethinking Intellectual History: Texts, Contexts, Language.* Ithaca, N.Y.: Cornell University Press, 1983.

Lane, Roger. *Policing the City: Boston, 1822–1885.* Cambridge, Mass.: Harvard University Press, 1967.

———. "Urbanization and Criminal Violence in the Nineteenth Century: Massachusetts as a Test Case." *Journal of Social History* 2, no. 2 (Winter 1968): 156–63.

———. *Violent Death in the City: Suicide, Accident, and Murder in Nineteenth-Century Philadelphia.* Cambridge, Mass.: Harvard University Press, 1979.

Laqueur, Thomas W. "Bodies, Details, and the Humanitarian Narrative." In *The New Cultural History,* edited by Lynn Hunt, 176–204. Berkeley: University of California Press, 1989.

Laurie, Bruce. " 'Nothing on Compulsion': Life Style of Philadelphia Artisans, 1820–1850." *Labor History* 15 (1974): 337–66.

———. *Working People of Philadelphia, 1800–1850.* Philadelphia: Temple University Press, 1980.

Lears, T. J. Jackson. "Beyond Veblen: Rethinking Consumer Culture in America." In *Consuming Visions: Accumulation and Display of Goods in America, 1880–1920,* edited by Simon J. Bronner, 73–97. New York: W. W. Norton, 1989.

————. *Fables of Abundance: A Cultural History of Advertising in America.* New York: Basic Books, 1994.

Le Goff, Jacques. *Time, Work and Culture in the Middle Ages.* Chicago: University of Chicago Press, 1980.

Lehmann-Haupt, Hellmut, Lawrence C. Wroth, and Rollo G. Silver. *The Book in America: A History of the Making and Selling of Books in the United States.* New York: R. R. Bowker, 1939.

Leonard, Thomas C. "News at the Hearth: A Drama of Reading in Nineteenth-Century America." *Proceedings of the American Antiquarian Society* 102, pt. 2 (1992): 379–401.

————. *The Power of the Press: The Birth of American Political Reporting.* New York: Oxford University Press, 1986.

Lerner, Gerda. "The Lady and the Mill Girl: Changes in the Status of Women in the Age of Jackson, 1800–1840." In *A Heritage of Her Own: Toward a New Social History of American Women,* edited by Nancy F. Cott and Elizabeth A. Pleck, 182–96. New York: Simon and Schuster, 1979.

Levine, Lawrence W. *Highbrow/Lowbrow: The Emergence of Cultural Hierarchy in America.* Cambridge, Mass.: Harvard University Press, 1988.

————. "William Shakespeare and the American People: A Study in Cultural Transformation." *American Historical Review* 89, no. 1 (February 1984): 34–66.

Levy, Leonard W. *The Emergence of a Free Press.* New York: Oxford University Press, 1985.

Lewis, Jan. "The Republican Wife: Virtue and Seduction in the Early Republic." *William and Mary Quarterly* 44 (October 1987): 689–721.

Lockridge, Kenneth A. *Literacy in Colonial New England.* New York: Norton, 1974.

Long, Elizabeth. "Women, Reading, and Cultural Authority: Some Implications of the Audience Perspective in Cultural Studies." *American Quarterly* 38 (Fall 1986): 606–10.

Loomis, Barbara Diane. "Piety and Play: Young Women's Leisure in an Era of Evangelical Religion, 1790–1840." Ph.D. diss., University of California, Berkeley, 1988.

Lovejoy, David S. "American Painting in Early Nineteenth-Century Gift Books." *American Quarterly* 7, no. 4 (Winter 1955): 345–61.

Lukacs, Georg. "The Phenomenon of Reification." In *History and Class Consciousness: Studies in Marxist Dialectics,* 83–119. Cambridge, Mass.: MIT Press, 1971.

Lund, Michael. *America's Continuing Story: An Introduction to Serial Fiction, 1850–1900.* Detroit: Wayne State University Press, 1993.

McCall, Laura. " 'The Reign of Brute Force Is Now Over': A Content Analysis of *Godey's Lady's Book,* 1830–1860." *Journal of the Early Republic* 9 (Summer 1989): 217–36.

————. "Symmetrical Minds: Literary Men and Women in Antebellum America." Ph.D. diss., University of Michigan, 1988.

McConachie, Bruce A. " 'The Theatre of the Mob': Melodrama and Preindustrial Riots in Antebellum New York." In *Theatre for Working-Class Audiences in the United States, 1830–1980,* edited by Bruce A. McConachie and Daniel Friedman. Westport, Conn.: Greenwood Press, 1985.

McCormick, Richard L. *The Party Period and Public Policy: American Politics from the Age of Jackson to the Progressive Era.* New York: Oxford University Press, 1986.

McDade, Thomas M., ed. *The Annals of Murder: A Bibliography of Books and Pamphlets on American Murders from Colonial Times to 1900.* Norman: University of Oklahoma Press, 1961.

McDannell, Colleen. *The Christian Home in Victorian America, 1840–1900.* Bloomington: Indiana University Press, 1986.

———. *Material Christianity: Religion and Popular Culture in America.* New Haven: Yale University Press, 1995.

McGaw, Judith A. *Most Wonderful Machine: Mechanization and Social Change in Berkshire Paper Making, 1801–1885.* Princeton, N.J.: Princeton University Press, 1987.

McKenzie, D. F. *Bibliography and the Sociology of Texts.* The Panizzi Lectures. London: British Library, 1986.

———. "The Sociology of a Text: Orality, Literacy and Print in Early New Zealand." *The Library* 6, no. 4 (December 1984): 333–65.

McLoughlin, William G. *The Meaning of Henry Ward Beecher: An Essay on the Shifting Values of Mid-Victorian America, 1840–1870.* New York: Knopf, 1970.

Mailloux, Steven. *Interpretive Conventions: The Reader in the Study of American Fiction.* Ithaca, N.Y.: Cornell University Press, 1982.

Main, Gloria L. "Inquiry into When and Why Women Learned to Write in Colonial New England." *Journal of Social History* 24, no. 3 (Spring 1991): 579–89.

Malcolmson, Robert W. *Popular Recreations in English Society, 1700–1850.* Cambridge: Cambridge University Press, 1973.

Mandrou, Robert. *De la culture populaire aux XVIIème et XVIIIème siècles: la Bibliothèque Bleue de Troyes.* Paris: Stock, 1964.

Marin, Louis. "Mimésis et description." *Word and Image* 4 (January–March 1988): 25–34.

———. "On Reading Pictures: Poussin's Letter on *Manna*." *Comparative Criticism: A Yearbook* 4 (1982): 3–18.

———. "Toward a Theory of Reading in the Visual Arts: Poussin's *The Arcadian Shepherds*." In *The Reader in the Text: Essays on Audience and Interpretation,* edited by Susan R. Suleiman and Inge Crosman, 293–324. Princeton, N.J.: Princeton University Press, 1980.

Martin, Henri-Jean, and Roger Chartier, eds. *Histoire de l'édition française.* 4 vols. Paris: Promodis, 1983.

Martin, Lawrence. "The Genesis of *Godey's Lady's Book*." *New England Quarterly* 1, no. 1 (January 1928): 52–65.

Martinez, Katherine. "'Messengers of Love, Tokens of Friendship': Gift-Book Illustrations by John Sartain." In *The American Illustrated Book in the*

Nineteenth Century, edited by Gerald W. R. Ward, 89–112. Winterthur, Del.: Winterthur Museum, 1987.

Marzio, Peter C. *The Democratic Art: Chromolithography, 1840–1900, Pictures for a Nineteenth-Century America.* Boston: David R. Godine, 1979.

Matthews, Glenna. *"Just a Housewife": The Rise and Fall of Domesticity in America.* New York: Oxford University Press, 1987.

Matthiessen, Francis O. *American Renaissance: Art and Expression in the Age of Emerson and Whitman.* New York: Oxford University Press, 1941.

Mauss, Marcel. *The Gift: Forms and Function of Exchange in Archaic Societies.* London: Routledge and Kegan Paul, 1974.

Mayo, Robert D. *The English Novel in the Magazines, 1740–1815.* Evanston: Northwestern University Press, 1962.

Melot, Michel. *L'Illustration: histoire d'un art.* Genève: Skira, 1984.

Mercer, Colin. "A Poverty of Desire: Pleasure and Popular Politics." In *Formations of Pleasure.* London: Routledge and Kegan Paul, 1983.

Merish, Lori. "'The Hand of Refined Taste' in the Frontier Landscape: Caroline Kirland's *A New Home, Who'll Follow?* and the Feminization of American Consumerism." *American Quarterly* 45, no. 4 (December 1993): 485–523.

Miller, David C. "Washington Allston and the Sister Arts Tradition in America." *European Romantic Review* 5, no. 1 (Summer 1994): 49–72.

Miller, Lillian B. "'An Influence in the Air': Italian Art and American Taste in the Mid-Nineteenth Century." In *The Italian Presence in American Art, 1760–1860,* edited by Irma B. Jaffe, 26–52. New York: Fordham University Press, 1989.

Miller, Linda Patterson. "Poe on the Beat: *Doings of Gotham* as Urban, Penny Press Journalism." *Journal of the Early Republic* 7, no. 2 (Summer 1987): 147–65.

Miller, Perry. *The Raven and the Whale: The War of Words and Wits in the Era of Poe and Melville.* New York: Harcourt, Brace, 1956.

Miller, Wilbur R. *Cops and Bobbies: Police Authority in New York and London, 1830–1870.* Chicago: University of Chicago Press, 1977.

Mitchell, W. J. T. *Iconology: Image, Text, Ideology.* Chicago: University of Chicago Press, 1986.

———. "Visible Language: Blake's Wond'rous Art of Writing." In *Romanticism and Contemporary Criticism,* edited by Morris Eaves and Michael Fischer, 46–95. Ithaca, N.Y.: Cornell University Press, 1986.

Monaghan, E. Jennifer. "Literacy Instruction and Gender in Colonial New England." *American Quarterly* 40, no. 1 (March 1988): 18–41.

Monkkonen, Eric H. *Police in Urban America, 1860–1920.* New York: Cambridge University Press, 1981.

Montgomery, David. *Beyond Equality: Labor and the Radical Republicans, 1862–1872.* New York: Knopf, 1967.

———. "The Shuttle and the Cross: Weavers amd Artisans in the Kensington Riots of 1844." *Journal of Social History* 5 (Summer 1972): 411–46.

————. *Workers' Control in America: Studies in the History of Work, Technology, and Labor Struggles*. New York: Cambridge University Press, 1979.

Montrose, Louis Adrian. "Gifts and Reasons: The Contexts of Peele's Araygnement of Paris." *ELH* 47 (1980): 433–61.

Moore, R. Laurence. "Learning to Play: The Mormon Way and the Way of Other Americans." *Journal of Mormon History* 16 (1990): 89–106.

————. "Religion, Secularization, and the Shaping of the Culture Industry in Antebellum America." *American Quarterly* 41, no. 2 (June 1989): 216–42.

————. *Religious Outsiders and the Making of Americans*. New York: Oxford University Press, 1986.

Morgan, Edmund S. *Inventing the People: The Rise of Popular Sovereignty in England and America*. New York: W. W. Norton, 1988.

Mott, Frank Luther. *American Journalism: A History of Newspapers in the United States through 250 Years, 1690 to 1940*. New York: Macmillan, 1941.

————. *Golden Multitudes: The Story of Best Sellers in the United States*. New York: Macmillan, 1947.

————. *A History of American Magazines*. 5 vols. Vol. 1, *1741–1850;* Vol. 2, *1850–1865*. Cambridge, Mass.: Belknap Press of Harvard University Press, 1966–68.

————. *The News in America*. Cambridge, Mass.: Harvard University Press, 1952.

Murder Did Pay: Nineteenth-Century New Jersey Murders. Introduced by John T. Cunningham, with a bibliography by Donald A. Sinclair. Newark: New Jersey Historical Society, 1982.

Nissenbaum, Stephen. *Sex, Diet, and Debility in Jacksonian America: Sylvester Graham and Health Reform*. Westport, Conn.: Greenwood Press, 1980.

Noel, Mary. *Villains Galore . . . The Heyday of the Popular Story Weekly*. New York: Macmillan, 1954.

Nord, David Paul. "The Evangelical Origins of Mass Media in America, 1815–1835." *Journalism Monographs* 88 (1984): 1–30.

————. "A Republican Literature: Magazine Reading and Readers in Late-Eighteenth-Century New York." *American Quarterly* 40, no. 1 (March 1988): 42–64.

————. "Working-Class Readers: Family, Community, and Reading in Late Nineteenth-Century America." *Communication Research* 13 (April 1986): 156–81.

O'Brien, Frank M. *The Story of the Sun. New York, 1833–1918*. New York: George H. Doran, 1918.

Ohmann, Richard. *Selling Culture: Magazines, Markets, and Class at the Turn of the Century*. New York: Verso, 1996.

————. "Where Did Mass Culture Come From? The Case of Magazines." In *Politics of Letters*, 135–51. Middletown, Conn.: Wesleyan University Press, 1987.

Palmer, Michael B. *Des petits journaux aux grandes agences. Naissance du journalisme moderne*. Paris: Aubier Montaigne, 1983.

Papke, David Ray. *Framing the Criminal: Crime, Cultural Work, and the Loss of Critical Perspective, 1830–1900.* Hamden, Conn.: Archon Books, 1987.

Pearson, Edmund Lester. "Lilies and Languors." *Scribner's Magazine* 75 (January–June 1924): 43–49.

Peiss, Kathy. *Cheap Amusements: Working Women and Amusements in Turn-of-the-Century New York.* Philadelphia: Temple University Press, 1986.

Perlmann, Joel, and Dennis Shirley. "When Did New England Women Acquire Literacy?" *William and Mary Quarterly* 48 (January 1991): 50–67.

Perrot, Michelle, ed. *From the Fires of Revolution to the Great War.* Translated by Arthur Goldhammer. Vol. 4 of *A History of Private Life,* edited by Philippe Ariès and Georges Duby. Cambridge, Mass.: Belknap Press of Harvard University Press, 1990.

Pessen, Edward. "The Egalitarian Myth and the American Social Reality: Wealth, Mobility, and Equality in the 'Era of the Common Man.'" *American Historical Review* 76 (October 1971): 989–1034.

———. *Jacksonian America: Society, Personality, and Politics.* Urbana: University of Illinois Press, 1985.

———. *Most Uncommon Jacksonians: The Radical Leaders of the Early Labor Movement.* Albany: State University of New York Press, 1967.

———. *Riches, Class, and Power Before the Civil War.* Lexington, Mass.: D. C. Heath, 1973.

Peters, Julie S. *Congreve, the Drama, and the Printed Word.* Stanford: Stanford University Press, 1990.

Pocock, J. G. A. *The Machiavellian Moment: Florentine Political Thought and the Atlantic Republican Tradition.* Princeton: Princeton University Press, 1975.

———. "The Machiavellian Moment Revisited: A Study in History and Ideology." *Journal of World History* 53 (1981): 49–72.

———. "Virtue and Commerce in the Eighteenth Century." *Journal of Interdisciplinary History* 3 (Summer 1972): 119–34.

Pred, Allan R. *Urban Growth and the Circulation of Information: The United States System of Cities, 1790–1840.* Cambridge, Mass.: Harvard University Press, 1973.

Prince, Gerald. "Notes on the Text as Reader." In *The Reader in the Text: Essays on Audience and Interpretation,* edited by Susan R. Suleiman and Inge Crosman, 225–40. Princeton, N.J.: Princeton University Press, 1980.

Pritchard, John Paul. *Literary Wise Men of Gotham: Criticism in New York, 1815–1860.* Baton Rouge: Louisiana State University Press, 1963.

Radway, Janice A. "Reading Is Not Eating: Mass-Produced Literature and the Theoretical, Methodological, and Political Consequences of a Metaphor." *Book Research Quarterly* 2, no. 3 (Fall 1986): 7–29.

———. *Reading the Romance: Women, Patriarchy, and Popular Literature.* Chapel Hill: University of North Carolina Press, 1984.

Ray, Gordon N. *The Illustrator and the Book in England from 1790 to 1914.* New York: Oxford University Press, 1976.

Reid, Douglas. "The Decline of Saint-Monday, 1766–1876." *Past and Present,* no. 71 (1976): 76–101.

Renier, Anne. *Friendship's Offering: An Essay on the Annuals and Gift Books of the Nineteenth Century.* London: Private Libraries Association, 1964.

Revel, Jacques. "The Uses of Civility." In *A History of Private Life,* edited by Philippe Ariès and George Duby. Vol. 3, *Passions of the Renaissance,* edited by Roger Chartier, translated by Arthur Goldhammer, 167–205. Cambridge, Mass.: Belknap Press of Harvard University Press, 1989.

Reynolds, David S. *Beneath the American Renaissance: The Subversive Imagination in the Age of Emerson and Melville.* New York: Knopf, 1988.

―――. *Faith in Fiction: The Emergence of Religious Literature in America.* Cambridge, Mass.: Harvard University Press, 1981.

―――. "From Doctrine to Narrative: The Rise of Pulpit Storytelling in America." *American Quarterly* 32 (Winter 1980): 479–98.

Richardson, James F. *The New York Police: Colonial Times to 1901.* New York: Oxford University Press, 1970.

Robinson, David. *Apostle of Culture: Emerson as Preacher and Lecturer.* Philadelphia: University of Pennsylvania Press, 1982.

Roche, Daniel. *The People of Paris: An Essay in Popular Culture in the Eighteenth Century.* Translated by Marie Evans and Gwynne Lewis. Berkeley: University of California Press, 1987.

Rodgers, Daniel T. *Contested Truths: Keywords in American Politics Since Independence.* New York: Basic Books, 1987.

―――. *The Work Ethic in Industrial America, 1850–1920.* Chicago: University of Chicago Press, 1978.

Roediger, David R. "The Movement for a Shorter Working Day in the United States before 1866." Ph.D. diss., Northwestern University, 1980.

Rogin, Michael P. *Fathers and Children: Andrew Jackson and the Subjugation of the American Indian.* New York: Knopf, 1975.

Rorabaugh, W. J. *The Craft Apprentice: From Franklin to the Machine Age in America.* New York: Oxford University Press, 1986.

Rosenberg, Charles E. "Sexuality, Class and Role in Nineteenth-Century America." *American Quarterly* 25, no. 2 (May 1973): 131–53.

Rosenthal, Bernard, and Paul E. Szarmach, eds. *Medievalism in American Culture: Papers of the Eighteenth Annual Conference of the Center for Medieval and Early Renaissance Studies.* Binghamton: Center for Medieval and Early Renaissance Studies, State University of New York at Binghamton, 1989.

Rosenzweig, Roy. *Eight Hours for What We Will: Workers and Leisure in an Industrial City, 1870–1920.* New York: Cambridge University Press, 1983.

Ross, Morton L. "What Happens in 'Rappaccini's Daughter.'" *American Literature* 43 (November 1971): 336–45.

Ross, Steven J. *Workers on the Edge: Work, Leisure, and Politics in Industrializing Cincinnati, 1788–1890.* New York: Columbia University Press, 1985.

Rothman, David J. *The Discovery of the Asylum: Social Order and Disorder in the New Republic.* Boston: Little, Brown, 1971.

Rowland, Benjamin, Jr. "Popular Romanticism: Art and the Gift Books." *Art Quarterly* 20 (Winter 1957): 365–81.

Ryan, Mary P. "The American Parade: Representations of the Nineteenth-

Century Social Order." In *The New Cultural History,* edited by Lynn Hunt, 131–53. Berkeley: University of California Press, 1989.

———. *Cradle of the Middle Class: The Family in Oneida County, New York, 1790–1865.* New York: Cambridge University Press, 1981.

———. *Women in Public: From Banners to Ballots, 1825–1880.* Baltimore: Johns Hopkins University Press, 1990.

Saisselin, Remy G. *The Bourgeois and the Bibelot.* New Brunswick, N.J.: Rutgers University Press, 1984.

Saum, Lewis O. "Death in the Popular Mind of Pre–Civil War America." *American Quarterly* 26 (1974): 477–95.

Saxton, Alexander. "Blackface Minstrelsy and Jacksonian Ideology." *American Quarterly* 27 (1975): 3–28.

———. "Problems of Class and Race in the Origins of the Mass Circulation Press." *American Quarterly* 36 (1984): 211–34.

———. *The Rise and Fall of the White Republic: Class Politics and Mass Culture in Nineteenth-Century America.* New York: Verso, 1990.

Schapiro, Meyer. *Words and Pictures: On the Literal and the Symbolic in the Illustration of a Text.* The Hague: Mouton, 1973.

Schiller, Dan. *Objectivity and the News: The Public and the Rise of Commercial Journalism.* Philadelphia: University of Pennsylvania Press, 1981.

Schlesinger, Arthur M. *Learning How to Behave: A Historical Study of American Etiquette Books.* New York: Macmillan, 1946.

Schlesinger, Arthur M., Jr. *The Age of Jackson.* Boston: Little, Brown, 1945.

Schneider, John C. *Detroit and the Problem of Order, 1830–1880: A Geography of Crime, Riot, and Policing.* Lincoln: University of Nebraska Press, 1980.

Schreyer, Alice D. "Copyright and Books in Nineteenth-Century America." In *Getting the Books Out: Papers of the Chicago Conference on the Book in Nineteenth-Century America,* edited by Michael Hackenberg, 121–36. Washington, D.C.: Library of Congress, 1987.

Schudson, Michael. *Discovering the News: A Social History of American Newspapers.* New York: Basic Books, 1978.

Scott, Donald M. *From Office to Profession: The New England Ministry, 1750–1850.* Philadelphia: University of Pennsylvania Press, 1978.

———. "The Popular Lecture and the Creation of a Public in Mid-Nineteenth Century America." *Journal of American History* 66 (March 1980): 791–809.

———. "Print and the Public Lecture System, 1840–1860." In *Printing and Society in Early America,* edited by William L. Joyce, David D. Hall, Richard D. Brown, and John B. Hench, 278–99. Worcester, Mass.: American Antiquarian Society, 1983.

Scott, Joan W. *Gender and the Politics of History.* New York: Columbia University Press, 1988.

Scribner, Robert W. *For the Sake of Simple Folk: Popular Propaganda for the German Reformation.* New York: Cambridge University Press, 1981.

Sedgwick, Ellery. *The Atlantic Monthly, 1857–1909: Yankee Humanism at High Tide and Ebb.* Amherst: University of Massachusetts Press, 1994.

Seguin, Jean-Pierre. *Les canards illustrés du XIXe siècle. Fascination du fait divers.* Catalogue d'exposition. Paris: Musée-galerie de la Seita, 1982.

———. *Nouvelles à sensation. Canards du XIXe siècle.* Paris: Armand Colin, 1959.

Seitz, Don C. *The James Gordon Bennetts, Father and Son: Proprietors of the New York Herald.* Indianapolis: Bobbs-Merrill, 1928.

Sellers, Charles G. *The Market Revolution: Jacksonian America, 1815–1846.* New York: Oxford University Press, 1991.

Shalhope, Robert E. "Republicanism and Early American Historiography." *William and Mary Quarterly* 39 (April 1982): 334–56.

———. "Toward a Republican Synthesis: The Emergence of an Understanding of Republicanism in American Historiography." *William and Mary Quarterly* 29 (January 1972): 49–80.

Shevelow, Kathryn. *Women and Print Culture: The Construction of Femininity in the Early Periodical.* New York: Routledge, 1989.

Shields, Rob. "The 'System of Pleasure': Liminality and the Carnivalesque at Brighton." *Theory, Culture and Society* 7, no. 1 (February 1990): 39–72.

Shipps, Jan. *Mormonism: The Story of a New Religious Tradition.* Urbana: University of Illinois Press, 1985.

Sicherman, Barbara. "Sense and Sensibility: A Case Study of Women's Reading in Late-Victorian America." In *Reading in America: Literature and Social History,* edited by Cathy N. Davidson, 201–25. Baltimore: Johns Hopkins University Press, 1989.

Siegel, Adrienne. *The Image of the American City in Popular Literature, 1820–1870.* Port Washington, N.Y.: Kennikat Press, 1981.

Siegert, Reinhart. *Aufklärung und Volkslektüre exemplarisch dargestellt an Rudolph Zacharias Becker und seinem "Noth- und Hülfsbüchlein" mit einer Bibliographie zum Gesamtthema.* Frankfurt am Main: Buchhandler-Vereinigung, 1978.

Silbey, Joel H. *The Partisan Imperative: The Dynamics of American Politics Before the Civil War.* New York: Oxford University Press, 1985.

Silverman, Kenneth. *A Cultural History of the American Revolution.* New York: T. Y. Crowell, 1976.

Sklar, Kathryn Kish. *Catharine Beecher: A Study in American Domesticity.* New Haven: Yale University Press, 1973.

Smith, David C. *History of Papermaking in the United States, 1691–1969.* New York: Lockwood, 1970.

Smith, Henry Nash. "The Scribbling Women and the Cosmic Success Story." *Critical Inquiry* 1, no. 1 (September 1974): 47–70.

Smith, Timothy L. *Revivalism and Social Reform: American Protestantism on the Eve of the Civil War.* New York: Harper and Row, 1965.

Smith-Rosenberg, Carroll. *Disorderly Conduct: Visions of Gender in Victorian America.* New York: Oxford University Press, 1985.

———. "The Female World of Love and Ritual: Relations between Women in Nineteenth-Century America." *Signs* 1 (Autumn 1975): 1–29.

———. "Sex as Symbol in Victorian Purity: An Ethnohistorical Analysis of

Jacksonian America." In *Turning Points: Historical and Sociological Essays on the Family,* edited by John Demos and Sarane Spence Boocock, 212–47. Chicago: University of Chicago Press, 1978.

Soltow, Lee, and Edward Stevens. *The Rise of Literacy and the Common School in the United States: A Socio-Economic Analysis to 1870.* Chicago: University of Chicago Press, 1981.

Spann, Edward K. *The New Metropolis: New York City, 1840–1857.* New York: Columbia University Press, 1981.

Spufford, Margaret. *Small Books and Pleasant Histories: Popular Fiction and Its Readership in Seventeenth-Century England.* Athens: University of Georgia Press, 1982.

Srebnick, Amy Gilman. "The Death of Mary Rogers, the 'Public Prints,' and the Violence of Representation." *Legal Studies Forum* 17, no. 2 (1993): 147–69.

Stallybrass, Peter, and Allon White. *The Politics and Poetics of Transgression.* Ithaca, N.Y.: Cornell University Press, 1986.

Stansell, Christine. *City of Women: Sex and Class in New York, 1789–1860.* New York: Knopf, 1986.

Stearns, Bertha Monica. "Before *Godey's.*" *American Literature* 2 (1930): 248–55.

———. "Early New England Magazines for Ladies." *New England Quarterly* 2 (1929): 420–57.

———. "Early Philadelphia Magazines for Ladies." *Pennsylvania Magazine of History and Biography* 64 (1940): 479–91.

———. "New England Magazines for Ladies, 1830–1860." *New England Quarterly* 3 (1930): 627–56.

———. "Southern Magazines for Ladies (1819–1860)." *South Atlantic Quarterly* 31, no. 1 (January 1932), 70–87.

Sterling, Dorothy, ed. *Speak Out in Thunder Tones: Letters and Other Writings by Black Northerners, 1787–1865.* New York: Doubleday, 1973.

Stern, Madeleine B. *Heads and Headlines: The Phrenological Fowlers.* Norman: University of Oklahoma Press, 1971.

Stevenson, Louise L. *Scholarly Means to Evangelical Ends: The New Haven Scholars and the Transformation of Higher Learning in America, 1830–1890.* Baltimore: Johns Hopkins University Press, 1986.

———. *The Victorian Homefront: American Thought and Culture, 1860–1880.* Boston: Twayne, 1991.

Stewart, Susan. *On Longing: Narratives of the Miniature, the Gigantic, the Souvenir, the Collection.* Baltimore: Johns Hopkins University Press, 1984.

Stone, Lawrence. "Literacy and Education in England, 1640–1900." *Past and Present,* no. 42 (February 1969): 69–139.

Stott, Richard B. *Workers in the Metropolis: Class, Ethnicity, and Youth in Antebellum New York City.* Ithaca, N.Y.: Cornell University Press, 1990.

Stout, Harry S. "Religion, Communications, and the Ideological Origins of the American Revolution." *William and Mary Quarterly* 34 (1977): 519–41.

Stout, Janis P. *Sodoms in Eden: The City in American Fiction Before 1860.* Westport, Conn.: Greenwood Press, 1976.

Stowell, Marion Barber. *Early American Almanacs: The Colonial Weekday Bible.* New York: Burt Franklin, 1977.

Suleiman, Susan R., and Inge Crosman, eds. *The Reader in the Text: Essays on Audience and Interpretation.* Princeton, N.J.: Princeton University Press, 1980.

Sutton, Walter. *The Western Book Trade: Cincinnati as a Nineteenth-Century Publishing and Book-Trade Center.* Columbus: Ohio State University Press for the Ohio Historical Society, 1961.

Tanselle, G. Thomas. "The Bibliography and Textual Study of American Books." In *Needs and Opportunities in the History of the Book: America, 1639–1876,* edited by David D. Hall and John B. Hench, 233–71. Worcester, Mass.: American Antiquarian Society, 1987.

Taylor, George Rogers. *The Transportation Revolution, 1815–1860.* New York: Rinehart, 1951.

Tebbel, John W. *The American Magazine: A Compact History.* New York: Hawthorn Books, 1969.

———. *The Magazine in America, 1741–1900.* New York: Oxford University Press, 1991.

Teichgraeber, Richard F. *Sublime Thoughts/Penny Wisdom: Situating Emerson and Thoreau in the American Market.* Baltimore: Johns Hopkins University Press, 1995.

———. "'A Yankee Diogenes': Thoreau and the Market." In *The Culture of the Market,* edited by Thomas L. Haskell and Richard F. Teichgraeber, 293–324. New York: Cambridge University Press, 1993.

Thiesse, Anne-Marie. *Le roman du quotidien. Lecteurs et lectures populaires à la Belle Epoque.* Paris: Le Chemin vert, 1984.

Thomas, Keith. "Work and Leisure in Pre-Industrial Society." *Past and Present,* no. 29 (December 1964): 50–66.

Thompson, E. P. *The Making of the English Working Class.* New York: Vintage Books, 1966.

———. "Time, Work-Discipline, and Industrial Capitalism." *Past and Present,* no. 38 (December 1967): 56–97.

Thompson, Neville. "Tools of Persuasion: The American Architecture Book of the Nineteenth Century." In *The American Illustrated Book in the Nineteenth Century,* edited by Gerald W. R. Ward, 137–69. Winterthur, Del.: Winterthur Museum, 1987.

Thompson, Ralph. *American Literary Annuals and Gift Books, 1825–1865.* New York: Archon Books, 1967.

Todorov, Tzvetan. "Reading as Construction." In *The Reader in the Text: Essays on Audience and Interpretation,* edited by Susan R. Suleiman and Inge Crosman, 67–82. Princeton, N.J.: Princeton University Press, 1980.

Toll, Robert. *Blacking Up: The Minstrel Show in Nineteenth-Century America.* New York: Oxford University Press, 1974.

Tompkins, Jane P. *Sensational Designs: The Cultural Work of American Fiction, 1790–1860.* New York: Oxford University Press, 1985.

———, ed. *Reader-Response Criticism: From Formalism to Post-Structuralism.* Baltimore: Johns Hopkins University Press, 1980.

Trachtenberg, Alan. *Reading American Photographs: Images as History—Mathew Brady to Walker Evans.* New York: Hill and Wang, 1989.

Truly Yours: One Hundred and Fifty Years of Play Publishing and Service to the Theatre. New York: Samuel French, 1980.

Tryon, Warren S. "The Publications of Ticknor and Fields in the South, 1840–1865." *Journal of Southern History* 14 (1948): 305–30.

———. "Ticknor and Fields' Publications in the Old Northwest." *Mississippi Valley Historical Review* 34 (1947): 589–610.

Tucher, Andie. *Froth and Scum: Truth, Beauty, Goodness, and the Ax Murder in America's First Mass Medium.* Chapel Hill: University of North Carolina Press, 1994.

Turner, Victor. *The Ritual Process: Structure and Anti-Structure.* Ithaca, N.Y.: Cornell University Press, 1977.

Van Every, Edward. *Sins of New York as "Exposed" by the Police Gazette.* New York: Frederick A. Stokes, 1930.

Vann, J. Don. *Victorian Novels in Serial.* New York: Modern Language Association of America, 1985.

Veyne, Paul. "Foucault révolutionne l'histoire." In *Comment on écrit l'histoire,* 203–42. Paris: Seuil, 1978.

Vincent, David. *Literacy and Popular Culture: England, 1750–1914.* New York: Cambridge University Press, 1989.

Vinovskis, Maris A. "Angels' Heads and Weeping Willows: Death in Early America." *Proceedings of the American Antiquarian Society* 86, no. 2 (1977): 273–302.

Waldstreicher, David. "Rites of Rebellion, Rites of Assent: Celebrations, Print Culture, and the Origins of American Nationalism." *Journal of American History* 82, no. 1 (June 1995): 37–61.

Walsh, John. *Poe the Detective: The Curious Circumstances behind the Mystery of Marie Roget.* New Brunswick, N.J.: Rutgers University Press, 1968.

Walters, Ronald G. *American Reformers, 1815–1860.* New York: Hill and Wang, 1978.

———. *Primers for Prudery: Sexual Advice to Victorian America.* Englewood Cliffs, N.J.: Prentice-Hall, 1973.

Warner, Michael. "Franklin and the Letters of the Republic." *Representations* 16 (Fall 1986): 110–30.

———. *The Letters of the Republic: Publication and the Public Sphere in Eighteenth-Century America.* Cambridge, Mass.: Harvard University Press, 1990.

———. "Textuality and Legitimacy in the Printed Constitution." *Proceedings of the American Antiquarian Society* 97, no. 1 (1987): 59–84.

Watson, Harry L. *Liberty and Power: The Politics of Jacksonian America.* New York: Hill and Wang, 1990.

Watt, Ian. *The Rise of the Novel: Studies in Defoe, Richardson and Fielding.* Berkeley: University of California Press, 1957.

Watts, Steven. *The Republic Reborn: War and the Making of Liberal America, 1790–1820.* Baltimore: Johns Hopkins University Press, 1987.

Weber, Donald. "From Limen to Border: A Meditation on the Legacy of Victor Turner for American Cultural Studies." *American Quarterly* 47, no. 3 (September 1995): 525–36.

Weinbaum, Paul O. *Mobs and Demagogues: The New York Response to Collective Violence in the Early Nineteenth Century.* Ann Arbor, Mich.: UMI Research Press, 1979.

Welter, Barbara. "The Cult of True Womanhood: 1820–1860." *American Quarterly* 18 (Summer 1966): 151–74.

———. *Dimity Convictions: The American Woman in the Nineteenth Century.* Athens: Ohio University Press, 1976.

White, Luke, Jr. *Henry William Herbert and the American Publishing Scene, 1831–1858.* Newark, N.J.: Carteret Book Club, 1943.

White, Robert L. " 'Rappacini's Daughter,' 'The Cenci,' and the Cenci Legend." *Studi Americani* (Rome) 14 (1968): 63–86.

Whorton, James C. *Crusaders for Fitness: The History of American Health Reformers.* Princeton, N.J.: Princeton University Press, 1982.

Wiebe, Robert H. *The Opening of American Society: From the Adoption of the Constitution to the Eve of Disunion.* New York: Knopf, 1984.

Wilentz, Sean. "Artisan Republican Festivals and the Rise of Class Conflict in New York City, 1788–1837." In *Working-Class America: Essays on Labor, Community, and American Society,* edited by Michael H. Frisch and Daniel J. Walkowitz, 37–77. Urbana: University of Illinois Press, 1983.

———. *Chants Democratic: New York City and the Rise of the American Working Class, 1788–1850.* New York: Oxford University Press, 1984.

———. "On Class and Politics in Jacksonian America." *Reviews in American History* (December 1982): 45–63.

Williams, Daniel E. " 'Behold a Tragic Scene Strangely Changed Into a Theater of Mercy': The Structure and Significance of Criminal Conversion Narratives in Early New England." *American Quarterly* 38 (1986): 827–47.

———. "Doctor, Preacher, Soldier, Thief: A New World of Possibilities in the Rogue Narrative of Henry Tufts." *Early American Literature* 19 (1984): 3–20.

———. "Puritans and Pirates: A Confrontation between Cotton Mather and William Fly in 1726." *Early American Literature* 22, no. 3 (1987): 233–51.

———. "Rogues, Rascals and Scoundrels: The Underworld Literature of Early America." *American Studies* 24, no. 2 (1983): 5–19.

Williams, Raymond. "Base and Superstructure in Marxist Cultural Theory." *New Left Review* 82 (December 1973): 3–16.

———. *The Long Revolution.* New York: Columbia University Press, 1961.

Williams, Robert V. "The Public Library as the Dependent Variable: Historically Oriented Theories and Hypotheses of Public Library Development." *Journal of Library History* 16, no. 2 (Spring 1981): 329–41.

Wilmeth, Don B. *Variety Entertainment and Outdoor Amusements: A Reference Guide*. Westport, Conn.: Greewood Press, 1982.

Wilson, Christopher P. *The Labor of Words: Literary Professionalism in the Progressive Era*. Athens: University of Georgia Press, 1985.

Wimsatt, William K., Jr. "Poe and the Mystery of Mary Rogers." *PMLA* 56, no. 1 (March 1941): 230–48.

Winkler, Gail Caskey. "Influence of Godey's *Lady's Book* on the American Woman and Her Home: Contributions to a National Culture (1830–1877)." Ph.D. diss., University of Wisconsin-Madison, 1988.

Winslow, Ola Elizabeth. "Books for the Lady Reader, 1820–1860." In *Romanticism in America: Papers Contributed to a Symposium Held at the Baltimore Museum of Art, May 13, 14, 15, 1940*, edited by George Boas, 89–109. New York: Russell and Russell, 1961.

Wolf, Bryan. *Romantic Re-Vision: Culture and Consciousness in Nineteenth-Century American Painting and Literature*. Chicago: University of Chicago Press, 1982.

Wolf, Edwin. *From Gothic Windows to Peacocks: American Embossed Leather Bindings, 1825–1855*. Philadelphia: Library Company of Philadelphia, 1990.

Wood, Gordon S. "The Democratization of Mind in the American Revolution." In *Leadership in the American Revolution: Papers Presented at the Third Library of Congress Symposium on the American Revolution*. Washington, D.C.: Library of Congress, 1974.

———. "The Significance of the Early Republic." *Journal of the Early Republic* 8 (Spring 1988): 1–20.

Wright, Conrad Edick, ed. *American Unitarianism, 1805–1865*. Boston: Massachusetts Historical Society, 1989.

Yeo, Eileen, and Stephen Yeo. "Ways of Seeing: Control and Leisure versus Class and Struggle." In *Popular Culture and Class Conflict, 1590–1914: Explorations in the History of Labour and Leisure*, 128–54. Sussex: Harvester Press, 1981.

Zboray, Ronald J. *A Fictive People: Antebellum Economic Development and the American Reading Public*. New York: Oxford University Press, 1993.

———. "The Transportation Revolution and Antebellum Book Distribution Reconsidered." *American Quarterly* 38, no. 1 (Spring 1986): 53–71.

Ziff, Larzer. "Upon What Pretext?: The Book and Literary History." *Proceedings of the American Antiquarian Society* 95, no. 2 (1986): 297–315.

Zonderman, David A. *Aspirations and Anxieties: New England Workers and the Mechanized Factory System, 1815–1850*. New York: Oxford University Press, 1992.

Zophy, Angela Marie Howard. "For the Improvement of My Sex: Sarah Josepha Hale's Editorship of *Godey's Lady's Book*, 1837–1877." Ph.D. diss., Ohio State University, 1978.

Index

Butler, Jon, 22
Bynum, Caroline Walker, 6
Byron, George Gordon, Lord, 137

Capitalism. *See* Marketplace
Card playing, 128, 137
Carey, Mathew, 156
Carey and Hart, 96, 142
Carey and Lea, 77, 96
Carnal imagery. *See* Body
Carnival, in print, 11, 25, 70, 103, 124, 126, 156–57, 159
Carnivalesque, 3, 7, 13, 35, 68, 71, 127, 154; ritual, 37
Carpenter, Edward Jenner, 69, 145, 148
Cash press, 37–38
Catholicism, 4, 53, 85, 116, 117
Celebrations, 9
Cenci, The, 92–93
Chamberlain, Thomas, 74, 174 (n. 43)
Channing, William Ellery, 138, 153
Character, 139, 158
Charlotte Temple, 19
Charvat, William, 25
Cheap and light publications, 13, 26–27, 35, 71, 101, 128, 153–54, 156, 157
Cheap books, 60, 101, 133, 136, 139, 141, 156; and competition, 61. *See also* Battle of books
Cheney, John, 88, 91–92, 93
Cheney, Seth Wells, 86–87, 88
Cherubim. *See* Angels
Child, Lydia Maria, 94, 96, 132, 153
Childhood, 87, 88, 90
Childhood, 88
Children's magazines, 75
Christmas, 81, 85; and New Year's presents, 79, 80, 98. *See also* Special issues
Churchgoing, 145
Circus, 8, 156
City gossip, 37, 51, 152. *See also* Gossip

City mysteries, 52, 58
Civic duty, 146
Civility, 135. *See also* Gentility
Class distinctions, 142, 150–51; and texts, 29; and gender, in *Godey's Lady's Book*, 114
Coleridge, Samuel Taylor, 91
Collective reading, 69, 133, 141. *See also* Family reading
Colored prints, 102, 103. *See also* Steel engravings, hand-colored
Coloring, and women, 109
Commercial culture, 27, 71, 152, 158. *See also* Popular culture
Commercialization, 78, 104; and literature, 30, 32, 71, 138, 154, 159; and gender, 34
Commercial papers, 38, 40. *See also* Newspapers
Commodification. *See* Commercialization
Commodities, 80, 83, 98, 99
Common public, 10. *See also* Reading—public for
Common Sense, 21
Community of readers: and daily newspapers, 48–49; idealized, 70, 141. *See also* Collective reading; Family reading
Comstock Act, 159
Concord Social Library, 147
Conduct-of-life books, 81, 85, 127–31, 136, 158; for women, 140
Consolation literature, 76, 90
Consolidation, 35, 153, 159
Conspicuous consumption, 84
Conspirator, The, 73
Constellation, The, 61
Consumerism, 36, 83–84, 98, 104, 121. *See also* Commodities; Objects
Consumers, and readers, 48, 98, 148
Contemplation, 78, 81, 82, 86, 141. *See also* Gaze; Reading—activity of
Contributors, 96, 103, 133

Popular media, 8, 12, 27, 62, 70, 154, 157; and gender, 34

Popular periodicals, 102, 133, 159

Popular publications. *See* Popular media

Popular reading, 10, 13, 31, 71, 125, 139, 148, 158–59; audience for, and *Herald*, 41; condemnation of, 128, 148, 157; representations of, 131, 141; control of, 131, 159
—discourse on, 32, 127, 139; in Europe, 154

Popular recreation. *See* Public recreation

Popular taste, 60, 67, 70, 72, 77, 103, 145, 147, 148, 157

Porter, Noah, 159

Portraits, 67, 88, 94; of women, 67, 91, 93–94, 95, 99, 103

Postal legislation, 60, 74

Practice of reading, 62, 74; reverential, 138. *See also* Popular reading; Reading—activity of

Prayer books, 124

Pred, Allan, 48

Prescriptive literature, 10, 127, 129–31, 140, 147, 151, 153–54. *See also* Conduct-of-life books

Presses, double-cylinder and ten-cylinder, 45; rotary self-feeding, 46; Napier-type Hoe, 65

Print: and fragmentation, 22; parody of, 60; transformation of, 60, 155; uses of, 62, 80, 99, 128, 132, 152, 153, 157; abundance of, 70, 127, 131, 133, 137–39, 144, 153, 157–58; and drama, 74, 77, 113; and consumption, 78, 83
—upheaval in, 9, 15; in antebellum period, 156. *See also* Popularization

Print culture: vernacular, 23, 47, 111, 114, 156; popular, 67, 108; and continuity, 70;
—traditional, 21, 105, 126; and penny papers, 47; demise of, 60,

61, 156; challenged, 60, 67, 124, 134, 156; appropriated, 70
—transformation of, 12, 76, 96, 100, 102, 103, 105, 136, 156, 160; and a separate sphere for women, 11, 94, 105, 114, 122; and diversification, 12; and feminization, 12, 94, 98, 100, 107, 114, 124; and women's emergence, 13, 113, 124, 158; materiality of, 25, 61; and publishing innovations, 30–31, 156; and commodification of, 78, 159. *See also* Carnival, in print; Material appearance

Print discourse, 32; public, 21–22; univocal, 29; of enlightenment, 154

Printing, 24, 72, 96, 97. *See also* Technology of printing

Print media. *See* Popular media

Private amusements, 151

Private life: in the press, 12; publicized in newspapers, 49, 50; tragedies of, 52

Private reading, 67, 141, 152, 153, 156, 158. *See also* Solitary reading

Private space, 113, 151, 158. *See also* Home; Public sphere—vs. private sphere

Productivity, 132

Proletarianization, 132

Prostitution, 130. *See also* Robinson-Jewett case

Protestantism, 85, 98, 116–17; as religion of the book, 21, 100, 157; softening of, 114, 117

Public amusements, 147, 148, 152. *See also* Amusements; Public recreation

Public demand: for lives of criminals, 51; for fashion plates, 107, 115; for paintings and images, 121. *See also* Taste

Public recreation, 128, 148–53; control of, 151

Public space, 64, 150

Public speaking, 141
Public sphere, 22, 124; and gender, 34, 124
—vs. private sphere, 36–37, 49, 84, 113, 123–24, 148, 150, 151, 152, 158; inversion of, 159. *See also* Separate spheres, ideology of
Publishers, 71; of giftbooks, 96, 97, 98, 152
Publishing, 59, 60, 72, 79, 97, 102; revolution in, 16–17, 45; in northeastern cities, 25–26, 156; industrialization of, 34; profit in, 97; golden age of, 126
Pulpit, 130; and the press, 23

Quadruple sheet, 61, 64
Quaker City, The, 52
Quarto editions, 61, 70
Quill, Charles. *See* Alexander, James W.

Raphael, 86, 88, 91
"Rappaccini's Daughter," 90, 93
Ray, Isaac, 139
Reader-response criticism, 31
Readers: self-absorbed, 25; and crime news, 41, 57; and consumers, 48, 97, 148, 159; poor, 70; viewers, 103, 105, 111, 113, 114, 117; working-class, 114, 147; and texts, interactions between, 132; male, 158. *See also* Women: as readers
Reading: aloud, 14–15, 133, 141, 153; and writing, 21; as emasculating, 25, 139, 145, 148; and concept of "reading formation," 31; of drama, 74; as beholding, 82, 93, 96, 98–100; societies for, 85; engagement with, 95; and intimacy, 113; of Scriptures, 124; as useful recreation, 126, 128, 131, 143, 145, 152; abuse of, 127, 152–53 (*see also* Omnivorous readers); critique of, in colonial

era, 128; dangers of, 128, 132–35, 139, 153; collective and individual, 128, 141 (*see also* Collective reading; Family reading; Private reading; Solitary reading); good and bad, 128, 141, 153–54, 159 (*see also* Bad books); at night, 132, 139, 154; as leisure activity, 132, 148, 153; and food metaphors, 136–37; and drinking, 137, 148; as strenuous exercise, 139–40, 153; usefulness of, 140, 142, 147, 153, 158; for women, 141; and learning, 142; moral value of, 142; on the Sabbath, 144 (*see also* Sunday newspapers); rooms for, 148; and private amusements, 151, 153, 158; as subversive, 152; public character of, 153; cheap and light (*see* Cheap and light publications)
—activity of, 10, 25, 31, 78, 94, 99, 116, 132, 156; and other cultural activities, 32, 147; as enlightening, 36; and crime news, 41, 57; representation of, 94–96; as private, 116, 139, 141, 153; as contemplation, 117, 123, 141; as controversial activity, 126, 152–53; and social improvement, 132; as feminine, 139, 158; and leisure time, 143, 146
—public for, 24, 29, 70, 130, 147; national, 9; plurality of, 10, 34; multifaceted, 17; in the eighteenth century, 22; segmentation of, 29, 101; and *New York Herald,* 37; in the city, 50–51; voyeurism of, 56; and differentiation of audiences, 69 (*see also* Gender—distinctions based on); and popular print culture, 108; and *Godey's Lady's Book,* 114, 123. *See also* Taste
—revolution in, 18–19, 100; elusiveness of, 20, 32